A Life in Middle East Studies

Roger Owen
Forward by Judith E. Tucker

T TADWEEN PUBLISHING

Printed in the United States of America
First Printing: November 2016
ISBN: 978-1-939067-23-4

This publication is produced in part with the support of the Middle East
Program at George Mason University, with which the Arab Studies
Institute is affiliated.

To my three children, Katey, Ben and Isabel,
that they should know more about their father's professional life.

CONTENTS

LIST OF ILLUSTRATIONS

FOREWORD

Roger Owen has written a captivating memoir that is at once personal, institutional, and intellectual, shaped at every turn by the momentous events of over fifty years of history in the Middle East. We are not often privy to the private thoughts of our colleagues about the people, ideas, and experiences that drew them to the region, suggested to them which research questions were the ones to ask, and forged in them the deep bonds and loyalties that seem to underpin much of the academic work in Middle East studies. So it is especially exciting, in this text, to have a front row seat on the formation of a "second generation" scholar in Middle East studies. And not just any scholar, but one who has played such a central role in the development of the field both intellectually and institutionally.

I first encountered Roger Owen when I was a graduate student at Harvard University in the mid-1970s. Many of us were feeling increasingly uncomfortable with our field, which seemed to be lagging badly behind the times, mired in academic Orientalism and seemingly immune to the seismic shifts taking place elsewhere—in Latin American studies for example—that were putting labor, class, gender, and social movements on their research agendas. We were delighted, and dare I say inspired, by the emergence of the "Hull group" in the United Kingdom, a loose association of faculty and graduate students who were shaking up Middle East studies by offering astringent critiques of Orientalism and modernization theory from a Marxian perspective in the *Review of Middle East Studies*. Owen was a historian we already admired for his writing on the economics of imperialism and colonialism in his book *Cotton and the Egyptian Economy,* and it was exciting to us that he lent his weight and intellect to this enterprise. It was my privilege to meet Owen soon afterward, when I was doing a leg of dissertation research that took me to Oxford University during his tenure there. He was known to be gracious and encouraging to graduate students, his own and passers-by like myself, boosting our spirits by taking a quite genuine interest in our work. In the years that followed, I have had the pleasure of talking with Roger on many occasions, of being made to feel welcome and well hosted by him and his wife Margaret during a term at Oxford, and of being treated each time we met to his incisive observations on the current political scene as well as the high-level political gossip that he has always so enjoyed. In addition to giving time and attention to younger scholars, Owen has made an enormous imprint on the field, helping to establish its priorities by playing pivotal roles in two of the leading centers for Middle East studies, St Antony's College at Oxford and the CMES at Harvard, as well as in the Economic and Business History Research Center at the American University in Cairo.

Owen does not dwell on his many such contributions in these pages, but rather allows his life to raise an intriguing question. How are our ideas and political alignments molded by the events we witness or we live through? In this memoir, we journey with Owen through years of tumultuous history in the Middle East as he remembers how certain moments shaped his consciousness and helped him formulate his questions. As a young man, British participation with France and Israel in the tripartite attack on Egypt in 1956 struck him as a wrongheaded move to reassert the privileges of lost empire, and no doubt helped make him the astute analyst of modern empire he was to become. In the heady days of the early 1960s in Egypt, Gamal Abdel Nasser's social policies inspired him, along with a generation of Arab intellectuals—many of them his friends—to look to Arab socialism for solutions to many of the painful legacies of the colonial period. Although a more sober accounting of the Nasser years would come, Owen's memories of the hopes and promises of this time continued to inform the position from which he analyzed the role of the military in some of his later work. He ran headlong into post-1967 popular movements, with the rise of the Palestine Liberation Organization (PLO) and its rocky history, first in Jordan and then in Lebanon, when he visited the region in the 1970s. These experiences have made him an astute and empathetic public intellectual who has commented on the Palestine question over the years. Although the sea change that was his move from Oxford to Harvard in 1993 slowed the pace of his visits to the region as a result of increased distance, his research continued to be guided by the pressing concerns of the day, including the crisis of authoritarianism in recent years.

We should not make the mistake, however, of thinking that the work of Roger Owen or any other scholar is legible as a simple and linear reflection of his or her experiences and times. Owen is quick to note the role of serendipity. We have the disarming admission that Owen was initially launched into academia because he failed to score high enough on the exam for the British Diplomatic Service and fell back on graduate study. Soon afterward, he came to study and write about Libya (and to spend his honeymoon there) thanks to a randomly obtained commission to update a chapter on its history and politics. When his plans to study for a semester in East Jerusalem were stymied by the 1967 June War, he ended up in Lebanon at the critical moment that it was becoming a microcosm of Arab politics. Owen recognizes the limits all of us face not only in controlling our lives but also in narrating them. He laments, "how limited and bare my descriptive vocabulary was" (150), and reminds us of how very unreliable memory can be. Although some of this memoir is based on journals he kept over the years, he seems to be warning us that he should not be fully trusted—this is not meant to be a work of social science.

The welcome lack of pretension in this text should not be allowed to obscure Owen's intellectual legacy, one that has shaped the research agendas of modern Middle East studies in significant ways. He taught us the importance of studying the nuts and bolts of empire in his detailed examination of the colonial economy in Egypt. He engaged both modernization and world systems theory in another masterwork, *The Middle East in the World Economy*, putting the former to rest as an explanatory paradigm and revising the latter to better reflect the specificities of economic development in the region in modern times. His textbook, *State, Power and Politics in the Making of the Modern Middle East*, brought a historian's sensibility to the vexing question of the trajectory of the state in the region, and integrated complex questions of political economy and the roles of the military and civil society. Finally, he turned his attention to political biography, to the examination of power by way of studying those who wield it. His book on Lord Cromer revealed the limits of power in a colonial context by way of tracking the development of the blinkered visions of this representative of Edwardian empire who made such a mark on Egypt. *The Rise and Fall of Arab Presidents for Life*, his most recent work, continued this exploration of power and the particularities of the Arab state through close analysis of the individuals who clung, and in some cases still cling, to personal power so tenaciously in defiance of many of our expectations. These projects entailed a way of writing political biography that has eschewed a psychological approach in favor of giving full attention to the workings of historical context and political economy that have been so much the signatures of Owen's scholarship.

The writing of this memoir is an act of generosity that allows his readers to place this extraordinary record of scholarship in its personal, historical,

11

and regional setting. I think others will join me in thanking Roger for inviting us into his life. He enriches our understanding of how Middle East studies, and intellectual endeavors in general, are not only embedded in past experience; they are, at their best, guided by our principles, our attachments, and our hopes for the future

Judith E. Tucker

PREFACE

My decision to write a partial memoir, involving what I call *A Life in Middle East Studies*, stems from two interconnected currents of thought. One was my growing realization as a young adult that the autobiographies of men and women involved in sustained intellectual activity, for example that of the philosopher Bertrand Russell, contained surprisingly little about how they came to hold the ideas that they taught and wrote about. The second was the interest that my Oxford University mentor, Albert Hourani, showed in listening to personal accounts of what he called the "intellectual formation" of leading Orientalists such as Oxford's Richard Walzer. Although it is also noteworthy that Hourani himself undertook no such exercise, leaving the genesis of his masterwork, *Arabic Thought in the Liberal Age*, an enduring mystery.

In my own case, I, too, have come to believe that students and practitioners of modern Middle East studies would be the better off for knowing something not only of the history of their field but also of the pioneers who established it as a separate enterprise within the wider field of modern area studies. Furthermore, it seems that there is much to be gained from seeing the field as more than just a set of ideas and ways of thinking—but also consisting of a set of institutions and practices that began to be created in the 1950s before coming to fruition in a number of key centers from the 1960s onward.

I was fortunate enough to find myself as a graduate student at one such center at St. Antony's College, and then as a lecturer there in the early 1960s. What follows is a very personal history of my experience of getting to know the Middle East as an object of study, along with the many pleasant (and on a few occasions, unpleasant,) experiences this involved, a journey I shared, in part, with two wives, Ursula and then Margaret, as well as, more recently, my partner Ruth. It also contains an analysis of the field from its early inception until the 1990s when, for reasons I set out in the general introduction, I consider it to have reached a self-sustaining maturity, followed by some thoughts as to its present state and where it might be headed in an inevitably contentious future.

Lastly, I should note that while I conceive the audience for this book to consist of all those engaged in the study of the modern Middle East, I trust that it will also appeal to those others who may be interested in the ways that the field's organization and practices are both like and unlike those in such adjacent studies: African, Latin American, or East Asian.

1   INTRODUCTION

One day in the summer of 1955, I heard a new and unusual sound. As part of my National (Military) Service, I was riding in a small open-top army vehicle at the head of a slow-moving convoy of signals vehicles heading from our Colchester headquarters to the Stamford Training Area in Suffolk. My unit provided the wireless and telegraph communications for the umpires who, every two weeks or so, monitored the mock battles fought there by members of the British Territorial Army, preparing them for a war with the Soviet Union that everyone prayed would never come. It was boring and often irritating work: the snail-like speed along narrow roads with high hedges on both sides, the pitching of tents in the latrine-infested clearing assigned to us, followed by the lack of sleep involved in making sure that the networks remained up and running for the thirty-six hours or so of the exercise. On this trip though, one of our signalmen, quite against the rules, switched his radio set to a BBC channel playing a hit song of the moment: "Stranger in Paradise" from the movie *Kismet*. The music was adapted from Alexander Borodin's "Polovtsian Dances" with their surging sense of a caravan setting off to the east, in bright mimicry of the wild sounds found in the land of the Muslim Cossacks and Tartars just opening up to Russian imperial expansion across the Central Asian steppes. It seemed like an urgent call, a tantalizing promise of experiences so much more exciting than anything I could possibly find in the rather stuffy England of the Churchill/Eden Conservative government that had replaced the reformist Labour government in 1951.

Of course, this was not my first encounter with notions of the far-away and the exotic that, some years later, were to be lumped together under the general title of "Orientalism"—a totalizing as well as patronizing approach to the East that I was later to do my best to undermine. Like any young English boy of my age and class, I had been exposed to a series of films and stories full of wicked viziers, captive princesses, magic lamps, and flying carpets.

These included an exciting World War II Soviet film called *The Firebird* and Michael Powell's mesmerizing *The Thief of Bagdad*, which contained practically every magical moment of the *Arabian Nights*, including an evil genie, a monster spider, and a mechanical horse. Later, after I had begun to read about T. E. Lawrence, I was even more excited by the idea of the desert, something I really took in for the first time when I saw the Korda brothers' spectacular version of *The Four Feathers*, which was filmed in Sudan and Egypt and ended with hundreds of soldiers fighting it out on horses and camels on a sandy plain across the Nile from Khartoum. My fascination with Eastern places increased again later, while I was living outside New York after my father had gone to work for the new United Nations in 1946, and where I learned something of the harsh realities of the Jewish insurgency against the British in Palestine, puzzling over new words like Kol Yisrael (Voice of Israel) and Irgun Zvai Leumi (National Military Organization).

Then, like another miracle, only a few weeks after I heard Borodin's call, I was heading east myself as part of a small signal troop hastily assembled to provide communications for a twenty-four-hour radar naval watch over the waters around the island of Cyprus. The goal was to prevent illegal arms shipments coming in for the National Organization of Cypriot Fighters, known to us as the EOKA guerrillas, who were struggling to get rid of British colonial rule. Although Cyprus was not technically part of the Middle East, it did feel significantly Eastern as we stepped out of the plane into the night sky at Nicosia Airport, with the day's heat still heavy in the air, sweet and unknown smells tickling the senses, and the insistent buzz of cicadas like so many tiny clocks ticking their way toward dawn.

I was soon to discover how close Nicosia was by plane to Tel Aviv, East Jerusalem, Beirut, and Cairo, journeys that I began to make during my Christmas leave in late December 1955 and early January 1956, and then again after I had demobilized from the army in Cyprus—not Britain—in May 1956 in order to take a longer eastern Mediterranean journey, including spending my twenty-first birthday in Israel followed by ten days in Egypt in early June. It was then that I got really hooked on the East as a result of the heady combination of the sweet early summer evenings, Biblical ruins, and the insistent hammer of contemporary politics. This ranged from hearing news in Israel of attacks by Palestinian *fedayeen* against people living and traveling in the Northern Negev, getting caught up in the anti-British riots in East Jerusalem against efforts to bring Jordan into the British-promoted Baghdad Pact, and, finally, experiencing the great political excitement in Egypt in anticipation of the evacuation of the last British troops from the Canal Zone under the Suez Agreement of October 1954. Nevertheless, all this ex-

An Army Signals truck in Cyprus, 1956.

citement was nothing compared to the moment I fell totally in love with the region: sitting with a friend of my father's in the open rooftop restaurant of the old Semiramis Hotel in Cairo with the warm air full of a cacophony of urban sounds, the inky black Nile sliding sedately below, and the vague shapes of the pyramids beyond.

Back in the United Kingdom events seemed to arrange themselves so that the Middle East, and particularly Egypt, were never long out of mind. While I could not actually study the contemporary Middle East when I got to Oxford University as an undergraduate in October 1956, there being no available courses on its history, I was immediately drawn back into an active interest in the region by the shock of the Tripartite Anglo-French and Israeli attack on Egypt, which took place only weeks after I entered university. The attack caused almost unprecedented divisions in British political life, which were exacerbated by huge demonstrations and other forms of protest. I myself felt so strongly about the sheer wrongness of trying to reoccupy parts of the postcolonial world that I am pretty certain that, if I had been recalled for National Service reserve duty in the Middle East, as some signals personnel were, I certainly would have had to resign my commission and take the consequences. No doubt, like the hero of Andrew Sinclair's Suez novel *The Breaking of Bumbo* (1959), it would have resulted in my spending some months in military jail.

Then for most of the rest of my three university years, I fondly imagined that I would return to the Middle East via a post in the Foreign Office, but this was not to be, as I did not obtain high enough points in my entrance exam to get in. Happily, and after only a frustrating number of months at home with my mother waiting for something to turn up, two opportunities did present themselves: the first was an interview at St. Antony's College,

17

which led to an offer to go back to Oxford as a graduate student to work on the modern economic history of the Middle East, the second was a commission to update a short Chatham House *Political and Economic Survey of Libya*, a country I knew nothing about whatsoever.

So it was that I determined to spend part of my approaching honeymoon in that country. A friend of my father who worked for the United Nations found my new wife, Ursula, and myself an apartment in Tripoli. Using this as a base, we spent our time talking to local experts and traveling around in a borrowed car as far as Cyrene in the east and, on one occasion, by plane to a desert drilling site in the south where the first oil had only recently been discovered. Magically, it seemed as though we had the whole country to ourselves, from the Green Mountain around Benghazi to the troglodyte pits at Gharyan, as well as the vast stretches of empty beaches with their Greek and Roman ruins—Leptis Magna, Sabratha, Cyrene—rising high above the dunes behind.

This was followed by a year in Cairo, in 1962, living with my wife in the posh suburb of Zamalek. We both taught English at the American University of Cairo (AUC). Once my permission had come through, I walked to the Abdeen Palace each day to comb through some archives I needed for my Oxford DPhil research on the cotton export sector in the nineteenth century. That winter we took a Nile trip to the Valley of the Kings and then went

Roger Owen in the courtyard of a 19th century house in Cairo in the early 1960s.

18

cruising on the Nile from Aswan to the temple of Abu Simbel just before it was raised to the cliff above to protect it from the rising waters of the new Lake Nasser created by the recently heightened Aswan High Dam. Finally, in the early summer of 1963, we made a quick visit to Beirut and East Jerusalem, then divided from West Jerusalem by a wall, before flying back from Cairo to London in June.

We spent the next academic year, from 1963 to 1964, in New York where I worked on my thesis before returning to Oxford to lecture on the economic history of the Middle East in the fall term of 1964. This post was something of an ordeal at first, particularly since the class included the Crown Prince of Jordan, Hassan bin Talal, an undergraduate at Christ Church College, who I rightly assumed knew much more about many aspects of the region's political and economic situation than I did.

For a short period, things were surprisingly quiet in the Middle East, and so it came as an almost complete surprise to all when the crisis of May 1967 quickly gave way to the June War, a dramatic event that in five short, breathless, and incomprehensible days changed the whole face of the region for good. The war forced me to revise the plans I had made to spend the academic year of 1967-1968 in East Jerusalem improving my Arabic. Instead, I made the impromptu decision to live in the small Lebanese hill village of Shemlan, the home of the British Foreign Office-funded Middle East Centre for Arabic Studies (MECAS). There, as we were soon to discover, conditions in the region in the aftermath of the war created a crash course in Middle East politics for me, a learning experience that began in Lebanon but also extended to Amman and Baghdad, and then later to Cairo, Jerusalem, and the Israeli-occupied West Bank, comings and goings now dimly recorded by a series of smudged Arabic date stamps in my old black British passport.

In this way, I was well positioned to witness how out of the thinly disguised triumphalism on the Israeli side, and the bitterness and humiliation on the Arab one, came a new sense of determination, expressed most directly by the upsurge of radical nationalism on the part of the Arab Left and its armed allies in the Palestine Liberation Organization (PLO) as they struggled to find ways to fight back against Israel and those they perceived as Israel's main allies: the United States and the leaders of most of the Arab states.

My wife and I encountered a similar sense of radical change as we made our way back to England from Beirut in the late spring of 1968. We took the car ferry to Nicosia and spent a week in Cyprus, where ethnic tensions between the Greeks and the Turks had escalated enormously since I had left the island in 1956. We observed Turkish invasion barges resting in plain sight as we drove along the south Turkish coast. Soon after, we witnessed quite another zone of revolutionary change as we passed through a Europe rocked by student uprisings in Paris and elsewhere. Gone was the sense of the Middle East as a separate region of wonder and delight. In its place was a cockpit of fierce contestation, linked directly to the rest of the world by global ideological currents focused on nationalism, revolution, liberation, and armed struggle, supported and intensified by the great Cold War rivals the United States and the Soviet Union. It was a situation that left little room for anyone like my previous self who wished to remain detached and friendly to all.

I returned to Cairo in 1969 to attend an international conference to celebrate the thousandth anniversary of the founding of the old city, finding it to be a drabber, drearier place than the one we had left. With its crumbling, sandbagged walls—to protect major buildings from possible Israeli bomb-blasts—the almost complete absence of foreign newspapers or other obvious links with the outside world, and the required visas and currency checks—first to get in, then to get out—the city seemed even more like a prison than it had been in 1962-63. Then, as I began to move into a much more political phase, I made visits to Kuwait starting in 1970 to attend a Palestinian student conference, with a return via Damascus where I visited the offices of the Popular Front for the Liberation of Palestine and Beirut. Even more dramatic was my return to Amman during the escalating violence that marked the beginnings of the fight to the death between armed Palestinians factions and the Jordanian army, which was almost immediately labeled "Black September."

Looking back on it now, I see this last experience as a particular personal turning point. In the short run, it put an end to a period of heady, if naïve, confidence during which I assumed I could go anywhere in the Middle East without great risk. My wife and I had just adopted a baby girl, and it was clearer to her than it was to me that I had no business putting myself in serious danger, given my new family obligations. Of almost equal importance was the highly political nature, not just of my visits to Kuwait and Amman, but also of the new friendships I had made there and my growing political reputation as a supporter of the progressive forces and their programs for radical political change.

So ended a phase of intellectual apprenticeship in which an initial interest in the Middle East was followed by a series of more or less random visits in the general interest of learning more about it, particularly its economic history. This was a period in which I used the conventional intellectual tools

Roger Owen and his friend Bob Sutcliffe on bridge across Barada River, Damascus, on way back from conference in Kuwait, 1971.

of the time, based largely on the grand theories of modernity, state building, and economic and political development. This was also a policy climate heavily shaped and supported by my father's work as a founding member of the United Nations Technical Assistance Board (UNTAB), with many of the people I stayed with in the Middle East in the 1960s friends of his and so-called UN Resident Representatives, there to facilitate the transfer of technical expertise.

I soon began to meet determined critics of the notion that the world was divided into "developed" and "underdeveloped" nations, with the latter destined to follow the exact paths laid down in the former, beginning with an accelerated process of industrialization. Prominent among them were also local critics of the neo-colonialist attitudes that were only flimsily concealed by this emphasis on the scientific and technical, including a mechanical adoption of certain key notions like "planning" and "raising the local savings ratio." And, at the margins, there were just a few voices condemning the essentializing view of Eastern peoples, summed up, as the Egyptian Marxist Anouar Abdel-Malek so trenchantly pointed out in 1963, by the notion of "Orientalism." Yet, it took people like me a whole decade to work all this out for ourselves and to begin to look for an alternative set of perspectives that would provide better accounts and better explanations for the major processes that gave rise to the modern world. Given the revolutionary temper of the times, and the fact that most of the Arab critics were leftists of one kind or another, it was more or less inevitable that this alternative should take the form of some type of Marxism, but it was one providentially divorced from Stalinism as a result of Khrushchev's 1956 "secret speech," itself given voice by the rise of the so-called New Left in both Europe and parts of the Middle East.

* * * * *

In what follows I propose to divide my story into three main sections. In the first I will give a country-by-country account of the three periods—1955-1956, 1962-1963, and 1967-1968—in which I was actually living in the region, first as a soldier in Cyprus, then as a graduate research student in Cairo, and finally in Lebanon as a new teacher at Oxford University, anxious both to improve my Arabic and to learn more about the politics of the region and how they had been affected by the comprehensive Israeli military victory during the June War of 1967. I will use the second section to provide a partial account of a number of much shorter visits to the countries not only at the eastern end of the Mediterranean but also in North Africa—Libya, Sudan, and Tunisia—and the Gulf—Kuwait, Bahrain, and the United Arab Emirates—together with a rehearsal of the thoughts I had then, and later, about their political and economic structures. Lastly, I will give a more general account of how I tried to understand the Middle East as a graduate student, teacher, and writer, followed by some more speculative thoughts on the creation of the field of modern Middle East studies—which I first encountered from 1960 onward while working with Albert Hourani at the Middle East Centre at St. Antony's College, Oxford—on the development of the field's particular organizational and intellectual practices, and on where they seem to me to have arrived at today.

In all this I rely largely on memory, supplemented when possible by the diaries I began to keep during my military service in Cyprus from 1954–1956, and which I then restarted during the latter part of my year in Egypt in 1962–1963. Kept originally as a form of talking to myself about each day's work when I had no one else to share it with, these later developed into something of a habit in which I simply jotted down ideas, opinions, and notes on each day's events whenever I felt the urge to do so, more often while traveling than at home in the United Kingdom. My diaries are, therefore, at once a check on memory and, at times, a record of its astonishing unreliability, both in terms of what actually happened, but also of the associated sights, sounds, and scenes that, when revisited or otherwise recovered, often seem so startlingly different to the way I remember them now.

As a scholar writing in the twenty-first century, I am also able to draw on the resources provided by Google and Wikipedia, not only with respect to facts, maps, and figures but also to the more fragmentary, yet often more vivid, memories of the songs heard at that time and the movies I watched. I have already mentioned the excitement produced by the echoes of the "Polovtsian Dances" in the Broadway musical, *Kismet*. There were many more to come.

2 LIVING IN CYPRUS, CAIRO, AND LEBANON

The foundation of my knowledge of the Middle East was laid down in the 1950s and 1960s. During this time, I spent the best part of three years first as a soldier in Cyprus in the Eastern Mediterranean, then as a graduate student in Cairo, and finally as a university teacher and researcher in Lebanon. It should go without saying that living in a place is different from visiting it as a traveler or a tourist. Living there means having your own abode and your own neighbors. It means going out to work every day. It means shopping for food and other necessities. It means being affected by the political temperature when listening to the local news or being out in the streets and squares. It means observing the passage of the seasons. And, in my case at least, it also meant being connected to the physical landscape, both in terms of being close to the earth in my army tent and in my Lebanese mountain village, and as a result of my academic interest in the annual harvest: of cotton in Egypt and the mulberry trees that provided the silkworms with their food in Lebanon.

Traveling is something else, and I did a lot of that too, using the close proximity of the countries at the eastern end of the Mediterranean to move quickly and easily from one to the other, as well as spending my honeymoon in Libya in 1960—although how I persuaded my wife, Ursula, to do this I cannot now remember. These were not only dramatic times but also highly significant years in which the region as a whole moved through the early post-colonial, post-independence period. The area had new structures of government to manage, new challenges to face in terms of economic and social development, and a whole variety of threats to each country's fledgling sovereignty to address. Not to mention the beginning of one of the most intractable international problems faced anywhere in the modern world: the wounds left by the division of the old state of Palestine between the new state of Israel and of Jordan and the consequent struggle between the Israelis, the Palestinians, and Israel's intransigent Arab neighbors.

Cyprus (1955–1956)

As a soldier in Cyprus, my political education involved a crash course in the anticolonial nationalism of the Enosis movement, which was determined to unite the island with mainland Greece. I also had to become familiar with its religious leadership by Archbishop Makarios III and the almost inevitable rise in ethnic tensions between the Greek-speaking, largely Christian majority and the minority of Muslim Turks. Egypt, as far as we could tell, was not only on the side of the Greeks but also said to be providing the anti-British EOKA guerillas with weapons. Hence my own presence on the island as part of an army signals unit; we provided a twenty-four-hour radar watch on all the shipping around its shores in the interest of preventing arms smuggling of the kind that had allowed the start of armed struggle in the spring of 1955.

As a result of the need to maintain regular contact with the seven radar batteries located around the island's shores, I spent long hours driving out from our base just outside the capital, Nicosia. I would head across the central plain and then along the coast or up into the mountains of the eastern panhandle past their Venetian castles, which had prevented invasion and occupation until they were overrun by the Ottoman Turks in the sixteenth century. As I generally carried a somewhat dry but useful guidebook with me on these trips—Rupert Guinis's Historic Cyprus (1936)—I soon got a sense of the separate layers of foreign occupation, ending with the British. These were manifest, for example, in the remains of the narrow-gauge military railway built by General Sir Garnet Wolseley in the late 1870s to connect Nicosia with the port of Famagusta; one of the old carriages had been put into new use as the premises of the washing and dry-cleaning establishment where we sent our uniforms, one colleague's shorts being returned with the letters E O K A across the back of the seat. Like Wolseley, I had made my own theatrical entrance through the sea gate of the Famagusta fortress at the head of a long line of one- and three-ton signals vehicles that had just disembarked from the deck of a British aircraft carrier. Given my youth, this experience, and my somewhat romantic nature it was easy to identify myself as one of the last in a line of military occupiers going back to the Hittites and the Assyrians, our presence just as transitory as theirs proved to be.

Moreover, when I left the island for my post-Christmas leave to Israel and Jordan, and then to Israel, Jordan, and Egypt after I was locally de-mobbed in May 1956, it was to states where the British presence had only recently been removed and where its influence was still being challenged. In Israel, the gallery of the squash court where I played with my local host still con-

The Cyprus Express at Nicosia Station in Cyprus, 1945. (Matson Photograph Collection, Library of Congress)

tained regimental files abandoned after the order given in February 1948 to be out by mid-May. In Jordan I ran straight into the anti-British "Templar" riots designed to prevent the young king from joining the British-sponsored Baghdad Pact. And in Egypt in June 1956 it was to see the streets full of Egyptian flags celebrating the evacuation of the last British troops from the Canal Zone. These perturbations even followed me to Oxford when I became an undergraduate in October 1956. The Suez Crisis erupted late that month as a result of the Anglo-French attempt to reverse President Gamal Abdel Nasser's nationalization of the Canal Company the previous June. No wonder that the British domestic politics of the stuffy Harold Macmillan era seemed so uninteresting beside all this excitement.

Egypt (1962–1963)

As a graduate student in economic history at Oxford in 1960, my interest in export sectors led me to propose a study of the role of cotton in the Egyptian economy, a subject I then narrowed down to the period from 1820—when the long-staple variety was first introduced—to 1914. This, in turn, involved a period of research in Egypt, including lessons in Arabic and work in various libraries and archives. To support ourselves, my wife and I both obtained jobs as teaching assistants at the American University; we were each obligated to give eight hours of lessons a week for the then princely sum of three thousand dollars a year.

We flew out via Athens in September 1962 and arrived, as almost all air travelers then did, at Cairo Airport after dark, with the heat of the day somewhat abated and the buzz of the never-sleeping city itself throbbing through the warm night air. A young man who was part of the famous Azzam family met us in a United Nations car. He drove us into town through the suburb

26

of Heliopolis and then across the Nile along an avenue that, though now renamed "The Twenty-Sixth of July" in honor of the Egyptian Revolution, was known then to most Egyptians by its prerevolutionary name: Fuad al-Awwal, or King Fuad the First.

Just before we reached our destination on the island of Zamalek, we passed an officers' club that I thought might have been the one in which the junior officers' first challenge had been made toward the soon-to-be-deposed monarch through the defeat of the king's candidate for president by the charismatic General Naguib. But when I tried to get young Azzam to confirm this, I was unable to get him to understand what I was saying. Looking back on it now, this may well have been the moment when I first learned a difficult lesson: while many Egyptians spoke English better than they understood it, for me—and I think most Europeans—it was the other way round; we were able to understand a foreign language more easily than we could formulate even the most simple of sentences. To make matters more complicated, the Arabic that I had just begun to learn was of the modern literary variety, designed to allow me to read government documents and the like, but of little use in asking questions, let alone ordinary conversation.

Ursula and I stayed the first few nights at the house of Osorio Tafal, the United Nations Resident Representative, a Spaniard who had escaped to Mexico after the Spanish Civil War. He and his staff were very helpful in finding us a duplex apartment located in a new building just across the street from their house, known as the Burg El-Zamalek, or Zamalek Tower. It cost only some forty US dollars a month and had the great advantage of being close to a number of shops, as well as close enough to the American University either to be able to walk or to take a short, cheap taxi ride. While consigning us to something of a foreign and expat ghetto, it had the great advantage of forcing us to cross the Nile every morning, and so to experience one of the wonders of the city: the bright blue freshness of a Cairo morning, with mist rising from the river and all the problems of the previous day seemingly wiped clean.

We soon established a daily routine. Ursula and I headed off to work together, spending our mornings teaching or sitting in the office that we shared with two other members of the English Language Institute. We returned home for a simple lunch of bread and soup that our maid prepared at about 2 p.m., after which we had an afternoon nap. Then we awakened for what was, in effect, a second start to the day. Often we went out for cocktails between 6 and 7 p.m. Other venues we frequented were the American University (where, in the New Year, Ursula had a singing and dancing role in the production of the musical *The Boy Friend*); the old opera house, a wonderfully decorated building put up to celebrate the opening of the Suez Canal in the late 1860s, to hear an Italian touring company perform *La Traviata* or *La Boheme*; a crowded cinema showing a low-budget and politically correct Egyptian film about Saladin or dancing peasants; or, perhaps one of the few restaurants like the Estoril that still served some semblance of French cooking, for dinner.

These were good days for foreigners in terms of cheap and easy living, but all the time there were reminders that we were living in an authoritarian and would-be socialist state. Legislation had just passed that nationalized or sequestrated large amounts of private property in land, banking, and commerce. Much of intellectual or cultural life was monitored or censored, the universities included, and the government did its best to control everything that crossed the country's borders, whether going in or out. Our phone was very obviously tapped—signaled by the whirring noise of an East German-made tape recorder when you picked up the hand piece. Our mail was examined, and we operated on the suspicion that members of the secret police, the *mukhabarat*—supposed to be identified by their black moustaches and shiny black shoes—were eavesdropping on our conversations in cafes like Groppis.

Much of the Nasser-period reforms I approved of, notably the transfer of wealth from rich to poor and the fact that no one was supposed to earn more than a flat five thousand Egyptian pounds a year, but I was well aware of the cost to friends who came from prominent ancien régime families like the

Roger and Ursula Owen at Cairo reception hosted by United Nations Permanent Representative Bibiano Osorio-Tafal, 1963.

Wahbas; they had lost much of their property, and Magdi Wahba had been more or less stripped of his citizenship and most of his rights. The same applied to his cousin, Boutros Boutros-Ghali, the future Secretary General of the United Nations. Like Magdi, his wife was Jewish, but in his case she also had close links to the Egyptian Jewish community in Israel. It took me a bit of time to realize that his somewhat clownish behavior on social occasions was an act designed to hide his true thoughts about the second stage of the Nasser revolution. Whereas Ursula and I had merely to be careful, for him it was literally a matter of life or a living death in the dreaded Torah prison.

One of the major symbols of the 1952 revolution was Tahrir Square (Maidan al-Tahrir), the site not only of the American University (AUC), housed in what was once an old tobacco factory at one end, but also the Foreign Office, the Arab League Building, the Hilton Hotel—where important guests of the regime were housed—and the Egyptian museum. Also present was the infamous Mugamma Tahrir, a Stalinist-looking building built in the late 1940s, which housed much of the control mechanisms of the government, including the offices responsible for issuing foreigners' residence visas and other necessary permissions. Fortunately for us, the American University employed a staff of "fixers" who went there on our behalf, leaving us with a Kafka-esque sense of a dusty bureaucratic labyrinth where people spent days trying to get their documents stamped in the company of other lost souls—such a change from the olden days when foreigners going there received special attention. Fortunately, I only had to visit the Mugamma once, long after its denizens had been mercilessly parodied in Adel Imam's famous 1992 film *al-irhab wal kebab*, or *Terrorism and Kebab*. But even for those like us who got our permits stamped there by the AUC fixer, it was still the subject of nervously funny stories of the kind that almost everyone likes to tell about its paper-shuffling bureaucrats and time-consuming procedures. So it came as something of a shock finally to learn that this dreadful building had actually been completed just before the 1952 revolution at the behest of the last of the civilian strongmen, Fuad Serag al-Din. This indicated that a civilian dictatorship might not have been so different from a military one, if that had been Egypt's alternative fate in the dark days after its humiliating military defeat in the 1948 Palestine War.

Once envisaged as the site of an annual festival in celebration of the Free Officers' July Revolution, Tahrir had now become something of a traffic nightmare of cars, buses, donkey carts, and other vehicles, whether we tried to negotiate it in a taxi or on foot. The only saving grace was that most of the cars themselves could not go very fast, being quite old and often in obvious need of repair. There were hardly any locally produced cars like the Nasr or the Ramses (obvious knockoffs of the Italian Fiat), and few people could afford the huge taxes levied on new ones from Europe. As I was later to find out, there had been one "festival" event to mark the first anniversary in 1953, where the crowd mobbed the column of tiny open cars carrying Abdel Nasser and his young colleagues. Thereafter, they only appeared on the balcony of the Abdeen Palace high above the people they ruled, a sinister development with dangerous authoritarian implications.

In the absence of political demonstrations of any kind, Tahrir had been given over to the occasional funeral procession of important persons, beginning in the small Omar Makram Mosque to one side and proceeding slowly across the square toward the cemeteries in the City of the Dead near the citadel. I saw two from a window of the American University, one for the distinguished intellectual Lutfi el-Sayed, the other for the ancien régime politician Mustapha Nahhas. Involving many tens of thousands of mourners, both seemed to worry the Nasser regime, which chose to see them, in part at least, as public protests against the new order.

The one mass demonstration the regime did allow, and no doubt did much to orchestrate, was an exuberant procession of largely youngish-looking men carrying Egyptian flags with four stars on them in anticipation of the short-lived acceptance of a political union between Egypt, Syria, Iraq, and Yemen, which was announced in April 1963. Only one time while I was in Egypt did some protesters burst out of Tahrir Square and into the university building itself, forcibly interrupting my class and ordering all my students to join them outside. It was a more annoying than frightening event and was marked with the rambunctious humor I associated with Egyptian working- and lower-middle-class youth. There was certainly no chance that the regime would allow matters to get out of hand as they had done on the famous Black Saturday in January 1952, in the last months of King Farouk's regime, when Muslim Brotherhood-led mobs burned down many of the hotels, cinemas, and smart shops of the modern city, leading to the deaths of fifty or so foreigners. One of the victims of Black Saturday, incidentally, was the elderly British economic statistician J. I. M. Craig, whose tables, calculations, and reports I was to rely on greatly when I came to try to reconstruct the role that cotton played in the Egyptian economy before the First World War.

For all the rest of our time in Cairo, the university remained an oasis of calm in an already overpopulated and always noisy city, with a quiet courtyard to sit in between classes, reading books and sipping tea with colleagues and friends.

Not that it did not have its own irritations, most of them stemming from a US-style of management by small-minded and unimaginative deans who had never lived abroad before. I kept a file of some of their more officious notes and memoranda,

Roger and Ursula Owen on camels behind Cairo pyramids, 1963.

the most lunatic being an injunction to post our own mail and not to give it to the *bawwabs* (doormen and university servants) who were allegedly removing the stamps we had put on the envelopes for resale to their own profit.

Founded by missionaries, the university had become a refuge for the sons and daughters of the old privileged classes—often with French and Greek names like Zoe and Calliope (Poppy). If they did not emigrate to the United States or France first, these young Egyptians were destined to work, not in government—for which their "foreign" degree went unrecognized—but in hotels and travel agencies where knowledge of some foreign language was at a premium. Or, in the case of the girls, to get married; all my male students were adamant that they did not want a working wife, particularly not one who showed any desire for an academic career. Many also had a very low opinion not only of Muslim Egyptians but of the land of Egypt itself, and so looked to Switzerland for their model of a romantic and, inevitably, mountainous scenery.

The American University also provided much of our social life, as well as guidance concerning some of my tentative forays in getting to know, as it were, ordinary Egyptians. Mostly Coptic Christians, our university colleagues were both well traveled and well aware that they suffered from certain disadvantages under the Nasser regime. Nevertheless, they were also well educated and well connected to people in the cultural and literary world. For example, it was through the good offices of a friend and fellow

31

teacher of English, Nadia Farag, that I had a short teatime meeting with the famous Egyptian author Taufiq al-Hakim in the Shepheard's Hotel, during which I asked a few cautious questions about his life. A small upright figure wearing a beret, suit, and tie, he seemed very French to me both in appearance and experience, as well as secure in his status as a major literary figure. Later he was to reveal how uncomfortable he felt during those Nasser years, particularly in the way his conscience had been lulled to sleep by his over-enthusiastic support for the revolution.

Contacts outside the university included a number of people connected in one way or another to the United Nations and the Egyptian economic development process, such as the experts employed at the Institute of National Planning. One was the director of the institute, a mathematician, who employed me briefly to teach a short weekly course on elementary economics in English to some of his student researchers. Another was the Danish economist Bent Hanson, who was on his way to becoming the scholar who best combined a sound theoretical approach with a desire to reconstruct significant aspects of Egypt's economic past. For example, he went to a huge amount of trouble to produce an index of prices and wages based on the daily information in the *Egyptian Gazette*, as a prelude to the larger and invaluable project of estimating the country's advance in national income since 1913.

Then, there was the task of getting to know something about Cairo and its history, about Egypt, and about the production of cotton. As far as Cairo was concerned, there was nothing like walking about it and trying to notice as much as possible about the architecture. This included the vital difference between the older buildings in the Fatimid city and the newer, nineteenth- and early-twentieth-century ones constructed when the city was extended toward the Nile, once its banks had been stabilized and European money began to pour in from the 1880s onward. Sometimes Ursula and I went by ourselves or with friends to places like Fishawi's, the old café hidden away on one of the narrow streets of the medieval part of Khan el-Khalili, the grand bazaar. At others we joined a US embassy tour conducted by a new friend, the historian of Islamic architecture George Scanlon, whose ability not just to explain the logic of mosque architecture and decoration but also to bring me to the beginnings of an understanding of what was then to me a totally foreign aesthetic of artistic balance, reticence, and subdued color was one of the greatest gifts I have ever received. Under his guidance, the high vaulted mosque of Sultan Hassan became as complex and holy a building as a Christian cathedral, and the gates of the old city a subtle combinations of eye-pleasing design and effective military architecture.

Outside Cairo, we visited the dark and forbidding Mokattam Hills where the *zabbaleen*, the Coptic rubbish-collectors, processed the city's garbage and where much of the city's stonework came from. We also saw the Barrage, just north of the city, where the Nile divided in two and where the first dam had been built to control its flow through the rich agricultural land of the desert. We then traveled further afield, by train to Alexandria to visit our friend Mahmoud Mazaloui, to the port of Suez where the British embassy had a rest house at the southern end of the Suez Canal, and then down the Nile to Luxor and the Valley of the Kings on our mid-year early spring break. This was followed by a cruise that took us from the elegant Cataract Hotel above Aswan, across Lake Nasser, to the soon-to-be-relocated temple of Abu Simbel, guarded by its huge statues of the Pharaoh Ramses II where we watched the sun's rays enter its central hall at dawn to illuminate almost as far as the smaller statues at its end. Like everyone who read anything about Egypt—in my case, James Henry Breasted's A *History of the Ancient Egyptians* (1908)—I knew about the importance of the waters of the slow-moving Nile and of the way the river divided the land of the living to the east from the kingdom of the dead toward the west. But it is one thing to encounter such information in books and quite another to be carried along by the river itself and to observe with never-ending excitement the juxtaposition of the dense hustle and bustle of agricultural life along its eastern bank and the largely desert emptiness on the other side.

Meanwhile, there was the need to attend to the main reason for my presence in Egypt: a study of the production and the economic influence of the world's strongest and silkiest cotton. This was partly a matter of libraries and archives. I worked my way through what books I could find in the French Institute—just across the street from the American University—the Egyptian Historical Institute, the Dar al-Kutub (Egypt's national library), the Library of the College of the Jesuit Fathers, and the offices of the Société d'Economie Politique. I also combed through those of Egypt's oldest surviving English-language newspaper, the *Egyptian Gazette*, while waiting for official permission to use the national archives housed in the Abdeen Palace. Sometimes I would strike gold in the form of a book or article that actually had the word "cotton" or "*coton*" or "*qutn*" (Arabic) in its title. But more usually it was a scrap of information or, perhaps, a tiny statistical table, printed on old paper that crumbled at the edges as I turned the pages. And, as this was long before photocopying of any kind, everything had to be painfully copied out by pen if allowed, by pencil if not, on the often sweat-soggy paper of my pad or notebook.

In any event, things did not greatly improve when I finally got permission to enter the Abdeen archives after seven months of waiting. The system of classifying documents in the card catalog had been changed a number of times, and I was not allowed to browse either in the stacks or among the cardboard boxes (known as "cartons") in the reading room itself, so I was never quite sure what I would find when I ordered each box and finally looked inside. And though what I was reading sometimes had some connection with the data to be found in Helen Rivlin's already published and indispensable *The Agricultural Policy of Muhammad Ali in Egypt* (1961), the legacy of her own research activity proved something of a mixed blessing. After a blistering attack on her as a US spy in the local press, both the archivists and state security were on the alert for anything fishy going on, if nothing more complicated than foreigners trying to make off with a few of the documents. Hence, any papers I took in and out were subject to search. Since I had no license to browse, it proved virtually impossible to follow through with any particular official correspondence or system of record-keeping from box to box.

Innocent of any knowledge of archival practice as I was, I could not even begin to formulate a set of ideas about why these archives had been created in the first place, or how they might relate to those in government offices elsewhere. Indeed, I only began to dimly understand these mechanisms many, many years later, after I had read Yoav DiCapua's pioneering study, *Gatekeepers of the Arab Past* (2009). I think that if I were to be honest with myself, my thesis (and then book) on cotton owed much more to material in the British archives, to books, to newspapers, and to privately owned material, than to the fragmentary pieces of documentation I found at the Abdeen.

Nevertheless, this did not mean, of course, that my academic year was at all wasted. For one thing, I profited a great deal from a passing remark made by my Oxford mentor, Albert Hourani, to the effect that Gabriel Baer's just-published and extremely useful work on *A History of Landownership in Modern Egypt* (1962) was dry enough to have been written by someone who had never been into a field or "seen a turnip." Determined to avoid the same accusation I made sure that I got into the countryside. I spent part of a day in a Delta village where I was able to examine the complex distribution system that brought water to the fields in smaller and smaller canals, to watch water-lifting devices like the wheel (*sakia*) and bucket on wooden swing (*shadouf*) at work, and to observe something of the pattern of mixed land use: one strip given over to the winter cereal crop (this was in the spring), one to clover (*birsim*) for the animals, and one was left fallow.

I also saw something of the division of labor; men used primitive wooden plows dragged by donkeys, and the children washed the village's water buffalos (*gamousas*) in a small stream.

Just as important were my two visits to the *ezba* (farm cultivated with service tenants) that my friend Mahmoud Manzaloui owned in the northern Delta province of Gharbia, especially since these visits were supplemented by a copy of the estate's account book (*kubi*) for 1907 to 1911, which he was generous to allow me to study. The Manzalouis had obtained their estate sometime in the mid-nineteenth century—Mahmoud always maintained this happened because one of his ancestors was a "boyfriend" of the ruler, Abbas I—and had developed it in the usual way: a combination of their own managerial and merchant skills and a Greek overseer (*nazir*) who looked after day-to-day affairs while they lived in nearby Alexandria. The money generated had been such that they were not only able to spend most of the First World War in London, but they had also been able to provide Mahmoud with a postgraduate education at Oxford, where he became a leading scholar of Medieval literature, before returning to teach in the English department at Alexandria University.

Mahmoud was a somewhat eccentric figure: hospitable, absent-minded, and subject to unusual accidents that circulated among his friends as "stories," like the time when he tried gamely to return a goose one of his students had attempted to give him as a bribe, or when all the exam papers he was correcting flew off his balcony into the street, pursued in a panic by Mahmoud and one of his house servants. His own stories were just as good, for example, the way in which one of his rakish uncles had married, successfully, two English chorus girls, Aunty Flora and Aunty Doris, each of whom owned fields on the family estate before they were expropriated by the land reform law of 1952. He was also deeply critical of the writer Lawrence Durrell's attempt to turn Alexandria, a place that Durrell had visited for only a few days during World War II, into a dream city of his own romantic imagination, in which foreigners led a gilded life that had nothing at all to do with the lived reality of its varied and mostly Arabic-speaking Egyptian population. Mahmoud was enormously helpful to me in my research.

The *ezba* building was a rather run-down and dusty place that had obviously seen better days before the two reform laws of 1952 and 1961 had stripped the estate of much of its land. But, as it existed very close to a small but densely populated group of shabby peasant houses, I got a good sense of the layout of this particular form of agricultural organization, developed in the late nineteenth century, in which the large landowners provided houses

35

for their service tenants in exchange for a certain amount of labor in their own fields. I remember in particular an aborted evening walk through a field of young cotton brought to an end by a peasant shouting to us that we should go back, apparently from an age-old suspicion that people out in the dark might be up to no good. Then there was Mahmoud, on a horse, throwing wrapped sweets to the little children during a Muslim feast, a reminder of the role once played by his more powerful landlord ancestors.

As for the *kubi*, it contained the day-to-day accounts of the estate, which had been written in Arabic and then pressed, while the ink was wet, onto an adjacent transparent page to allow at least one extra copy. This made it difficult to read in those parts where the ink had run in the heat. Nevertheless, it provided a wonderfully detailed example of estate practice, with its careful tabulation of how much land was allocated to cotton; how much was paid to those who planted it, weeded it, and finally picked it; how the raw cotton bolls were dried and cleaned; and how the crop was then sold to Alexandria merchants for export. It was this hands-on account of the actual production process that, I think, did much to provide the 1969 book of my doctoral thesis with some of its continued worth. Readers, it seems, responded well to the sense it gives of material life and of the effort put into producing something as basic, and yet necessary, as the fiber used to clothe much of the European and Middle Eastern world. It also provided me with the type of approach I was to use five years later, when I began to study the production of silk thread in neighboring Lebanon.

* * * * *

Ursula and I left Egypt in a state of some confusion. For one thing the Egyptian plane that was to take us on a scheduled morning flight to Beirut for a brief visit was suddenly withdrawn from service in order to take a party of Egyptian schoolteachers on an internal flight to Aswan, thus causing us to miss our own connecting flight from Beirut to Amman. For another, I was worried that my research notes might not get through the customs inspection on the way back to England, an eventuality I tried to guard against by giving them to a United Nations friend to take, since she had diplomatic immunity. Both provided important personal lessons for which I was later to thank the Middle East itself: the value of a kind of stoic patience in the face of the unexpected, and the capacity to think around possible problems on the assumption that, if you persevered long enough, there would always be an answer.

Lebanon (1967–1968)

We did not return to the Middle East until the autumn of 1967, and then under very changed circumstances. I was now a lecturer at Oxford, where I had been teaching Middle East economic history for three years, following my year in Cairo and another working in New York. More importantly, Israel's lightning and totally surprising victory in the June War had changed the whole regional landscape. We had been planning to spend 1967–1968 in the old city of Jerusalem as part of Albert Hourani's personal program for me to take a year off to improve my Arabic. Now, with East Jerusalem under Israeli military occupation, it seemed wiser to go somewhere else, and Lebanon seemed the obvious choice. Particularly since there was already an Arabic school for British diplomats—the Middle East Centre for Arabic Studies (MECAS)—in the village of Shemlan above Beirut, where I had been told that it was quite easy to find a private tutor. Though not an ideal decision, in that we were, inevitably, surrounded by too many English-speakers, it did prove to have a number of other advantages: notably those of living in a new and unfamiliar Arab country that, after the June War, had become a listening post for all the changes that were going on as the Arab world adjusted to the fact that Israel was not simply going to abandon the territories it conquered, as it had been forced to do in 1956–1957.

So it was that in August 1967 we set off in our newly bought Volkswagen to drive across Europe to the Port of Piraeus in Greece where we had the car lifted on board a boat bound for Beirut. It was an interesting ten days, the more so as we got to Yugoslavia and began to notice the changes that indicated that we were crossing the old dividing line between the West, as represented by the Austro-Hungarian Empire, and the East, as represented by the Ottoman invasion. The border was somewhere between Zagreb and Belgrade and was demonstrated, if only a little imprecisely, by the mosques, bullock carts, and the black baggy trousers of the men working in the fields. As we crossed the well-fortified border into Greece, we immediately had the sense of a country under the rule of a military junta—which had taken power the previous year and ruled over a proud people who, at least in their whispered conversations to us, felt deeply humiliated by this assault on their democracy. I remember with some vividness an evening spent around a fire in a campsite near Mount Athos listening drunkenly to a young man with a guitar singing and playing the banned songs by Mikis Theodorakis that had suddenly become the anthems of the popular opposition.

Arriving in Beirut on a bright summer morning, we disembarked with the car and drove with great caution through the chaotic streets of Beirut to Martyrs Square and then up the Damascus Road to Aley where we turned south to the village of Shemlan and its inviting Melcom Hotel. It was there, in the gardens of the hotel, that I corrected the proofs of my book on Egyptian cotton, which had somehow reached me in Lebanon; there that I started my Arabic lessons with Wadi Khouri, a Palestinian who lived in the neighboring town of Suq al-Gharb; and there that, with the help of a Shemlan-based American/Canadian couple, Peter and Erica Dodd, we went on to rent a small garden flat just below the main road known after its proprietress as Bayt Miladi. It all could not have been easier.

Shemlan turned out to have quite an interesting history for somewhere so small. It was the site of one of the country's largest silk factories, which had fallen into ruin after the dramatic collapse of the industry in the early 1930s. In the 1960s, it was also beginning to obtain global attention as a result of the Arabic school, which, so it was widely believed, was a place where several notorious British spies had been trained, most notably George Blake and Kim Philby. The village was also the home of Druze Shaykh Najib Alamuddin, the director of Lebanon's Middle East Airways and the father of a young woman, Layla Baalbaki, who had just written what was regarded as a scandalous novel about young love. Up the hill, and more or less out of sight, was the gated estate of the veteran Palestinian leader Ahmad Shukairi, the first chairman of the Palestine Liberation Organization (PLO) and then the most prominent member of the pre-Yasser Arafat PLO.

As I had also learned from Albert Hourani before leaving Oxford, Shemlan was the native home of the famous Lebanese/Arab historian Philip Hitti, the doyen of the first group of men who had laid the foundation of modern Middle East studies in the English-speaking world. I was to learn the first part of this story from one of the remaining Shemlani Hittis later in my stay. When he was nine or so, Philip had badly broken his arm when falling off a donkey; since he was no longer fit for agricultural work, his family sent him to the missionary school in neighboring Suq al-Gharb. From there he proceeded to the American University of Beirut (AUB) and then the United States, where he wrote his influential *History of the Arabs* (1937), probably the first book in English to focus on the Arabs as an important race in its own right and not simply as the carrier of Islam. Given the role of the largely Christian Lebanese Arabs in the nineteenth-century revival of Arabism, it was not surprising that, for Hitti, Shemlan could be identified as the center of the modern Arab world.

Last but not least, the village had a most spectacular view. Shemlan was set at eight-hundred meters above sea level, just below the crest of the first line of Lebanese hills. You could look down along the line of the coast south toward Saida to the slight curve of the Bay of Jounieh which took the eye in the direction of Tripoli to the north, with the five-thousand-meter mountain of Jabal Sanin just above. Directly down below lay not only Beirut but also its airport, where you could observe, regular as clockwork, the morning arrival and departure of Pan Am One, the only regular round-the-world air service. Flying in from Istanbul and departing for Cairo, Pan Am One was a daily reminder of the country's connections with the wider Middle East and beyond. Whether in the clear light of morning, the heat haze of the day, or at night when the lights of the plain began to twinkle below as the sun fell into the sea beyond, there was always something to observe, something to talk about, something to marvel upon.

* * * * *

Days quickly fell into a certain routine. On weekdays, I worked on my Arabic before the weekday journey to my teacher's house, the purchase of the local paper from Nimr's "Tiger" store in the village, and then, whenever possible and as a wonderful relief from having to become an anxious student again, a drink with Ursula and friends toward sundown on a terrace with a view of the sea. For a real treat, we had a simple supper consisting of a mezze, grilled chicken, and, in my case, a glass of whiskey at the Cliff House Restaurant, converted from an Ottoman-period structure built originally as a stable and rest stop where riders could change horses. Or, as an alternative, we took a quick drive down to Beirut, some forty minutes away, for dinner or a party with a growing circle of mostly expatriate friends. When they were not engaged in local gossip, these friends were a wonderful source of information not only about Lebanese politics but also the growing tensions in the Arab world as it digested its almost total defeat at the hands of the Israelis. For instance, in early 1968, news began to arrive of the rise of a new force: the freedom fighter or guerilla, with his AK-47 assault rival and *keffiyeh*, the very opposite of the uniformed soldier who had put up so futile a resistance to the Israeli blitzkrieg. Indeed, the city proved a wonderful listening post, full of journalists, oilmen, adventurers, and others, many just back from the nearby trouble spots in Jordan, Egypt, and elsewhere.

Weekends were often used to travel about the country, particularly when we had friends, or sometimes relatives, from home. Being so small, Lebanon was very easy to get about once you had mastered the local code of the road, which seemed to consist of doing exactly what you liked on the spur of the moment without any preliminary signal, whether it was a service taxi coming to a sudden stop to pick up a passenger or the three or four cars trying to overtake one another on a bend in the main Damascus road, hooting furiously on their horns as they raced along. I soon found it an exhilarating experience, a constant test of reflexes and good temper with so many daily surprises that I often wanted either to whoop in delight or simply to clap my hands in applause at the unbelievable maneuvers taking place in front of me. As someone in Lebanon soon advised me, you had to imagine that the young men were showing off their cars and their driving skills as they once would have done with a new horse.

Nevertheless, there was always a lurking sense of danger, spread among the foreign population by stories, some of them undoubtedly true, of drivers who had hit a child or a donkey by accident while passing through a crowded village street, only to be held for ransom by the enraged population. In one version, the driver was immediately incarcerated in Beirut's notorious underground prison for many years. For reasons unknown to me, one of the Druze villages we had to pass through on our way up and down to the coast had a particularly dangerous reputation for allegedly pushing children in the way of passing cars—whether true or not, these stories were alarming enough to ensure that we always proceeded through it with the most extreme caution.

Albert Hourani had made his own disturbing contribution to the lore surrounding the local hazards. He shared his brother's story of the necessity of the regular services of a local type of fixer, called a *simsar*, who would come to your aid if you were involved in an accident. According to legend, the *simsar* would throw a bottle of whiskey over the other driver in an effort to persuade the police that he was drunk. In the event, and only as a result of great good fortune, we entirely avoided accidents. Our only brush with the dangerous-looking traffic police was an occasion when I made my usual illegal left turn up to a mountain road just south of the airport and was stopped and interrogated, but not charged, by a stern-looking highway patrolman in jodhpurs and a peaked cap.

One place we never managed to visit was Damascus in Syria, the home, we were told, of enormous bargains; the old well-to-do families were forced to sell off their precious rugs, porcelain, and other treasures to meet the voracious tax demands of the newly installed radical wing of the Ba'th party. In spite of having obtained a one-day visa in Beirut, we were denied entry at the frontier by a border guard who seemed to find my name, or rather a vague Arabic equivalent, blacklisted in a set of enormous registers that looked to me as though they went back to Ottoman times. There could be no appeal. Later, I was to hear from one of my father's Arabic-speaking friends that he had seen a sign at one of the border crossings stating that, "The Ba'th

Arab party recognizes no frontiers"! And that when he pointed out the incongruity of this to one of the guards engaged in searching the luggage of some passing travelers, the latter replied, "Oh, that is just Arab talk."

Later in the year, more hazards arrived in the form first of rain, then of ice, snow, and a low mist that draped the higher elevations and made visibility difficult. As Ursula and I were to discover, Shemlan, as well as the towns we had to drive through to get to the main Beirut/Damascus highway, was exactly on the snow line, coating the roads into a sheet of ice when nighttime temperatures dropped, causing cars to slide into each other with alarming ease. As this was the only way down to the airport in the late winter, we developed a sense of entrapment, of being stuck up in our village with no way out. Meanwhile, the house itself, a summer place with only a wood-fired heater to warm it, often seemed colder inside than it was outside; we lay in bed at night with all our clothes on watching our breath steam out in front of us. Trying to wash ourselves—in a few inches of hot water at the bottom of a large tin tub we had brought up from Orozdibeks department store down in Beirut—was even worse. It was a great relief when someone like my father turned up in Lebanon on an official visit with a warm room, or, better still, a warm bathroom in the wonderful St. George Hotel down in Beirut by the sea.

All in all, we were made very much aware of the passage of the seasons, in a way very unlike living in Egypt. And if there were frustrating moments, as with the arrival of first rains in October, which turned the streets of Beirut into rivers of mud, there were also ones of pure sensuous delight, like the evening we returned from Tripoli along the coastal road and the setting sun turned the water in the separate salt pans along the beach into differently colored mirrors. Or the sparkling days of late February when the first spring flowers lit up the hillside terraces with specks of yellow and white and the air offered you a light perfumed embrace, producing what I described in my diary as a "wonderful feeling of physical well-being."

Lebanon also contained a number of men whom I used as my teachers about the country and its history. One was Professor Zeine Zeine who came to MECAS to give what I was later to learn was a standard explanation of Lebanese particularity in terms of the country's role as both a mountain refuge and a crossroads. He also described its many different sects and the problems created by its enlargement under the French Mandate, which added enough extra Sunni and Shi'i Muslim population to make the creation of a single national identity very difficult, the more so because of what he termed "outside interference" in their affairs. He, like many others at this time, was disappointed by the way the country's universities had failed

41

to produce a modern-minded collection of students; instead, the students thought only "with their hearts" in a political crisis.

Very much the same analysis was found in AUB Professor Kamal Salibi's influential article on the legacy of President Chehab, which had come out in *Middle Eastern Studies* in 1966. Salibi, though, differed in placing blame more squarely on the system by which the centralizing and modernizing activities of Chehab were put at risk by his retirement from office as required by the constitution in 1964 and his replacement by a less energetic successor, Charles Helou. Being a "modernizer" myself at the time, I was much taken with this argument, even while noticing some of the less attractive aspects of the Chehab regime, notably the extra power it had given to the members of the security services, the so-called "Deuxieme Bureau" to use its official French name, and the intense opposition that this had created even among what I regarded as my more "enlightened" Lebanese friends. What was also evident was the continued weakness of many of the country's most important institutions. Notable among these was the army, which was to prove no match for the local armed militias, and the banking system, which had been so severely rocked by the collapse of the huge Intra Bank in 1965 that the economy had still not recovered two years later—everywhere one could see many unfinished buildings whose owners had simply exhausted their existing lines of credit.

In other circumstances all this might have been a staple of dinner party conversation as well, but given a combination of Lebanon's particular geographical position and the fact that it had managed to stay out of the 1967 Middle East war—as it had been unable to do in 1948—the most heated topic of the day remained the new wounds created by the Israeli victory and, as we got into the spring of 1968, the possibility of an aggressive Palestinian response. This first appeared in Jordan, as I heard from my Arabic teacher on his return from a visit there in early March 1968 with his talk of armed "freedom fighters all over the place." Soon, in Beirut, posters showing photos of martyrs killed in action along the border with Israel began to appear tacked to the city's lampposts.

Not that I did not have opportunities to find out something of what was going on in the rest of the Middle East firsthand; I visited Jordan in December 1967 and April 1968, Cairo and Alexandria in February 1968, Baghdad in April, and Israel on the way back to the United Kingdom in May/June 1968. Some of this was little better than tourism. But, as I will relate when I come to my separate sections on each particular country later in the book, I was able to get some sense of the larger picture of those times simply by visiting the royal palace in Amman in December and talking to Crown Prince

Hassan about his June 1967 experience; or just being in Cairo shortly after Gamal Abdel Nasser's significant Helwan speech when, for the first time, he experienced serious heckling from the local military factory workers; or, later, of finding myself in a now forcibly united Jerusalem. In the case of Israel, I was able to compare what was being said and thought and felt in the Arab world to that on the Israeli side. So it was that when a message came from Albert Hourani in April of that same year asking me if I could add an analysis of Middle East politics to my next series of Oxford lectures, I felt both excited and reasonably well prepared.

More difficult to work out was my own personal position with respect to what I was studying when everything in the Middle East itself was so highly charged in terms of competing nationalism, competing ideologies, and competing political programs. Not only was I British and so open to charges of both postcolonial imperialism and being party to a Western colonialist alliance, but I was also still something of a "moderate" in the sense that I remained anxious for compromise and for negotiation at a time when reasonable dialogue was almost impossible. Looking back on it, I see that this was partly due to my own personality, partly due to my growing sense of myself as an academic historian, and partly due to a desire for a quiet life in which I did not have to take sides. So it was that I often found myself very much on the defensive in public, while adopting the private position of "a plague on both your houses." As I wrote in my diary, I observed both Arabs and Jews going on in "the same old way," using "the same arguments," and clearly uninterested in compromise of any sort.

Had I realized it at the time, this position was not too far from that adopted by Albert Hourani's brother Cecil, in the soon-to-be notorious article "The Moment of Truth," first published in Arabic in the Beirut newspaper *al-Nahar* and then reprinted in English in the November 1967 edition of *Encounter*. Not having read either version myself, I was witness only to the extreme anger that it aroused among many of my Beiruti friends, being taken as a call to renounce any hope of ever defeating Israel. That it was written by someone who was technically British and who had previously acted as an adviser to Habib Bourguiba of Tunisia, the most accommodating of the Arab leaders as far as the Israelis were concerned, only made matters worse, the more so after it had appeared in English in what was then regarded as an Anglo-American Cold War publication.

What I said at the time I now cannot remember, apart from having a general feeling that I, as a friend of the Houranis, was being accused of some sort of guilt by association. What I realize having finally read the article now is that, whatever its merits, Cecil's argument was no more likely to

43

have won significant intellectual support than a similar article would have done if it had appeared in the United Kingdom in the dark days of 1940 just after the fall of France. There are times of national crisis when, reasonable or unreasonable, it is simply impossible to accept defeat. While in this particular case, when the Arab regimes and the Arab armies were held in particular contempt, hopes were quickly transferred to the *fedayeen* and the men with the AK-47s.

One saving grace was that I was not called upon to engage in any instant punditry about contemporary trends and events during my Beirut year, writing no articles and not being asked my opinion by anyone but friends. This stood in marked contrast to the period just before Ursula and I had left the United Kingdom in the summer of 1967 when I had begun doing some interviews for the BBC from the small studio it then maintained in Beaumont Street in Oxford. These had started all right but then become spectacularly embarrassing during the opening of the June War when I had asserted that the Israelis could not possibly have destroyed nearly four hundred Arab aircraft in a few hours. This opinion was based on a childhood memory of the inaccurate figures provided for air battles during the Second World War; I had not noticed that almost all the planes that Israel had claimed were in fact bombed and strafed on the ground! My second assertion—that Israel would soon be forced to withdraw from the territories it had conquered as it had been in 1956–1957—proved equally unsound. Given the fast-moving and rather confused situation in the Middle East in the spring of 1968, I almost certainly got a great many things wrong in just the same way.

I should also note that, at about the same time, I was finding a form of personal satisfaction in terms of my growing interest in the hundred-year history of Lebanon's silk industry. This history was so evident all about me: from the terraces where the mulberry leaves were picked for the worms to feed on, to the remains of the factory where the workers, mostly women, dipped the cocoons in hot water pans so as to be able to unravel the single thread—up to nine hundred meters in length. They then twisted it together with others to form a stronger skein of raw silk for export to the weaving mills in France and elsewhere. At its peak, just before World War I, there were two hundred such factories in Lebanon, but their numbers dwindled away to a handful after 1945. As for the buildings themselves, very few remained when we got to Lebanon in 1967. The large sheds were sometimes put to other uses, like the short-lived chicken hatchery on the banks of the stream at Jisr al-Qadi, several miles south of Shemlan, or as potteries. For the rest, the only visible signs of this vanished craft consisted of the activities of the government-sponsored Silk Office in Beirut, established in 1956, with its valuable library. It also promoted an expensive line in silk ties and other such products for sale at the airport and the city's large hotels. It was only much later that members of the Asseily family reconstructed the family-owned factory in Bsous, near Aley, as both a museum and an educational center for those interested in remembering the central importance of silk in the country's social and economic past.

For me, it was the testimony to the past "industry" of Shemlan's inhabitants that was most striking—I use the word in the sense of the endless backbreaking work required to maintain the yellowy-brown walls that underpinned the terraces where the mulberry bushes had grown. As I took an evening walk below the village in March 1968, the five or six feet of earth along the terraces was covered in green grass full of yellow, white, and occasionally red flowers, along with some old olive trees and a few bare twigs of mulberry. Not surprisingly, there were places where the no-longer-tended walls had given way, as a result of the pressure from the winter rains, producing a muddy pile of stones below. All in all, as I wrote in my diary, it had a "deserted air," but I did not feel at all sad walking along a hillside upon which "so many feet, so many donkeys had trod." And it was with great pleasure that I encountered "an old man with pack-donkey," perhaps one of the few agriculturalists left, making his way down carefully to the next village. Except for that, I had the terraces to myself, feeling completely at home and at one with those who had gone before: a rare moment when past and present combined to produce a timeless sense of belonging to a world containing both the living and the dead, so very much larger than my single self.

Studying the production of silk in all its aspects proved a perfect complement to my previous study of the growth and processing of Egyptian cotton: each was subject to an unvarying annual agricultural cycle; each involved a chain of producers from peasant farmer to merchants, brokers, bankers, and exporters; each stood at the heart of a much larger economy on which its well-being depended. Now, much later, I also see that it must have been these same concerns, writ large, that account for the continuing popularity of my textbooks on the economic history of the Middle East: their combination of a concern with the nuts and bolts of how things were actually done and the political economy of the context in which this took place.

Nevertheless, for all the attractions of the simple life in Shemlan, Ursula and I found ourselves spending more and more time in Beirut, finally moving down there in April for our last month, taking a flat near the American University. This gave me the opportunity to extend my range of acquaintances and informants from the ones who had summerhouses either in the village or nearby to a wider set of academics, foreigners, and Lebanese. I would often meet these new contacts, who were usually connected with the American University, for lunch or a coffee in Faisal's Restaurant on Bliss Street just across from the university's main gate.

One such contact was Kamal Salibi who had been educated, in part, at London University and who talked to me about his own teachers. These included the influential Sir Hamilton Gibb, who employed what Salibi called the "Orientalist" paradigm—the idea that the organizing principle of nineteenth-century Middle Eastern history should be the impact of West on East. By way of personal illustration, Salibi described his own father's "shock and humiliation when he first wore Western clothes." He also spoke of the particular role of Beirut in this whole process: for example, the Sursock Cabaret, which was the first center of entertainment to introduce European artistes into Lebanon.

Other nicely talkative persons I met at this time, either at Faisal's or in their university offices, had Oxford connections: for instance, the Palestinian scholar Walid Khalidi, who was extremely well informed about local Lebanese politics, and the rather infamous Joe Malone, who was widely reputed to be a CIA agent. From Walid I heard stories about the recent parliamentary elections that had taken place just before we moved down to the city. One involved his wife, Rasha, congratulating the father of the Protestant candidate who had stood as part of Pierre Gemayel's list on the success of his son and being told that "he is not my son, he is the son of the nation." Walid added that being part of that list was an honor that had cost the father one hundred thousand Lebanese pounds. Also according to local gossip, this was fifty thousand Lebanese pounds more than the distinguished Greek Orthodox economist Paul Khlat had had to pay to get onto the list in Tripoli, which was in the gift of the Sunni Prime Minister, Rashid Karami.

Other political conversations I recorded in my diary concerned the local elation after the so-called "battle" of Karameh, which my Lebanese and Palestinian interlocutors presented as a significant victory; Palestinian guerrillas clashed with an Israeli force advancing into Jordan in March 1968, which lost two of its tanks in the process. As Jamil Abu-Nasser—a former Oxford graduate student—and I quickly agreed, this was a good example of the way the old rules were changing: though the Israelis were the real winners, they were wrong to suppose that this would be followed by the submission of their Palestinian or Jordanian adversaries, rather the reverse. I was later to make another version of the same point when Ursula and I visited Israel two months later, arguing to Jewish friends that Israel had now reached the limits of its expansion into Arab lands and, hence, that any significant movement from now on could only be in the form of a withdrawal.

Then there was the local university gossip and the talk about the dismissal of Sadik al-Azm from the philosophy department in 1967, allegedly by the veteran Lebanese politician and intellectual, Charles Malik, who disapproved of both his left-wing politics and his view on religion—Sadik was a free thinker. But Lebanon being Lebanon, the charges against Sadik were left deliberately vague so as not to embarrass the leader of the Sunni community to which Sadik, in theory, belonged. Additionally, he was immediately offered a good job outside Lebanon so as not to make a fuss.

We soon found ourselves in a widening circle of new friends and acquaintances. Many were what were then called "old Middle East hands" like the veteran journalist and writer, Tom Little, who kept popping back with reports from Cairo and other areas, and Tom Mullins, from Pittsburgh, who had spent two decades working in the oil fields of Saudi Arabia and other Gulf states; he was to become one of my best friends after I found him working at the Center for Middle Eastern Studies when I got to Harvard in 1993. Others were more colorful types like Bushrod Howard, a somewhat shady US lawyer working for the Yemeni royalists and the man responsible for a minor propaganda coup when he produced some extremely dodgy evidence to suggest to the British and the Americans that Soviet planes were being used to support the pro-Egyptian republican side. When I asked him what had led him to put on stunts of this kind, he replied that it had much to do with his boyhood reading of the adventure stories of G. A. Henty. Being something of a romantic myself, I just about believed him.

Lastly, there were a few interesting people whose social life straddled the English and Arabic-speaking worlds, like Majid Arslan, the tall, broad Druze politician dressed habitually in suit and tarbush. My favorite of all, however, was the charismatic Lebanese poet Yusuf al-Khal, who began his first conversation with me by asking why I was interested in the Middle East, with the rider that you can only study another culture "if you love it." My honest reply, that I only had a mixed bag of feelings about it— "affection, respect, friends, memories"—was clearly insufficient. So too was my pronunciation of Arabic. I remember him taking me severely to task for my lackluster rendering of the name of God in the conventional phrase *insha'allah*, or "God willing." Altogether he made a formidable impression on me, taking me seriously enough to provide stern, if ultimately helpful, criticism in such a way that he soon became one of a small band of Middle Easterners whose respect I really wanted and which I knew I would have to work very hard to earn. I remember how flattered I was when he said that I looked more like a poet than an economist. But looks, clearly, were not enough.

Roger Owen and Thomas Mullins at Center for Middle Eastern Studies, Harvard University, mid-1990s. (CMES Archives)

We left Beirut by boat on 24 May 1968, once again watching our car swinging uneasily from a crane as it was hoisted on board the ferry, and arrived in Famagusta harbor in Cyprus to spend several days touring the island before flying to Israel to visit friends in Jerusalem and Tel Aviv. Then we headed back to Cyprus for another boat that took us to Mersin in southern Turkey, via a short stop in Latakia on the Syrian coast where we were unable to land as Syria was refusing to issue visas to Britons. It was there, sitting on deck with nothing to do, that I wrote out Cavafy's famous poem, "Ithaka," in John Mavrogordato's 1951 translation with its injunction not to "hurry" your journey but to "ask that your way may be long... so that when you reach the island you are old / rich with all you have gained along the way." I found this to be a nice conceit. Then along the beautiful southern coast of Turkey on the winding road between the Taurus Mountains and the sea, and across to Istanbul and back through the Balkans to Belgrade and Vienna where we made a brief stop to see my father who was there on United Nations business. This time the division between the Eastern and Western worlds seemed to have moved north to somewhere on the Austrian border.

More to the point, parts of Europe seemed in an uproar from the few glimpses we saw of the television news in towns like Plovdiv and Zalena, with noisy crowds attacking the police, throwing up barricades, and disappearing in clouds of teargas. It was only when we finally returned to England, after four weeks of driving and camping, that we learned of the wholesale challenge to authority launched by the student revolutionaries in Paris and elsewhere, which soon also disturbed the peace in our own university world in Oxford and London. These events introduced me to a new breed of British and Middle Eastern leftists who were to become my friends, colleagues, and often my teachers, in my own efforts to make sense of the new world of post–June 1967 Arab politics that I had begun to encounter in Beirut, Baghdad, and Amman.

3   VISITING THE MIDDLE EAST

Living in Oxford, an hour or so journey by bus or car to Heathrow Airport, and then only another five hours to Cairo or Beirut, it was easy to visit the Middle East whenever there was a reason to do so and money was available to pay the fare. Indeed, sometimes it seemed too easy, lying in bed early on an Oxford morning, and knowing that, by the end of the day, I would be in Egypt or Lebanon, Israel or Jordan, arriving almost always at night, and finding myself in another world of sounds and smells; of the stamp of visas; of the search for a taxi—there was hardly ever a bus—or a waiting friend to take me to my hotel, my friend's apartment, or wherever I was to stay the first night. Being wakened by the morning light or some loud motor horn. Hurrying to open the curtains to a bright world of bustle and the business of getting to work. And then up early for the flight back some days—or a week or so—later, words ringing in my ears, full of new information, new experiences, and as often as not, new answers to new puzzles concerning the latest happenings, the latest political news, the latest gossip.

After a while I began to think of these visits as the equivalent of what the Arab tribesmen used to call "raids" in earlier centuries: a quick grab at something, a quick get-away with the loot. They were a necessary—but certainly not sufficient—way of keeping in touch. For instance, I stayed mostly in houses, hostels, or hotels in the capital cities, with only rare trips into the countryside. But they were exciting nevertheless, because of their intensity, the opportunity they gave me to notice change, and how easy it usually was to obtain a great deal of information in such a short space of time. The capitals of the Middle East were remarkable for their small elites of largely Western-educated individuals, most of whom knew one another, most of whom were willing to talk to foreigners, to pass you on from one to another, to provide networks of trust. There was also a subtle flattery involved. Talk was almost always about Egypt, Lebanon, or whatever country they came from, never about politics in England or the United States, and, just as I wanted to learn what they were thinking about local events, they seemed to want to find out what I was thinking too. This was the result, I now believe, of life in societies where, more than most other places, official political news was assumed to be both censored and not to be trusted. In such a context, facts, where they could be established as more or less true, were the coinage of the realm, eagerly passed from person to person as part of the endless puzzle of trying to work out what was really going on.

Fear, I realize, also had something to do with it. When I started to visit the Middle East in the 1950s and 1960s, the states were relatively new. Their societies were only recently wrenched from the predictable if often humiliating circumstances of the colonial period; they had only just plunged into the exhilarating but challenging process of postcolonial socio-economic and political experimentation, called for and then carried out by new men using a muddled rhetoric of nationalism, freedom, and necessary change. This was a primer in the heady, almost textbook sense of a set of theoretical ideas that informed local thinking about development, popular mobilization, and national planning. For those actually involved as observers or participants, it was something much more worryingly connected to their own well-being; the situation provided opportunities, challenges, and the ever-present possibility of danger to their wealth, their property, their children's futures, even to life itself, whether from sudden coups and revolutions or attack by some outside power. For me, and for others like me, there was always the road to the airport, whereas for them there was usually no option but to stick it out.

Then, when I went to live on the East Coast of the United States in 1993, the whole world of the Middle East seemed so much further away. Gone was the proximity of the huge Arab community in London, with someone who knew someone who was just back from somewhere to answer questions about the latest events. Middle Eastern visits took on the aspect of an expedition rather than a raid, to be planned well in advance, to be coordinated with stopovers in the United Kingdom to keep up with relatives and friends. Also, as it seemed to me when I contemplated what I had lost, from what was otherwise a wonderful move from a professional point of view, there was none of the well-remembered buzz when something important or exciting happened in the Middle East. Phones did not ring to make anxious inquiries about whether everyone you knew in that particular locale was all right. It is true, of course, that in the new world of the Internet and the twenty-four-hour news cycle, information got to the United States just as quickly as it got to Britain. Nonetheless, it took some time for me not to regret the personal touch that networks of Middle Eastern friends and colleagues once used to provide.

Change also came to the Arab states. Sometime after the political turmoil that marked the end of the 1970s, we began to realize that a number of regimes—in Egypt, in Syria, in Iraq—had been in power for quite a considerable time. Ergo, the period of regular coups and forced changes of government had more or less come to an end, with both the military and the street now well under presidential control. At one level, this made for an easier life when planning trips. At another, something was lost in terms of the sheer exuberance of political ideas and of the possibility of alternative political futures. "Do not talk to me of freedom, revolution, and Arab unity," said a young man to me in Khartoum in 1982, "these are just empty words that mean absolutely nothing at all."

It is against this historical backdrop that I would now like to tell the story of my many visits to the Arab countries east and south of the Mediterranean, beginning with Israel and Palestine, Egypt and Sudan, and going on to the rest of the countries of the Fertile Crescent and North Africa, and finally, the Gulf Arab states.

Part I. Israel and Palestine

1955–56

I first flew to Israel—from Cyprus in late December 1955 in the noisy, British European Airways Dakota—only seven and half years after the country's declaration of independence, an event about which I was only distantly aware from half-remembered news broadcasts and a jumble of, mostly British, resentments about the way it had taken place and the killings of British soldiers involved. And, although Tel Aviv seemed peaceful enough, there were instant signs of some of the fighting that had taken place in 1948–49.

My multi-person taxi, known as a *sharut*, passed the heavily contested stronghold of Kastel where the 1948 Arab siege of West Jerusalem was finally broken by Jewish forces and made its way up the narrow road to the divided city of Jerusalem. The edges of the wooded sides of the road were littered with remains of some of the trucks and half-track vehicles ambushed by their Arab Legion and Palestinian attackers, who had been intent on denying the Jewish part of the capital city food and weapons. Fighting had stopped with the provisional truce agreement negotiated in 1949, but, to all intents and purposes, both sides were still in a state of war.

My destination was the Tel Hai apartment of Hart Schaaf, an American friend and colleague of my father's, who was also what was called the "resident representative" of the United Nations Technical Assistance Board. He was living there with his English wife, Barbara, and their two highly intelligent but very boisterous and, as I thought, ill-disciplined boys. As Hart's job was to act both as a sort of UN ambassador as well as the conduit between the Israeli government and a number of international aid experts at work in the new state, he was well placed not only to show me around but also to teach me something about the planned development of that young country. This was a subject about which he was enormously enthusiastic and, so it seemed to me, very proud. All in all, I could not have had a nicer or better introduction.

West Jerusalem was not a very impressive place at the time. It mostly consisted of the western suburbs of the city, which had been largely built in the twentieth century and which were divided from the older, eastern part either by the Crusader-period wall or an open strip of land that only foreigners were allowed to cross at the famous Mandelbaum Gate. Nevertheless, as I was soon to discover with the help of Hart, it was full of interesting juxtapositions of the old and the new, the religious and the secular, as well as a highly varied population. This ranged from the ultra-Orthodox residents long-established in what seemed to me the medieval squalor of Mea Shearim to the out-and-out secularists who went to watch the national football league on the Sabbath and to buy sausages from the pork butcher housed underneath the Israeli parliament building.

Hart himself was an amused spectator of all this. He happily pointed out all the oddities and anomalies as he drove me around: Theodor Herzel's tomb, where we noted the space left for "future heroes" whom he said "they confidently expect"; the village where John the Baptist was supposed to have been born, now full of Russian immigrants; and the Montefiore Windmill, testimony to an interesting pre-Zionist movement to provide the economic support thought necessary to settle English Jews in the Holy Land in the 1840s. He seemed to take a particular delight in showing me the stones on the road used as barricades by the inhabitants of Mea Shearim to try to dissuade cars from passing their quarter on the Sabbath. I saw this for myself when we passed the same way again on my last Saturday in Jerusalem, when the Orthodox residents shouted insults at us.

More interest and excitement was to follow as we set out into the no-man's-land around the old British government house for a New Year's Eve party hosted by the Canadian General Burns, head of the United Nations Truce Supervisory Organization. The wide dome of the black night sky was scattered with twinkling stars as we left Israel to cross what had been Mandatory Palestine's one golf course toward the brightly lit building, with sounds of music growing louder as we approached. It was an extraordinary scene: few signs of other habitation, the Jordanian-occupied West Bank somewhere beyond, the peace, the sheer unexpectedness of it giving way to the impression of wandering into a time warp between different worlds, different times, perhaps out of time altogether.

General Burns—who seemed in something of a bad temper—met us at the door and then we moved on into a round, pillared ballroom full of well-dressed people. The soldiers, like Burns, were in full dress uniforms of blue and red, the men in suits, the women in long dresses. All were talking, dancing, and finally coming together at midnight, some to kiss, all to raise their champagne glasses to wish each other a good new year—1956, the year of the Middle East War, as it was later to turn out. All the while, a military band played "Old Lang Syne." I think it must have been all too much for me: the rich theater, my crumpled suit, belonging and not belonging, contemplating the distance from my army tent in Cyprus where colonialism still reigned, and the fact that I had never learned any of the dances, all jumbled together in a way that made me urgently want to return to the darkness outside, and on to bed.

Back in Israel, Hart and I were off early the next morning on a northern tour, driving down toward Tel Aviv and then up the narrow coastal plain to Nazareth with its smelly streets full of garbage and its open butcher shops full of raw meat. As we made our way to the ornate church that covered the cave of the Annunciation, our guide told us that the Holy Family, like almost everyone else, had lived in a tent, before retiring to a cave each winter. Later, we passed the Sea of Galilee and spent the night in a room at a kibbutz, Ayalet Ha-Shakhar, close to the green and biblical Mount of Beatitudes where Christ is said to have preached what I think of as his most influential sermon: the Sermon on the Mount. As at many other times, I found myself much closer to being a believer down in the streets of the old city of Jerusalem, or by a blue lake, or out in the bright air than in the over-decorated churches that have become Jesus's modern-day monument.

Staying in the kibbutz and being taken on a guided tour by its official spokesmen before we left the next morning gave me my first insight into the particular and practical form of hardworking communal living that some of the Israeli settlers developed, both a fortified outpost and an exercise in a new type of social organization. The grown-up inhabitants lived in two sparse rooms with a shower but without their children, who were quartered elsewhere. The families spent time together for only two hours a day. Meals were taken together as a group, and there were few public buildings, just

54

a library and a carpenter's shop, and no synagogue or religious meeting place, with religious observance regarded as old-fashioned. Management was left largely to experts, assisted by a general weekly meeting, which, we were told, only about half the members attended. Money was handed out once a year, and the kibbutzniks were allowed a tiny holiday once every two or three months. It was not a life for me, I thought. I was willing to acknowledge the guide's obvious pride in the kibbutz's insular life, but I also remember my increasingly sharp questions and my growing annoyance at his air of smugness and the sense he gave of having found "perfection."

We could find no local guide when we got to Acre the next morning. Its massive soft-stone, grey fortifications surrounded a city of old, and it seemed, decaying buildings connected by narrow streets full of dirt and smells, all so different from the neat white houses climbing up the steep slopes of Haifa only a mile or two away. What my diary does not record, and what I now cannot remember, is what meaning I gave, if any, to the obvious differences between modern Jewish/Israeli and Palestinian Arab life when we visited the Arab camel market at Be'er Sheba several days later. Knowing so little about the structure of their relationship, I certainly had no way of thinking about the one as in some way a consequence of the other. I had also become aware of pockets of Jewish life—the heavily-dressed families of Mea Shearim, the muddy chicken market of Ben Yehuda where blood-soaked rabbis supervised the ritual slaughter, which seemed just as squalid as those on the Palestinian-Arab side. As I began to read more, for example, of Arthur Koestler's *Thieves in the Night*, I had my first whiff of the unequal power relations involved, as well as the sheer racism that lay at the basis of many encounters between people coming from Europe and people who had long lived in the Middle East.

More generally, however, I was much under the influence of Richard Crossman's book *Palestine Mission*, with its very rosy view of the whole Zionist project—string quartets playing in the shade of olive trees and all. I was also becoming aware of the effect that Crossman was having in Israel, addressing a crowded meeting of five hundred just the day before, as I was told by Dean Alfred Bonne of the Hebrew University at a dinner just after we had returned from our northern trip. Also, at this stage, I was at least as interested in Palestine's long past, from biblical through Crusader times to the last imperial occupation by the British. Traces of this last presence were still to be seen in the red pillar boxes engraved with "GRVI" (George Rex, the Sixth) and in the spectators' gallery of the squash club where I played with Barbara Schaaf and which was full of abandoned files from the former British Officers' Club nearby. I was also reading Arthur Koestler's allegations of the anti-Jewish bias of many of the British colonial officers and the recent use of the castle at Acre to house and execute men the British regarded as Jewish terrorists.

My last trip with Hart Schaaf and his son Timmy took us to Be'er Sheba through fields full of green cereals planted just after the first winter rains in November and early December. The town itself had many of the characteristics I was now beginning to recognize: a small Palestinian Arab section near the animal market next to a "new," or Jewish, town with factories, a magnificent auditorium, and small box-like houses with plastered walls for the settlers. Then we headed further south into the Negev where we went to inspect a few houses built under the instruction of an enthusiastic UN expert using bricks made out of what was called "stabilized" earth: local soil compacted in wooden troughs. This simple and inexpensive process seemed like an immediate answer to the Third World housing problem. But Hart and the UN expert talked more about the practical problems, of "chipping" at the corners and whether such houses would stand up well to winter storms, and more generally, about the market in Israel formed by the small number of Jewish immigrants who had arrived in 1955—less than forty thousand.

We had lunch at Ashkelon by the sea near another development town built in a grid pattern with more "cheap, boxy houses" financed by money from South Africa. Then we paid a quick visit to the Weizmann Institute at Rehovot where we were told that they were willing to conduct free research "into anything." Then I went back home up to West Jerusalem.

I spent my last day in Israel on that trip—6 January 1956—reading more of Crossman's *Palestine Mission*, food shopping

Roger Owen being toasted at his 21st birthday party on the beach at Ashkelon, Israel.

with the family, and eating squash and lobster for dinner. Then, armed with a certificate to say that I was a "Christian," which I had obtained some days earlier, I crossed the small strip of land bristling with tank traps known as the Mandelbaum Gate. Someone from the Israeli side accompanied me with my suitcase to the middle; then he returned, and I had to wait for a similar person to appear from the Jordanian side to complete the process.

Fortunately, I was able to spend the rest of the day using a guide to take me to the Mount of Olives; the Garden of Gethsemane, where I could see the whole of the old city spread out in the sun; Bethlehem, where we had lunch; and finally, within Jerusalem, the Via Dolorosa, the Pool of Silwan, the narrow alleyway that was the Wailing Wall, and the Church of the Holy Sepulcher. Being on my own, with just one guide to guard me against beggars, postcard sellers, and warring priests, I had a bit of freedom to take in the sheer intensity of lived experience in mosque, church, and street. The marks of the chariot wheels and of the dice games of the Roman soldiers scratched in to the stones of the Via Dolorosa pulled me back nineteen centuries while the groups of contemporary pilgrims and tourists and shoppers pushed by.

There were other, more disturbing things in the air as well. As I had heard before leaving Israel, there might be "trouble"—a word that I got well used to during the EOKA uprising in Cyprus. The British General Templar had arrived in Jordan to try to persuade the young King Hussein to enter the British-sponsored, and obviously anti-Nasser, Baghdad Pact. I mentioned this to my guide on the day of my arrival only to be told that it was "nothing but a malicious Jewish rumor," yet I heard the dull thud of tear gas canisters that same night: rioting had begun in spite of the king's declaration of martial law. This was enough to prevent my proposed drive down to Jericho, always a hotbed of Palestinian opposition to the monarchy, although we did drive a few miles through streets that were beginning to fill up with stone-throwing boys and young men. I can well remember the driver's annoyance as some of the stones clanked against the bonnet of his shiny new American taxi and the fear among my fellow foreign hotel guests that the hotel itself might be subject to attack.

As it turned out, the road to the old Qalandia (Jerusalem) Airport was open—these days, it is completely destroyed by the imposition of a huge Israeli checkpoint at the same place. Although there was no sight of any planes on the ground at all, the handful of other passengers and I soon heard the approach of yet another Middle East Airlines DC-3, which taxied up to the tiny terminal and then flew us through the valleys of the southern Lebanese mountains to Beirut. I cannot remember if it was then, or on a similar

Passengers embarking/disembarking from plane at Qalandia, pre-1967.

bumpy flight some years later, that I was first comforted by the relaxed Australian voice of our pilot crackling over the intercom; it was conventional wisdom among the local foreign community in the Middle East that Australians could fly, and then land, their DC-3s safely in the most extreme of circumstances.

I returned to Israel only five months later, after I had myself demobilized from the army in May 1956. Once again, I flew to Lydda, or Lod, Airport, spent the night in a hotel in Tel Aviv, and took a *sharut* up to West Jerusalem. This time, however, I was in the company of a UN expert who, on hearing that I had just come from Cyprus, reminded me that many Israelis remembered it as the place they had been placed in internment camps after their ships had been intercepted by British warships on their way from Europe in the years before 1948.

My program was also much more relaxed. I spent much more time in the Schaafs' comfortable new house talking to their guests and either reading to myself or to the boys about the Crusaders' century-long rule over Jerusalem and a diminishing part of the coastal strip, before they were driven out by the armies of the Muslim hero Saladin. We all very much appreciated Steven Runciman's efforts in his three-volume *History of the Crusades* not only to paint a favorable picture of Saladin but also to demonstrate that, in many ways, he was a much more civilized and learned man than his rough and ready Crusader opponents, who were forced to adopt Eastern ways as the only passport to survival. There was none of the same level of interest and excitement in the book I had chosen as a birthday present from the famous Steimatzky's Bookshop, Richard Llewellyn's *Mr. Hamish Gleave*. This novel turned out to be a disappointingly unsatisfactory fictional exploration of the life of someone like one of the "Cambridge Spies," Burgess and McClain, who had defected to Moscow in 1951 after having been tipped off by a mysterious "Third Man," later revealed to be the sometime Middle Eastern journalist Kim Philby.

By living what was much more of a domestic life than I did in Cyprus, I learned much more about Israeli manners and customs as well. Much of it I found both irritating and somewhat comical: the people who pushed past you to get to a food counter first, with a spirited cry of "Shalom!" as they did so; the dithering of the many bad drivers coexisting with the very large number of driving schools (often with what seemed to be the learner's whole family gathered for an outing in the back seat); and the difficulty of obtaining pasteurized milk. Then there were the foreign experts whom I met at dinners and parties with their own take on what was wrong and how to make things work better.

During this trip, I went to a church that I was told had "formerly been used by 'Christian Arabs,'" who were no longer around. I drove down with Barbara Schaaf to Tel Aviv to play tennis on a May day so humid that I was soaked to the skin before making the elementary dietary mistake of asking for a glass of milk with my juicy beef steak for lunch. I was also taken for a birthday treat—my twenty-first—back to the beach at Ascalon; a photo shows me posing with Barbara above a cake with a number of candles. What the photo does not show was how crowded it was on the Sabbath, with swimmers herded into a very restricted bathing area by whistle-blowing lifeguards. Given the biblical associations of the site—the place where Samson pulled down the temple on the Philistines—it was about as memorable an entry into adulthood as I could possibly have imagined.

Equally memorable was my second visit with Hart to Mea Shearim, to a classroom where boys with small ringlets—sometimes singing, sometimes swaying back and forth—were studying the Talmud by way of puzzling out certain recondite problems reminiscent of those that occupied the infamous European "schoolmen:" "when X's donkey strays into Y's field, how much recompense should be paid for whatever wheat or barley the donkey has eaten?" The boys, used to the presence of curious visitors, seemed to find our presence a somewhat amusing diversion. For their part, the teachers were happy to provide us with the proper answers, for example, when a thief must pay back two times the value of a stolen oxen—when he has been given the beast to hold—as opposed to five times when he has not.

I crossed over to East Jerusalem once again by the Mandelbaum Gate on the day after my birthday. This time I had a letter from Cannon Jones of the Church of England, for which I had thanked him with a small donation. Then I headed straight to Qalandia Airport and was off by DC-3 to Amman—and on to Cairo.

May-June 1968

My second visit to Israel took place just after my year in Lebanon, which was in 1967–68, and involved going to Cyprus in order to get there. There were now a number of reasons for making the effort to return. First and foremost, not only had the country obviously changed a great deal in the last ten years but it had also grown much larger as a result of the occupation of the West Bank in the beginning of the June 1967 War. Now, too, my own Middle Eastern interests had expanded from those of an economic historian to a more general concern with the political economy of the different states of the region, as was required for my new Oxford teaching postition. And then there were the many new links I had formed with Israelis, some through the time they had spent at Oxford as graduate students and researchers, others through various networks like those of my father's branch of the United Nations.

My wife and I stayed our first two nights at the beautiful, but expensive, American Colony Hotel, before moving to more austere quarters in the guesthouse of the Anglican cathedral. Both represented aspects of Old Jerusalem as it was before its forcible reunification during the June War. The building housing the American Colony dated back to the early 1880s, and the Anglo-American family that still ran it, the Vesters, was well known to many British travelers of older generations than myself. We had drinks with Horatio Vester, the manager and owner, on our second evening. We sat at a table in the flagstone courtyard, fountain splashing, dark colors relieved by the occasional blue-white of the Turkish tiles—a peaceful backdrop to our conversation about mutual friends, as well as, more guardedly, about the changes brought by the Israeli victory. The guesthouse had a more melancholic aspect. It had been home to decades of religious pilgrims but now was more or less empty, and it was in an area that was almost completely deserted at night, leaving the streets to the occasional Israeli military patrol. Just as disconcerting was the way the evening air echoed with the hugely amplified sound of Tom Jones singing his latest hit from the nearby YMCA, its unhappy residents perhaps strangely comforted by the song's endless repetition of the question "Why, why, why, Delilah?"

Those in the eastern part of the city seemed in a state of obvious shock, which was exacerbated by worries about an uncertain future, in spite of the general assumption that the territories would soon be returned to Jordan. Our Israeli friends in the West, on the other hand, could not contain the excitement and sense of relief that they still felt after the unexpected victory and their sudden ability to get out to see what life was like on the other side of the old Green Line. I felt this in particular with an Oxford student friend, Moshe Maoz, who took us on a brief tour into the Jordan Valley toward Jericho. On the way, we stopped for lunch at an outdoor café where he addressed the proprietor, politely, in Palestinian Arabic. Perhaps I read too much into this exchange, but it seemed obvious to me, as a result of my Cyprus experience, that although both men were on their best behavior, there could be no hiding the fact that one represented the occupier and the other a people still reeling from shameful and humiliating defeat.

Having said that, I found Israeli Jerusalem full of people to talk seriously with about matters economic, from officials at the Bank of Israel such as the president, David Horowitz, and David Krevine, an economic reporter for the *Jerusalem Post*. Another set of meetings were in the new Knesset building to which we were taken by an Oxford friend, Gaby Cohen, a recently elected Member of the Knesset (MK) on Yigal Alon's Ahdut HaAvoda list. We saw the chamber itself, in session, and were introduced in one of the lounges to the courageous, charismatic, and piratical-bearded Uri Avneri, the editor of the mass circulation magazine *HaOlam HaZeh* ("The New Force") and a longtime political activist whose recently formed party, also called HaOlam HaZeh, had won one seat in the 1965 elections. Apart from Moshe Maoz, I also began to make contact with Arabic-speaking members of the Hebrew University's Department of Oriental Studies, notably Gabriel Baer, the doyen of modern Middle East studies in Israel, and the author of a book on landed property in Egypt that had been one of the most important sources for my Oxford DPhil thesis.

After a few days in Jerusalem, we had a sadly memorable journey down to Tel Aviv in a *sharut*; somewhere along the way, we heard the almost unbelievable news of Bobby Kennedy's assassination on a political trip to Los Angeles. We had to wait until we arrived to share it with a former St Antony's graduate student, Neville Mandel, now working for the British Foreign Office as one of its very few Hebrew speakers. We stayed in his apartment and accompanied him on his various official duties, to a trade fair and to an Israeli wine tasting during which I got quite drunk by neglecting to spit out each sip of what proved to be a somewhat over-sweet and generally insipid collection. Not an Israeli forte, or so it seemed to me.

Then, after other visits to the university and back to the port city of Jaffa, we took a plane back to Nicosia. Our car was parked there in a compound used by British members of the UN peacekeeping force monitoring the truce established after the latest outbreak of intra-communal violence. Later, as we drove back to the United Kingdom along the Turkish coast near Antakya, we were to see hordes of the invasion barges that would have brought Turkish troops to Cyprus if they had not been stooped by the firm diktat of US President Lyndon B. Johnson.

1970s

As far as I can recall, I made only one trip to Israel in the 1970s, a very short one to testify in a Jerusalem court on behalf of a relatively new British organization, the Council for the Advancement of Arab-British Understanding, or CAABU. CAABU had been founded in 1967 and was already the target of many verbal attacks in both Britain and Israel, one of the most pernicious being the charge that its leading officers were anti-Semitic. This had led, in turn, to a countersuit for libel against an Israeli publication. As a result, I was asked to testify as an "expert witness" that there was a huge difference between being anti-Zionist, which the editors certainly were, and anti-Semitic, which they were not.

I flew to Tel Aviv alone, where the Israeli defense lawyer hired by CAABU looked after me. This included taking me out to dinner in Jaffa in a restaurant on the ground floor of a house that had previously been the home of what must have been a relatively well-to-do Palestinian Arab family before the exodus of 1948–49. As I was soon to discover, the lawyer himself, a very nice man, knew very little about the real rights and wrongs of the Israeli-Palestinian conflict and saw nothing odd in dining in what had previously been someone's home. Whereas, for me, the place was clearly full of ghosts from the past, with the port-city of Jaffa more or less as it has been three decades or so before. This must have been my first experience of what later turned out to be a common phenomenon: different groups of people seeing and experiencing quite different landscapes and histories. Some might only see the present; others like me saw a place of absences and abandonment and the often difficult-to-discern traces of plowed-over villages.

The lawyer drove me to Jerusalem the next day to a courthouse just over the old division between East and West Jerusalem. I had the great advantage of being able to testify in English, sometimes using words and phrases that the defense attorney could not understand. Thinking about it afterward, it seemed to me that the lawyer and I had done quite well, not that it really mattered. Even though the judge was a man of the old school, having started off his career in Mandate times, he turned down CAABU's suit, and that was that.

1980s

My next visit to Israel was in August 1986 at the invitation of Ilan Pappé and others to attend a conference at Haifa University that had been organized to discuss Joan Peters' notorious new book, *From Time Immemorial: The Origins of the Arab-Jewish Conflict over Palestine* (1985). This had caused a huge political and academic stir due mainly to its argument that "there was little settled Arab population" in nineteenth-century Palestine and so no proper "Palestinian identity" to speak of. Peters herself had been invited, or so I was told, but chose not to show up, leaving no one to defend her views, which were almost universally condemned by those in attendance, mostly Israeli academics like Yehoshua Porath. Most of the papers presented at the conference were later published in the September 1987 edition of *Cathedra* 45. My own contribution was to point out the phenomenon that, whereas the bulk of the Palestinian population lived in the hill villages and towns north and south of Jerusalem in the early part of the nineteenth century, later, as the coastal plains became more secure, many agricultural workers came down to help work the land there, creating satellite villages in the process.

It was also an opportunity to visit old friends and to make new ones, as well as to learn more about the surrounding area and its history. One night, I was taken to dinner in a Druze village just to the south by Butrus Abu-Manneh, to a second dinner in Acre, and then to a pub on the Haifa seafront where the Middle East political historian P.J. Vatikiotis had earned money playing in a small band in his student days in 1942. It was on this trip that I was also introduced to the historical sociologist Gershon Shafir and liked the topic of his thesis so much that I was later able to get it published. His book became one of the first volumes in the new Cambridge University Press series on the Middle East that I was helping to edit with Albert Hourani and Michael Gilsenan, under the title *Land, Labor and the Origins of the Israeli-Palestinian Conflict: 1882-1914* (1989). Not only was its political economy approach greatly to my liking but it was also one of the first serious academic studies that put the whole issue of land and labor in the perspective of a particular type of settler colonialism, a concept then applied almost exclusively to the history of South Africa.

After the conference, Ilan Pappé drove me back to Tel Aviv and then took me to the university's Dayan Center—formerly the Shiloah Institute, established in 1959 but renamed in 1983—where Ilan was working as a student assistant. Though the center was run largely as a source of information about the Arab world for Israeli military intelligence, I knew little or nothing about this at the time. I was allowed to see only the rooms where information obtained from Arabic newspapers was copied laboriously onto thousands and thousands of index cards. Nor was I particularly suspicious of the fact that there seemed to be a file on me that the clerk in charge first said I could, and then said I could not, see. Nevertheless, it was clear that Ilan, as well as two of his Tel Aviv university colleagues, Israel Gershoni and Ehud Toledano, were of the straightforward opinion that such a center had no place within an academic setting.

However, if I try to think back to my own position at the time, this seemed no more than an obvious aspect of Israeli life where the links between military intelligence and academia were bound to be very close, just as they had been in the United Kingdom both during World War II and the Cold War that followed. It is only now, as I begin to compose these memoirs, that I have begun to wonder about the implications of this relationship in its Israeli setting. I particularly wonder this after reading Gil Eyal's wonderfully incisive *The Disenchantment of the Orient* (2006), with its detailed account of the creation of the center as a place where the academic and the official were united in a common effort to understand certain aspects of the contemporary Arab world. I also wonder about the way in which certain key members of the center—several of whom I met for lunch at Tel Aviv's Café Jardin at the invitation of a former San Antonio friend and colleague, Gabriel Cohen—may have been using me as a kind of academic cover to help legitimize historical work that drew upon classified material, some of it captured during the course of one of Israel's wars. But this is now. At the time it did not occur to me to question any of this; nor, I should note, did my Israeli friends make much of an effort to enlighten me.

My visit ended in Jerusalem with lunch at the Orient Palace Hotel and a tour of the city conducted by a former Oxford student, Thomas Friedman, now an enormously influential correspondent at the *New York Times*. With his help, I tried to orient myself in terms of the city as I had first seen it in 1955–56. But there had been so much building since then, and so many new spaces opened up between the old East and the old West that, apart from the Mount of Olives and the Dome of the Rock, I was more or less lost. Tom,

I was both surprised and interested to find out, was now the confidante of many of the most important people in Israel, all anxious, I supposed, to use him to pass on their point of view to his readers in the United States. He did not just meet people like the prime minister, Simon Peres, he was also invited to their homes, an astonishing ascent for someone who had been an Oxford student only a decade before. It was also, it seemed to me, a rich reward for the dangerous years he had spent in Beirut during the Lebanese Civil War. He had already won the first of his Pulitzer Prizes from his fine reporting on the Israeli involvement in the Sabra and Shatila Palestinian refugee camp massacres in 1982, information about which had come, in part, from another St Antony's graduate student, Stuart Cohen. He had quickly proved to be an excellent journalist with a wonderful eye for a story, and he certainly knew his US audience, even if his style was sometimes a bit too folksy for me—large issues were often reduced to encounters between stock characters like a Moshe and a Mohamed. I also have to admit to myself that if he really believed that Arab states consisted of no more than "Tribes with Flags," the title of one of his latest pieces, he had not taken in the thrust of much of what I had said in my Oxford lectures about the creation of modern political communities in the Middle East and the dangers of explaining everything in terms of age-old categories and rivalries.

Later that same day I had another memorable encounter: a dinner with friends of Clinton Bailey, whom I had met at the Haifa conference, at the marvelously situated residence of Lia van Leer, the director of the Jerusalem Cinematheque, in a small valley below the Jaffa Gate and close to the Montefiore Windmill. Clinton—he had chosen his new Israeli name from a street crossing in his hometown in Upstate New York—was an ethnographer with strong views about the Israeli treatment of the Bedouin of the Negev, whose tribal history he knew well. Another guest was the well-known Israeli writer and journalist Amos Elon, the author of *The Israelis: Founders and Sons* (1971), who I discovered shared the same views as I about the very unholy behavior of the inhabitants of the city around and above us.

1990s

My March 1992 visit owed its origin to a meeting I had with an Israeli journalist, Yona Hadari-Ramage, at a conference at the Centre for Post-Graduate Hebrew Studies at Yarnton Manor near Oxford where we discussed Ilan Troen and Noah Lucas's *Israel: The First Decade of Independence*. For reasons I never properly understood, she decided that I should be invited to her country to be the focus of an article to be published in the mass Tel Aviv daily *Yedioth Ahronoth*. Perhaps it was partly a piece of self-advertisement, partly hopes for a minor scoop. Cooperating in the project was Professor Ilan Troen of Ben-Gurion University—an expert in the links between professional architects, town planners, and others in the early Mandate period—who entertained me and showed me around.

The highlight of the visit was an evening party arranged so that I could meet General Ehud Barak, then chief of the general staff of the Israel army, a highly intelligent man known locally to my Israeli friends as "Mr. Brilliant." It was a somewhat uncomfortable occasion eased just a bit by a rare, for Israel, bottle of whiskey: a soldier's drink that, I was happy to note, Barak, in his military uniform, seemed to enjoy as much as I. Not really knowing what to say in these strange circumstances, I gave a short presentation about how Israeli historians seemed to have failed to notice the impact that the creation of the new state had on its Arab neighbors: a series of military coups in Syria and Egypt that immediately put a halt to the fledgling democracies in those countries, in Egypt's case multiparty elections going back as far as 1923. How much better, I somewhat naively suggested, if the victors in the war of 1948–49 could have behaved with greater magnanimity toward those defeated Arab states in which there was some chance that democracy might have been preserved.

This was then translated to Hebrew by Ilan Pappe, to which the general replied, "water under the bridge," or something to that effect. Then, he asked me a few questions in return, one about why Abdel Nasser had allowed the Egyptian press to attack Israel so much, followed by two interesting comments: that he did not know that there had been any sort of democracy in Egypt before 1952 and that, according to Professor Bernard Lewis, the Arabs were "unfit for democracy" anyway.

The rest of my trip was much less demanding. I had several meetings with Yona's friends and former students from a course she had given to Israeli fighter pilots, and then went on another tour of the country, from Metulla on the Lebanese border in the north to the beginnings of the Negev desert in the south. There was also time to meet friends and colleagues in Middle East studies at Tel Aviv and to give a lecture at Ben-Gurion University on "What Was the Colonial State?" Since it was March, the countryside from Tel Aviv up to the blue waters of the Sea of Galilee and beyond was carpeted in flowers. The high hill where Christ is said to have preached the Sermon on the Mount was a picturesque and wholly believable origin for the Christian world's basic ethical prescriptions: "Turn the other cheek" and "Do unto others as you would have them do you." As always, there were also other landscapes as well: the "Crusader" one as we passed by the site of the Battle of Hittin where the Christian army was annihilated by that of Saladin, the empty Palestinian one, and the Zionist one, from Degania Alef, the site of the first kibbutz, to the former outpost of Tel Hai with its memorial to Joseph Trumpeldor, a Zionist hero, killed there in a battle with armed local people in 1920.

Among the people I met through Yona was a former air force pilot, Jacob (Kobi) Richter, who had established a successful high-tech company in the Tel Aviv version of Silicon Valley. It made computer software that could read the countersignatures on the back of checks electronically, thus saving banks thousands of hours of manpower. As he told me, he was glad to be doing something more constructive than dropping bombs. He also told me that most of his workforce had received their technical training in the air force, and that he believed in a strong Israel, because the only way in which his fellow countrymen would make peace was if they were assured that they would not be in any danger if the deal went wrong.

Another was the famous Israel novelist Amos Oz, living in a cottage-like building in Arad on the northern edge of the Negev. We had a general chat about the huge variety of colorful people who had washed up in Jerusalem during World War II. He laughed a great deal at my description of what I had imagined the country looked like before I paid my first visit in December 1955, full of men playing string quartets under the olive trees of their kibbutzim.

A third memorable encounter was with Arif Abu-Rabieh, a Bedouin student studying agriculture at Ben-Gurion University who took me to lunch with his uncle, an elder of his tribe, where we sat on the floor eating chicken and vast amounts of rice. The Negev Bedouins, as I had also learned from Clinton Bailey some years before, were being progressively deprived of their tribal grazing land, fenced off with barbed wire while being confined to a smaller and smaller area in the hopes that they would settle down and roam no more. But it was one thing to hear about it and quite another to get a real sense of the anxiety experienced by people who felt such a severe threat to their traditional way of life.

Apart from Tel Hai, I also visited other places I had never been to before, including the southern end of the Dead Sea. Here, Ilan Troen showed me a potash company, which obtained not only the potash from the salt waters of the sea but bromine and magnesium as well. Another drive from Beersheba took me east to the grim grey hills at the southern end of the Dead Sea where Ilan Troen and I climbed up the near vertical path to the mountain redoubt of Masada. Myth has it that the last few fighters and their families involved in the Bar Kokhba Revolt against Roman rule had holed up there in a cave in the rocks, with the Roman soldiers, in their encampment on the flat top above, content to see them starve to death. No wonder it has such a powerful echo in Zionist mythology, the more so as the British Mandatory authorities had banned organized tours in 1943, which made the struggle to get there part of the struggle against the British in general. For many years, as well, numerous Israeli combat units took their oath at the top, a practice begun when Moshe Dayan was commander-in-chief.

Yet another trip took us south past the secret Israeli nuclear facility at Dimona—which no one was supposed to notice—and on to Ben-Gurion's old house in Sde Boker, which looked like a US suburban dwelling of the 1950s, with its huge GE refrigerator and clanking air-conditioning. Lastly, we went to see the nearby Desert Research Institute, a rather rundown-looking place with few signs to support the oft-stated claim that Israel could make "desert bloom." My final stop was back at Yona's apartment in Tel Aviv. From there, we ventured to the Museum of the Diaspora and to the famous Dizengoff Street for last-minute shopping and tea with an Israeli pilot, Yigal Shofart, who had been shot down by Egyptian antiaircraft fire on a mission over Helwan in 1968. Sadly for Yona, and to her obvious annoyance, my plane back to the United Kingdom the next morning left too early for her to give me that day's *Yedioth Ahronoth*, which had her account of my visit. I was only able to read about it much later when it had been translated into English by one of my Israeli friends.

May 2000

A brief visit to Israel at the end of a Harvard alumni Arabian cruise started with a somewhat lunatic moment when we landed at Aqaba at the top of the Red Sea. Because it was so early, we had to carry our own luggage across to the Israeli border outside Eilat where female officers were completely unprepared for any travelers coming from the East with passports full of Arab visas. Nor did they speak any language but Hebrew. All this took a bit of time to sort out before we got onto a plane at the small airfield and flew up the Rift Valley, passing the Dead Sea to our right, and into Ben-Gurion Airport before transferring to a flight to Frankfurt and back to the United States.

December 2007

Visits to the Middle East were rarer after I had moved to the United States, but one of the more memorable, and most uncomfortable, was just before Christmas in 2007. I was to give one of the two keynote speeches in a conference honoring Edward Said organized by the Palestinian Birzeit University in a small town close to Ramallah. I was met at Ben-Gurion Airport by two Palestinians driving a car with Israeli plates, as those with West Bank ones were prohibited for security reasons. We passed through the Qalandia checkpoint, a huge circle of roads made from the old airfield, tiny bits of its old runway now all that remained, and were finally taken to the almost empty Best Eastern Hotel, an experience made more dismal by the constant rain and cold outside. Then, after a brief pause, we set off to the university along a straight road covered with homemade speed bumps—designed to prevent cars speeding so fast that they endangered the lives of children and others forced to walk along its edges to keep out of the mud.

My speech was well received in both English and then an Arabic translation but was delivered to only a small audience of thirty-five to forty people. It was followed by the most desultory of receptions back at my hotel at which no alcohol could be served and the music was provided by the only two tapes the establishment seemed to possess: "Lara's Theme" from the film *Doctor Zhivago* and Ravel's "Pavane for a Dead Infanta." Fortunately, my Palestinian friend Salim Tamari lived close by, and I had been able to fortify myself with some of his whiskey. Just as fortuitously, the weather cleared the next day for a personal tour organized for me by the wonderfully knowledgeable Birzeit geographer Kamal Abdul Fattah. This trip took us northwest to Qalqilya, past the peaceful, flower-filled glade housing the tomb of Shaykh Qatrawani, a holy place if ever there was one, with a long view of the Mediterranean Sea. And then across a landscape dotted with olive trees accompanied by more and more Jewish settlements, some large, like Ariel with its thirty-five thousand to forty thousand inhabitants, others consisting simply of rows of white trailers staking out a piece of land for future extension. Not for the first time, I thought about the sheer beauty of this small piece of land, deserving of so much more than to be divided by a hideous concrete wall and the source of an undying struggle by the two warring sides.

I spent the second part of the day on a special tour of the Old City of Jerusalem guided by Albert Aghazarian, an Armenian Palestinian who taught at Birzeit. From the Jaffa Gate, he took an accompanying French travel journalist and me to a room in the house of a rich Palestinian friend of Edward Said. This room provided spectacular views of one of the most significant landscapes in the whole world: from the golden dome of the al-Aqsa Mosque on the old Temple Mount to the Mount of Olives where Jesus spent his last night while his disciples slept. Then we did something much more unusual: a tour of the old Armenian Quarter, including the magnificent Cathedral of St. James, which was built in two parts in the fifth and eleventh centuries and richly decorated with glazed blue/white porcelain tiles brought by Armenian craftsmen from Iznik from their potteries in Anatolia.

I spent my last evening in Ramallah with Salim Tamari dining with him at an Italian restaurant and learning something more about this unusual town. Ramallah was the political headquarters of the Palestinian administration and full of money from the European Union and other donors, but it could not expand in any direction but up toward the sky because it was almost entirely surrounded by Jewish settlements. The result was a community of wealthy bureaucrats with little work and only limited opportunities to spend their money other than in cafes and fancy boutiques. Perhaps by the same token, it was also the home of daring criminals with connections across the border into Israel. As an illustration, Salim told me a typical story of a car hired in Israel, stolen while its driver was being processed at the Qalandia checkpoint, and then offered back for money. This was easily done because the rental company could claim insurance if they could prove it was taken away in Jerusalem. Even more surprising, according to Salim, was the trade in advanced weaponry by criminal gangs active on both sides of what was supposed to be a secure border.

The next day, I was taken back through the Qalandia crossing and then via a roundabout route allocated to non-Israeli vehicles to Jerusalem's Jaffa Gate. There I was met by an Israeli friend who escorted me to the Van Leer Jerusalem Institute in the west of the city. Before an audience of many local friends and colleagues, I gave the same talk about Edward Said and his legacy that I had given at Birzeit—a new policy of mine, aimed at favoring neither side in the conflict. Just how and why I came to do this I am not now sure, but I think it may have been partly the result of moving to the United States while still retaining a strong British identity, and then using that same identity to negotiate the "tribal" feel of the Middle East where everyone I met seemed to belong to some community or another. In the case of this particular visit it may also have been a response to the brief British presence in Jerusalem, something that had left almost no traces inside the old walled city. There was, however, a remnant in the bar of the King David Hotel, once the headquarters of the occupation authority. The hotel had been partially blown up by Zionist terrorists in 1946 and was now nicely restored with photos of British soldiers leaving hastily that same year. Whether I liked it or not, by the mere fact of being born in 1935, I was not only a child of late Empire but also, for a brief period in Cyprus, one of its military servants. By the same token, too, the unhappy, and in some cases, disastrous

British period was now so far away in time that its memory had been so completely overshadowed by subsequent wars and local hatred. The British occupation was remembered, when it was remembered, as a time when the local elites learned English, obtained professional qualifications in London, lived in British or European-style houses and villas surrounded by gardens, and we were now free to exercise a powerful nostalgia for those more comfortable times.

Odd for me, but somehow not surprising, to find myself part of such a history and to be welcomed as a witness as well as some kind of emotional tourist, rather than a one-time colonial conqueror. So, under warm, sunny skies, I was able to spend a little time walking parts of West Jerusalem that either I had not seen before—like the many beautiful late Ottoman/early Mandate villas in Rehovia—or which had changed greatly since I had first been in those parts, when I had stayed with the Schaafs over fifty years ago. Flying out of Ben-Gurion Airport, having my passport stamped with an Israeli stamp that would prevent me from using it in many other Middle Eastern countries, I found myself thinking that my passage from outsider to insider to outsider again was finally complete.

Part II. Egypt and Sudan

Egypt: Frequent Returns

After the year I spent doing research in Cairo in 1962–63, I kept returning for a variety of reasons, sometimes on an almost annual basis, and watched the country go through the various stages of its modern history. I witnessed Egypt go from the defeated and somewhat paranoid Nasserism of the late 1960s, to Anwar Sadat's economic opening and his surprise visit to Jerusalem, to the elections of the early Mubarak years and the disappointed hopes that followed once he began the consolidation of his crony-dictatorship in the 1980s. Being a visitor, and sometimes little more than a tourist, I was, of course, only tangentially related to these events, although often sharing the hopes and anxieties of my friends in Cairo. Most of these belonged to the Nasserite Left—many of whom I had first gotten to know while they were living in a kind of political exile in the United Kingdom—and were fiercely critical of the threat that Sadat's innovations seemed to pose to the public sector. Though sometime in the late 1980s or early 1990s, they (and I) began to take a darker view of the great man as an autocrat and lifelong conspirator. Looking back on it now, I begin to think that if Abdel Nasser had lived into the 1970s, we might well have begun to be more critical of him much earlier. But, as it were, the senior ex-Nasserites seemed to think of themselves as a kind of government in exile.

THE ACADEMIC
1974: The Old Nasserites

I remember one particular evening in April 1974 when I had been invited to a party in Dokki, Cairo, which included the economist Ismail Sabri Abdullah, the former leftist Khalid Mohieddine, and the novelist Yusuf Idris, whom I had met first during a year he spent in Oxford and of whom I was particularly fond. There was a lot of anti-Sadat talk concerning his so-called "October" working paper—just issued to take advantage of his partial victory against Israel in the 1973 October war—in which he set out his ideas about the need to encourage foreign investment and to promote private sector enterprise for the first time. There was also talk about Sadat's invitation to Ismail Sabri to join his cabinet as minister of development, a move that was generally welcomed by all those present as a way of ensuring that there was someone in government who would be able to defend such a central tenet of the Nasser-period economic architecture. What I particularly liked about such occasions was the general camaraderie of a group of men and women who had mostly learned their Marxist ideas abroad, had often been jailed by the Nasser regime as communists, but who still agreed that its economic and social programs were worth fighting for.

The fact that I was made to feel so much at ease among them was an added bonus. I was later driven back through the warm spring air to my Nileside apartment in Yusuf Idris's large open American car, which had been bought, he said, with dollars from writing a film script, and of which he was inordinately proud. Feeling a great surge of love and affection, I gave him a great thank you hug as I said goodbye, one of the very few times I had ever done such a thing. It was the perfect end to one of the most purely "Egyptian" evenings of my life.

The late 1970s and early 1980s were also a time when secularists had to come to terms with the rise of political Islam as it invaded first the university campuses and then the whole political field. Most of them were deeply suspicious of it, but just a few, like my friend Adel Hussein, sought to use it. He calculated that the "masses," as Muslims, were more likely to be swayed by a kind of religious populism than by Marxism. He had acquired this view, as he told me in a hushed conversation by the Nile in 1974, from his study of the Euro-communist alliances in places like Italy, where Christian democrats and communists had proved able to work together on the basis of a shared program of social reforms so long as they were willing not to confront each other with their all-too-obvious ideological differences. Not that it worked in practice; I later learned that members of the "real" Muslim movements were quick to condemn Adel's apparent reconversion to their faith as simply opportunistic.

I also watched while other Nasserite friends whom I had gotten to know while there and who were living in exile in the United Kingdom made their own peace with the Sadat regime. Some found employment as journalists at papers like the new English-language *al-Ahram Weekly* or began to think of starting a new leftist political party. Others combined academic employment with the development of small vegetable and fruit gardens, often with a small house or hut for weekend living. This was an interesting return to the land by urban Egyptians who had previously shown no interest at all in rural life but who had decided to take advantage of a Sadat initiative allowing people to claim desert land for free, provided that they brought it into some sort of cultivation.

I remember in particular two of these new *ezbas*, as they began to be called, created by friends at Dashour, a cluster of villages on a canal that ran along the edge of the desert just south of Cairo. Though it was, as I described in my diary, a "beautiful and peaceful place" by day, it was also an important nighttime distribution point for illegal goods being imported from Sudan and Libya. To sleep there one was required, in the words of an old English nursery song about smugglers, "to watch the wall, my darling, as the gentlemen go by."

May 1983: The New Private Farms

For many reasons, Dashour was also a good place in which to observe Egypt's reconnection with the world economy. Sadat's liberalization had brought money pouring in from remittances from local peasants who had gone to work in the rich Arab oil states to the east and west. When I visited it in May 1983, there was already an acute shortage of labor. Although a nearby factory, for instance, made mud bricks using the topsoil from the local fields, there was no one to build with them. This, in turn, had encouraged the greater use of labor-saving machines, including water pumps imported from India, and often financed by the village co-op established during Nasser times. Also underway was the return of a form of sharecropping, banned under Abdel Nasser, as a way of working land that might otherwise have lain fallow. Meanwhile, the remaining peasant population, now grown much more well-to-do as a result of both remittances and a surge in day

73

wages, was able to purchase videos for their evening's entertainment from the private-sector village shop, which was also financed with loans from the same co-op.

One of my friends, Adel Bishai, had a special interest in agriculture, having worked for a while as an assistant to the Egyptian expert Said Marei when he was chief of the United Nation's Food and Agriculture Organization in Rome. Not only did he experiment with new ways of cultivation on his own Dashour plot, but he had also taken part in AUC experiments into reclaiming marginal land, planting clover (*birsim*) and sesame straight into the sand and then plowing in the clover in such a way that, after four to five years, the sand became much like regular soil. Like me, Adel knew that clover had long been an essential part of the system of crop rotation and that much would be lost if farmers were encouraged to drop it in favor of other crops. President Sadat had suggested just such a misguided strategy as part of what he had famously called his "war on donkeys." Those animals were mainly the eaters of clover and, he urged, should be replaced by small tractors. Given the fact that, for my friends, the president was regarded as little more than a "donkey" himself, a basic Egyptian insult, it is easy to understand the merriment with which this whole episode was discussed.

THE PERSONAL

Cairo remained a kind of second home, full of friends, as well as buildings, nooks and crannies, and old mosque complexes yet to be explored. I loved the way it was possible to walk between its two main worlds: the old walled Fatimid city built a thousand years before and the Westernized sector. This last part had been created in the mid-nineteenth century as a kind of Paris by the Nile and had a hub of avenues stretching out from various sml circles, as well as a cluster of nineteenth- and twentieth-century hotels. One of these was the Shepheard's, situated close to the Ezbekiya Gardens. Along the river, there was also the much newer Hilton, the Semiramis, and Marriott, the last of which was on the grounds of what was left of the Gezira Palace, originally constructed to house the French empress Eugenie when she came to the opening of the Suez Canal in 1869. I particularly loved the shabbiness of the palace's older buildings, which were often decorated in wrought-iron faux-Oriental style, their discolored facades and blocked-up entrances hiding bright treasures, if only you could find a way to get in.

Over time, I also took great pleasure from learning to "read" a building's age from its facade, from the rather barrack-like Greek-style of the

Mohammad Ali period to the more ornate buildings of his son, Ismail, and then the secular monuments of the twentieth century. These last included the great museums, the grand palaces of the notables, and the magnificent British Embassy masterminded by Lord Cromer with gardens that, until the construction of the riverside corniche in the mid-1950s—built, it was said, by the Free Officers as a deliberate affront to its imperial pretensions—ran right down to the Nile. Hidden behind trees and high walls, many of these buildings provided oases of a green calm against the bustle and noise and dirt of the streets outside.

An even more personal reason for visiting Cairo was that one of my British Foreign Office friends, Michael Weir, had been sent to Egypt as British ambassador. I hoped to take advantage of this opportunity to spend a day and night at the embassy in 1983 looking for signs of Lord Cromer, whose biography I had begun to think about writing. Those were the days when, under the influence of Michael Holroyd's marvelous biography of the poet Samuel Taylor Coleridge and of Lytton Strachey, it was de rigeur to follow your subjects around the world to get a feel for the places in which they had lived their working lives. Not that I was able to find any trace of the "spirit" of Cromer even in the room that I knew he had used as his study, but it did help me imagine his life a little better, as well as his isolation from the people of Egypt over whom he exercised his control. It also had the additional effect of making me an expert on the building itself. Later, in 2007, I was invited back to talk about it with a subsequent ambassadorial couple, the Plumleys—and I found myself shocked by the way they had allowed the beautiful green lawn on which so many glittering summer parties had been held to be invaded by a carpet of various unsightly weeds. It was here, if anywhere, that it was possible to imagine ghosts from the past, including that of the bumptious Ronald Storrs, who, as first secretary at the embassy just before the First World War, tried to kiss my friend Katie Antonius (then Katie Nimr) in the dark shadows down by the river, only to have his face slapped for his temerity.

For most of my visits to Cairo I stayed at least part of the time with my friend George Scanlon in his various residences. The first of these was the University of Chicago's houseboat, moored on the Giza side of the little Nile. Scanlon used it as the headquarters for his own excavations at Fustat, the site of the first city of Cairo but at the time a sort of ruined medieval rubbish-heap, soon to be built over by a new government that wished to use the land for an extension of a local public housing project. These were in many ways perfect days. We started with a communal breakfast and then proceeded in George's jeep to the site, some twenty minutes drive away, for

75

a morning of digging and uncovering with a team of white-robed workers known as Guftis; they were named after the village that had provided such services for a host of foreign archaeological teams for many decades. As I was to quickly learn, they provided a kind of chorus of comment on whatever was new and interesting to them, my own first approach being heralded by a rhythmic rendering of a song beginning "*Ya Habibi Salamah*," ("Oh my beloved Salamah") which then yielded to other, more ribald, interjections.

George Scanlon directing excavations at Fustat, Old Cairo, 1965.

The work was painstaking but rather dull, consisting as it did of the uncovering of a well-built sewage and drainage system that ran along the contours of an outcrop of rock with occasional square structures that must have been public baths or latrines. To George this all proved that the Islamic water engineers had been at least the equals of their Roman predecessors—high praise indeed, but the main excitement came from the fact that coins and other precious objects had sometimes slipped into the system, as well as shards of a lusterware almost as fine as Chinese porcelain and slivers of colored glass from vases and lamps.

We all broke off, if I remember, for lunch at about two in the afternoon, followed by a siesta and then an early evening drink at dusk to the rich melodies of Tomaso Albinoni's "Fugue" as the music turned our bit of the river into a huge cathedral of sound as it swelled slowly toward its almost impossible final crescendo. Then back, briefly, to the general cacophony of the Cairo night—the hum of radios, the staccato bleat of horns, the cries of dogs and cats, the call to prayer—before Albinoni again, or perhaps some Bach. We then had supper from the expedition's local cook, usually followed with George and me by a game or two of Scrabble. My large (as I liked to think) vocabulary was more than matched by his knowledge of sets of little two-, three-, and four-letter words from a number of different technical vocabularies—architectural, archaeological, etc.—almost all to be discovered in his battered dictionary, few of which I had ever heard before.

Nothing was ever quite the same again, although we tried as best we could to recover the atmosphere of those evenings in several others of his subsequent flats. These were along the Nile, in Garden City, or eventually in one of the smart ends of Zamalek near the old Yugoslav Embassy and the new Pub 26. By day, when neither of us was working, we would go on architectural walks. On these, we combined old favorites like the Mosque of Sultan Hassan or the fortified gates of the Fatimid city with my growing interest in the smaller and more refined mosques and fountains of the early Ottoman period, in which the Egyptian builders were learning to build in a style that, after a while, seemed to me almost Mozartian in the combination of its structure and decoration. As these treasures were often hidden away in quarters of the city that had fallen on hard times, like the interior of the once-bustling riverside port of Bulaq, they took on more of the character of an adventure. Indeed, we found ourselves sandwiched into a slow tide of sweaty humanity before scrambling into the relative quiet of a fenced-off graveyard or a saint's tomb.

All of this was George's great gift to me, along with the beginnings of the architect's "eye," that is, the vision needed to see the way that architects had been forced to improvise buildings on the unevenly shaped plots produced by the uneven development of urban land ownership, or had used new motifs to decorate different combinations of domes and minarets. But luckily for me, we were more equal when it came to our discoveries among the city's late-nineteenth- and early-twentieth-century buildings, such as the rich mélange of Bauhaus and other European modernist styles to be found in the once-fashionable quarter just outside the Fatimid city's northern gates.

Walking around like this over many years was part of the larger process of making the city mine, something of which I first became sharply aware when I sat with my friend Mona Anis in the new revolving restaurant constructed at the top of the elegant Nasser-period Cairo Tower, just across the Nile from Tahrir Square. There, as the dining room made its ever-so-slow 360-degree turn, we were able to identify many of the most significant places in both our Cairo lives: where we had each lived, where we had worked, where we had had our separate political and emotional adventures. These included a little garden of shrubbery at the base of the tower, where thirteen- or fourteen-year-old Mona had first kissed a young Russian visitor, as well as the place where, in the mid-1970s, I had tried desperately to be alone with an attractive former student of mine, Farida, only to be defeated by the prying eyes of those who thought it their duty to monitor the activities of

77

any young Egyptian female out without a chaperone with any foreign male. In my case, it was a sharp insight into the frustrations of anyone trying to court: a friend of Farida's family popped up in the restaurant in which we had just been eating, the taxi driver put on the dome light so that he could watch what was going on in the back, and voices hissed angrily out of the dark as we took our first tentative steps into the shadows.

THE UNIVERSITIES

There were other reasons to keep coming back to the city as well. One was the contact I tried to maintain with its universities, notably AUC, but also, on a few occasions, Cairo University. This school stood in its once-grand stone buildings across the river in Giza, Cairo, which for most foreigners was largely a world apart, given that the explosion of Egypt's university population under Abdel Nasser had led to a sharp decline in academic standards, in libraries, and in professors' abilities to organize international conferences. I had used this university catalog during the time I lived in Cairo in order to check its holdings of books related to the cultivation and processing of cotton. Later, I was very pleased to be invited to give a eulogy at a meeting held there to memorialize my dear friend Ahmed Abdulla, a student and social activist, who had worked himself so hard that he had finally collapsed of a heart attack while standing, unsuccessfully, for election to parliament in June 2006.

I had first met Ahmed in Oxford in 1974. He was sent to me, as so many other young political refugees were, by my London-based friend Fred Halliday. Fred acted as a kind of distribution point for those fleeing from imprisonment in the Middle East. In Ahmed's case, he had been a student militant in a very incendiary public protest against the Sadat government's apparent indecisiveness about confronting the Israeli occupation of the Sinai, which took place around a small pillar in Tahrir Square in 1972. I remember the quiet knock on my office door and the appearance of this tall, strikingly intense young man, looking every inch a leader, and the conversation we had about where he might continue his studies in the United Kingdom. Ultimately, he secured a place at Cambridge to study for a DPhil on the history of Egyptian student activism in the modern period.

Ahmed and I then met regularly in Oxford, London, and, later, North America. I also always made sure to look him up in Cairo, in spite of the perennial pre-Internet problem of contacting someone when the only postal address is of the most rudimentary "near to this," "behind the mosque" type. Being regarded as politically dangerous, he never managed to get a permanent academic job in Egypt. Instead, he made do as the no-doubt largely unpaid director of the al-Jeel Charitable Center for Youth and Social Studies, which he created in the mid-1990s to provide working children with a hot meal and a place to play at the end of the day. In addition, he did some freelance writing and lecturing abroad.

The shock of learning about his sudden death at the age of fifty-six encouraged me to try to make sure that his selfless life would be properly remembered by all those who knew and loved Egypt. I helped to organize a memorial session at the Boston meeting of the Middle East Studies Association (MESA) that November. To this event, I invited his daughter Bushra (meaning "good news" in Arabic)—then just becoming well known herself as a television presenter and popular singer—to come talk about her father. I also got her to talk about her career to an overcrowded meeting at the Center for Middle Eastern Studies, as well as to sing one of my favorite Egyptian popular songs of the prerevolutionary period, "*Ya Mustafa*," with its Levantine mixture of English, French, and Arabic. She stayed with a great admirer of her father, Michal Goldman, who also knew her mother, and spent a happy time shopping for clothes to take back to Cairo.

Ahmed's much-delayed Cairo University memorial was finally held the following May. Some fifty to sixty friends and relatives attended, including Bushra and her mother, Ebtehaj. I spoke for about forty minutes and was followed by spontaneous tributes and stories from Bushra and others. Then, just at the end, some al-Jeel children, mostly brightly dressed little girls, managed to get in to the hall; they were in a bus that had been held up, needlessly, by the university security police until almost too late. Their timid, loving, respectful but excited presence was just what the occasion demanded: a vivid reminder of the impact of this big-hearted, courageous man on the lives of so many.

I was to learn more about his remarkable life at a small dinner in the Nile Hilton with Ebtehaj, Bushra, and an Egyptian friend of theirs who had been living in Germany for the past twenty-five years. They told me of the way he had tried to organize the impoverished, illegal Egyptian migrant workers he had found working in the outdoor cafes of London's Hyde Park, when Ebtehaj and he were living in England, and how he had invited the poor of Cambridge to Sunday meals of rice and beans cooked by his long-suffering wife. They also told me of the time he took two suitcases of vodka and caviar that he had bought in Moscow as presents for the students attending a conference in Havana, only to fly into a rage when he found that it had all been stolen. "He loved life," someone said, and this was certainly true in every possible respect.

I met Bushra again on my last evening in Cairo. She drove me (rather unsteadily) in her new car to a fashionable new restaurant, BoraBora, on the Little Nile. This restaurant happened to be just across from the place where the University of Chicago archaeologists' houseboat had been moored when I slept in it in 1965. It had the great advantage for her that it was dark inside; she was less likely to be recognized by a fancy crowd that included a set of handsome young men in silk suits who looked to me like well-paid professional football players. Bushra talked about her newfound fame as a television personality—and how she was looking forward to the transition from a popular singer who wrote many of her own songs to being the female love interest in films and television serials like the Egyptian version of America's *ER*. It had all began, she said, because her adoring father had insisted that she take ballet lessons when she was little and later encouraged her not to go straight to university but to start her career as an entertainer first.

ACADEMIC CONFERENCES

Another reason for visiting Egypt was the invitations I received to academic conferences like the one to mark the city's millennium in 1969 or the one to celebrate the work of Egypt's first major chronicler, historian Abd al-Rahman al-Jabarti, which was organized by the Egyptian Historical Society in 1974. It was at the first that I met Gamal Abdel Nasser for the one and only time. I watched him enter the front door of the Arab League building, where we had been taken to be introduced to him: a charismatic figure with an electric smile who seemed both taller and more alive than all around him. Then I lined up to be presented to him with a brief handshake and a few muttered words of welcome.

There were more personal reasons for visiting Egypt, such as the desire to show the new warden of my Oxford college, Raymond Carr, a staunch supporter of Israel, something of the Arab side of the great Middle Eastern divide in 1971. This was a somewhat antic event as we flew unsteadily via Paris—where we touched down in the grass besides the runway—in one of the United Arab Airways' Russian Ilyushins, which had been lent to it after most of its planes had been destroyed in the 1967 war. When we arrived, we were given an official welcome that involved, in Raymond's case, being interviewed on television in the honeymoon suite of the new Shepheard's Hotel (his own room being considered insignificantly grand), followed by a visit to the National Stud, given his love of riding horses.

It was on this same occasion, and in the company of one of my Oxford colleagues, the poet and literary critic Mustafa Badawi, that I attended one of the most important cultural events in Cairo's weekly calendar: the open house held on Saturday mornings at the *al-Ahram* newspaper's new headquarters. Many of the country's leading intellectual and literary figures came together at this function to discuss the week's news. Sadly, on the day I was there, the great writer Naguib Mahfouz, a usual attendee, was absent, but I did meet many figures well known to me by name or previous acquaintance, as well as aspiring young writers like the influential critic, Sabry Hafez.

The American Unicersity in Cairo (AUC) and the Economic and Business History Research Centre (EBHRC)

My two other major reasons for visiting Cairo were my association with the American University, which I first got to know when my wife and I taught in its English Language Institute in 1962–63 and then through my role in a Middle East history records project that, over time, turned into an economic and business history research project focusing mainly on Egypt. It was the AUC that brought me to Cairo in April 1975 to give a "distinguished lecture" on the management of agricultural land in nineteenth-century Egypt. This trip included, as one of its perks, a drive with George Scanlon through the eastern part of the Delta to spend a night in Port Said, which had still not recovered from its battering in the 1967 war and the subsequent closure of the Suez Canal, and so was almost empty of tourists. Indeed, so desperate had things become that we were offered—as one of the traditional "filthy pictures" so often mentioned in travelers' tales—an obviously pre-World War I woman with her breasts just visible above her corset, as well as what the seller told us was a bottle of "Spanish Fly" of an equally venerable-looking vintage. The next day we drove south along the western side of the canal to Ismailia where there were all kinds of signs welcoming President Sadat's ceremonial reopening of the canal two months or so later. We then headed back to Cairo along the Ismailia Canal, which had been built to provide the county between Cairo and the Suez Canal with water from the Nile.

As for the business history project, this was an idea I had for many years. I received some money from the British Social Science Research Council (SSRC) in the early 1970s to create a list of the whereabouts of the records of British firms that had traded with or established enterprises like banks in various parts of the Middle East in the modern period. Yet it was not until 2004 that I got the opportunity to take the project further and explore Egyptian and other local firms. I did this in association with a small group of other economic historians interested in the region, including Cairo University's Abdel-Aziz Ezzel-Arab, a man with invaluable business experience through his previous job as a banker in the Gulf.

We started off with an opening ceremony at the American University's Tahrir Square campus at which the three American friends who were at the core of the initiative—Bob Tignor, Bob Vitalis, and Ellis Goldberg—and I spoke under two headings, "Why Economic History of the Middle East? Why Business History of Egypt?" and "Middle East Studies in the United States." This was followed by a session with invited Egyptian guests, most of who had been personally involved with the Nasserite attempt to develop heavy industry, such as economists Aziz Sidki (who had studied at Harvard in the early 1950s) and Abel-Aziz Hegazy. There was also a memorable excursion to Alexandria by train with Abdel-Aziz and five of his students who were working on the business history project, looking out at the newly plowed fields in the Delta and then walking around the city itself. This trip included a visit to the newly reopened Alexandria Library, an extravagant effort supported by Suzanne Mubarak to revive the glories of the famous library of antiquity in a new and electronic guise.

Three years later, in May and June 2007, I returned to Cairo twice to do two things. One was to attend another mini-conference to discuss Egyptian business history, as well as to sign an agreement of cooperation between Harvard University and the AUC as far as the collection of records was concerned. This was a rare privilege, since usually only the president of Harvard was allowed to sign on behalf of the whole university. There was a little ceremony with a pleasing speech of introduction by my former student Khaled Fahmy, who talked about my long-term engagement with Egypt, after which I spoke on my own time in Cairo in the 1960s. Finally, we had dinner with some of the former Egyptian politicians who were associated with the project, including Aziz Sidki and Fuad Sultan.

The second visit, a month later, I received an honorary AUC degree along with Mohammad Hassanein Heikal, the former editor of the official newspaper, *al-Ahram*, and close confidant of President Gamal Abdel Nasser. As an extra perk, I got to visit Heikal beforehand at his farm at the southern end of al-Minufiya Province where he grew melons, a property which, according to a well-informed Egyptian friend, he had originally purchased at a knock-down price from its hastily departing Lebanese owner.

Heikal, it seemed, had wanted to get some sense of the kind of person I was before the degree ceremony itself, at which both of us were to make speeches. And so it was that we sat drinking tea in his study, which was lined with some of the books he had collected about Egypt, the Middle East, and the international system, as well as photographs showing him meeting an enormous range of presidents and other world statesmen. Not sure of how the conversation would go, I had not prepared anything very much either to ask or to say. But as it soon dawned on me that I was being presented with the rare opportunity to ask any questions I liked, I decided, on the spur of the moment, to find out more about Abdel Nasser's personal habits when it came to entertaining foreign guests, starting with his use of the Nile Hilton Hotel, opened in 1958, to put up foreign heads of state or to invite visiting foreigners to dine, there being no presidential palace or other residence available for the purpose.

At first, according to Heikel, neither Abdel Nasser nor any of his military colleagues had had any idea of what to do in the evenings other than hang out together to smoke, talk, and tell jokes. But under Heikal's guidance, so I was led to infer, Abdel Nasser soon learned to feel comfortable around a dinner table with ladies present, such as when he met the visiting British Prime Minister Sir Anthony Eden at the British Embassy. Eden, he said, had set out to charm, speaking the Arabic he had learned at Cambridge University complete with flourishes and proverbs, and then giving the game away by the obvious way he showed off his skills by translating the conversation into English for his wife. As for the Hilton, Heikal told me he kept a permanent room there in which he stayed while his wife and family were away in Alexandria to escape the summer heat. He liked it so much that, on one occasion, he misguidedly suggested that Abdel Nasser himself come and take a look, only to regret it when the whole hotel was closed down by security for the visit. After that, Abdel Nasser's fondness for the place had to be exhibited at a distance, so he sent tanks to guard it any time there were anti-US demonstrations, just in case some fanatics tried to burn it down in an excess of zeal.

Heikal's other, and more important role, was to guide Abdel Nasser and his colleagues through some of the intricacies of foreign relations, explaining how the international system worked and how it might best be manipulated to Egypt's advantage. Being slightly older than they were, a social class or so above most of them, and with some experience of the outside world through his journalism, it is possible to imagine him playing a role as an important Nasser adviser that has yet to be properly understood. No doubt some of it can be found in his own personal papers, which he was then guarding in jealous fashion while, at the same time, worrying somewhat obsessively where they could be safely stored after his death. One option he mentioned was at AUC, where they would be properly cataloged and looked after—protected, he hoped, from any official attempt by the Egyptian government to squirrel them away in either the national or the presidential archives.

The AUC commencement exercise proved to be in two parts. One was at the university where I had a short talk followed by a grand dinner at the Garden City Sheraton Hotel. There I sat at a table with the president of the university, the British ambassador and his wife, Heikal, and an Egyptian judge, and close to another table that had some of my invited guests, including friends and former students. The other was at the huge Cairo convention center on the airport road where degrees were awarded to the graduating students after Heikal had given the major address.

It was during this visit, too, that I gave a long interview to the new Egyptian newspaper *al-Masry al-Youm* and in which I described what I took to be the unsatisfactory nature of Mubarak's one-man rule. I used language with which I tried to walk a fine line between making critical points that I knew Egyptians were unlikely to be able to make themselves and not saying anything that would get the journalist herself in trouble. What worried me most in the days that followed, however, was a light aside I had made to the effect that, given Egypt's system of presidents for life, the country was lucky when someone like President Sadat was suddenly removed from office before his time. What pleases me now is the sense I managed to give of the country as being in some kind of prerevolutionary condition.

I was back in Cairo again for business history meetings in 2008 and 2009. These had now begun to assume something of a regular form. Programs included general discussions of major topics like policies of industrialization under Abdel Nasser, led by some of the architects of such policies, such as Aziz Sidki; presentations by the young scholars associated with the initiative; and meetings with important business constituencies like men from the Egyptian Businessmen's Association. This was an invaluable opportunity to meet, and then to question, some of the key players involved in masterminding policies and projects that I knew only from books. Also there was the charming Adel Gazarin, a pioneer of the local automobile industry who had been charged by the Nasser regime in the 1950s to assist in the establishment of a new factory for the production of military trucks. The first of these models, the "Nasr," came off the assembly lines in 1962.

Of perhaps even more significance was the ability to watch these key players talking among themselves. I observed how, on occasions, members of the same cabinet seem to have known very little about what their ministerial colleagues were up to. They would collectively, and spontaneously, start to work out the history of basic attempts at policy realignment of which most, at the time, had been only dimly aware. This was especially true, it seems, of the role of Yusuf Wali, Sadat's longtime minister of agriculture. He had been secretly tasked to institute a program of privatization, beginning with the state-owned hotels where labor unions either did not exist or were not strong enough to protest, as they would certainly have done in the big factories.

I was unable to attend the final set of meetings in 2010. This was at first due to the huge disruptions caused to air travel by the dense smoke from the erupting Icelandic volcano in May of that year, then, due to my desire not to get stuck in Cairo and miss the celebrations that had been planned back in Cambridge for my seventy-fifth birthday. A year later, in 2011, Abdel-Aziz parted with the project, leaving all the records of meetings and of the many interviews he and his staff had conducted with senior businessmen, politicians, and managers, as well as all the accumulated material referring to the running of individual enterprises to the Economic and Business History Research Center established at the new desert campus of AUC.

Thinking back over the six years of the project, I see it not only as a valuable learning experience in institution building but also the best chance that I ever had to make a permanent contribution to Middle Eastern economic history. First, there was the collection of business records and of finding them a permanent home where they could be accessible for a wide variety of different uses—intellectual, pedagogical, and as a magnet for foreign researchers. Secondly, our work was inspirational in the sense of encouraging business groups and others to value the practice of recordkeeping.

Of course, none of this could have been achieved without Abdel-Aziz's superb organizational and motivational skills. He created a team of dedicated young researchers, persuading businessmen and others to talk and to share their experiences, and he carried his own university along with him on the back of his own obvious enthusiasm. Although my American colleagues and I assisted in a number of smaller ways, for instance, by helping him to persuade his fellow Egyptians that it was a worthwhile enterprise, it was very much his show. It was he who really got the whole thing going, he who arranged the annual meetings, and he, above all, who created that vital sense of trust between the participants without which they would have been unwilling either to share their knowledge or, more importantly, to come to see the significance of what we were all doing for a proper understanding of their own country's history.

Not the least of the project's virtues is the way it can be used to throw light on one aspect of the late-Mubarak period: the tremendous growth of what was coming to be called crony-capitalism. That this had always been a feature of Egyptian political life was reasonably well known. Often the phenomenon appeared with particular clarity at times of turmoil and discontent, as in the late 1940s when it became part of the wider accusations of corruption and moral wrongdoing. Nevertheless, it is my belief that the cronyism to be found in the late Mubarak period was of a somewhat different character in terms of the huge sums of money involved—now billions rather than millions of dollars—as well as the role it played in the uprisings that overthrew the regime. On the one hand, you had stories of the president rubbing one of the cronies' large stomachs and asking him "How much money is in there?" On the other hand, there was the public sense that it was all getting worse and that if his son, Gamal, were to succeed him, there would be kleptocracy for ever.

Though the subject was impossible to research in Egypt before 2011, for obvious reasons, I was fortunate enough to gain some small insight into what was going on during a visit I paid to Washington, DC, in 2003. My old friend and student Jon Alterman of the Center for Strategic and International Studies had set up a meeting with the young Gamal Mubarak and his entourage. Even then, the Mubarak family's strategy to acquaint Gamal with the Washington power establishment was obvious. Fortunately for me, the master of ceremonies was none other than my old acquaintance Osama El-Baz, someone whom I had met at the British Embassy in Cairo many years before and whom I had always regarded as the cleverest man in Egypt. A pity, I thought, that he was applying his great intelligence to such a task. But interestingly enough, after I had caught his eye on one occasion he winked back as though to say, "We both know it is all a bit of a game."

Of even greater interest was the opportunity to learn much about the men who were close to the young Mubarak, who had helped him streamline his father's National Democratic Party and who would, if he managed to succeed his father, have played an enormously significant role in Egypt's political economy. One of these was the steel magnate and Member of Parliament, Ahmed Ezz. Also present was the second "cleverest" man, Youssef Boutros-Ghali, then minister of trade and later to become known in the British press as the "fugitive financier" after he fled to London to avoid charges of corruption in 2011.

Looking again through the internal transcript of this event, I am impressed by the obvious signs that Gamal had received a lot of good coaching from his team. He knew something of the questions that were going to be asked and repeated over and over again in the same formula—Egypt's economic and political progress toward openness and free trade—and he never went beyond the agreed script. It was exactly what, I suppose, those in Washington who harbored doubts about the country's future policy wanted to hear. But by 2003, this message flew in the face of what was known even then concerning the great sell-off of state property in the early 1990s; as in Margaret Thatcher's Britain, this had merely converted public monopolies into private ones like Ezz's steel business, at great cost to everyone else.

Sudan, *2002*

Sudan was part of my Oxford life long before my one visit to Khartoum in January 1982. Both the university and the city were full of people and institutions with Sudanese connections, often going back into the colonial period well before the country became independent in 1956. Notable among these was the professor of social anthropology, Edward Evans-Pritchard, who had first visited there in the early 1920s, followed by a number of his students. Sudanese visiting professors and students had been coming to St. Antony's since the 1950s, often meeting for long evenings of drinks and noisy discussion at one of the local pubs such as the Horse and Jockey, a peripatetic venue that in the late 1970s was just opposite the college. Then, over time, I also got to know friends and colleagues at Hull and Durham universities who were connected with Sudan. Of these, far and away the most important was Talal Asad, who had done his anthropological field-work there in the 1960s and who arranged for the first meetings of what we called the "Hull Group:" British-based critics of the prevailing orthodoxy in Middle East and Oriental studies.

One of the most regular and the most convivial of the St Antony's Sudanese visitors was Mohammad Omar Bashir ("MOB" to everyone), who was both anxious to improve links between Oxford and the new institute of Asian and African studies he had just helped to found at the University of Khartoum and unusually adept at finding money to finance exchange visits. It was he who invited me to spend two weeks in Sudan in January 1982, with all expenses paid by the British Council. It was a not-to-be-missed opportunity to extend my range of experience of the Arab world. Although, when I set out for Khartoum on New Year's Day, I had no idea of the "troubles" ahead as a result of the increases that had just been announced in the price of petrol and sugar—two of the most important staples in such a large country now connected more by its rivers than its roads and containing inhabitants with a particularly sweet tooth, judging by the vast amounts of sugar they poured into each large glass of green tea.

I took the daily overnight British European Airways (BEA) flight that arrived at three in the morning, to find no one at Khartoum Airport to meet me due to some mix-up over dates. This was worrying, but soon turned out to be something of a blessing in disguise. Not knowing where I was supposed to stay, the taxi driver took me to the Nile Hilton Hotel. There, I was given a room from which, waking up in the bright light of day just a few hours later, I was able to look down at the quite extraordinary and completely unexpected sight of the confluence of the White and the Blue Nile just below my window. The two Niles—one rising in the mountains of Ethiopia, the other sliding slowly out of the lake region of East Africa—melded silently together to form the one great river whose steady, predictable presence had informed my life in Egypt. This, in a landscape that also contained the dome of the Mahdi's bright, light-green tomb shining away in the old city of Omdurman to the left and the gleaming white North Korean-built Friendship Hotel on Khartoum North to the right. The grand panorama held extraordinary beauty and was also a view of much of what had come together to create modern Sudan.

MOB soon came to collect me from the hotel for a walk along the Nile and to fill me in on some of the country's many difficulties under the increasingly authoritarian regime of President Gafar Nimeiri. Economically, Sudan was more or less bankrupt and unable to service its international debt. Politically, the recent elections had only attracted an apathetic turnout of some twenty percent, and their other noteworthy feature was the success of the Muslim Brotherhood candidates standing for constituencies in Greater Khartoum. MOB's own cynical response was that, "If elections changed anything, they would make them illegal." The next day he helped me move to the university guesthouse near the Koba prison. He then took me to his institute at the University of Khartoum where I met his co-director, Yusuf Fadil Hassan, along with William Abu-Zaid, an attractive man with movie-star looks who was also the vice chancellor of the recently opened southern University of Juba, many miles up the Blue Nile.

Then followed a number of happy days in which I was introduced to many of MOB's other colleagues and friends at lunches, dinners, and parties. I was also able to meet up with my Oxford friends Thomas and Dorothy Hodgkin, who had their own long connection with Sudan and who had recently taken to wintering there in a house belonging to the veteran nationalist Babiker Bedri, because the dry warm air was better for Thomas's chronic emphysema than the damp atmosphere of the Thames Valley. One fixed social point was when friends got together to watch the best entertainment on Sudan's one television channel: the evening showing of the Egyptian serial *Nour My Brother*. The program was remarkable for its dramatic plot, its over-the-top acting—what Thomas and I learned to recognize as Egypt's "*Matbouli*" style, so named after one of its leading male exponents—and the fact that it was made in modern studios in Dubai with props and furniture then quite unknown to middle-class Cairene life, ostentatious white leather sofas and all. Indeed it was so popular that, as I was told by a visiting British female development expert, honeymooners at Wad Medani's Honeymoon Hotel were said to get up from the beds in which they had spent the day to dress up for the occasion. They would then sit in front of the hotel's communal television set, women on one side of the room, men on other, and once the program was over they would quickly return to bed with trays of food.

Parties were everywhere but sometimes difficult to find. They often took place in brand new establishments out on Khartoum's dusty desert fringe where there were no roads, no numbers, just white-walled compounds with doors that opened to reveal a garden full of men in snowy white gowns and turbans drinking whiskey, and going in turns into the desert to pee. It was on such friendly and jovial occasions that I learned the local gossip as well as much about local lore and practices and political and university problems. I think of William Abu-Zaid, getting more and more drunk and complaining about the way that the University of Juba's first graduation had been mostly ignored in the north—including by President Nimeiri—even though it included the award of an honorary doctorate to the imprisoned Nelson Mandela, the first by any African university. Or of listening to Shagara poems and songs and being told that one was addressed to the singer's mother back in the village and another was about a man who came back to his village from Khartoum and who everyone thought was rich. Or Thomas Hodgkin himself explaining that, in a wedding dance, the bride closed her eyes and whirled around and around until she became dizzy, to be caught by her husband just when she was about to fall over.

Plans also went ahead for my lecture, although under the shadow of an approaching showdown between the Niemeri regime and the demonstrating schoolchildren and students. On 4 January, after I had a talk with people at the university's Institute of Extra-Mural Studies, I was taken shopping on one of Khartoum's main streets, Gumhuriya Avenue, by one of the institute's members, Dr. Fatima Babiker. Fatima became increasingly anxious as we passed riot police armed with wooden laths and small round shields at a number of the main intersections. She thought she could smell teargas. Many shops were pulling down shutters. Later that evening, the Hodgkins, the Abu-Zaids, and I watched pictures of the demonstrations on television. On the next day I went to the university to visit its library, bookshop, and cafeteria. And on the following one I was taken by university students to Omdurman to visit the Khalifa's house, now a museum, with interesting reminders of the mixed natures of the forces under his command at the great 1898 battle with Kitchener's army, ranging from flintlocks to a Gatling gun captured at the annihilation of Hicks' column in 1884. Meanwhile, my student guides talked excitedly about the role that their grandfathers played during the Mahdiya movement against the Egyptian-backed local government: one was an Ansar, a militant follower of the Mahdi and another was from an anti-Mahdi tribe. Back in Khartoum, there was the now-usual smell of teargas, while the remains of branches, torn down from trees to use as weapons, littered the pavements. More disturbingly, there was the first news that the popular forces were beginning to be drawn into the struggle via a demonstration in the main souk. By now the power was likely to fail at any time of the day or night, and we saw longer and longer queues at the petrol stations with women drivers allowed straight to the front by the police, or so I was told.

To a certain extent, normal life continued in the form of things like the *mawlid* (a festival to mark the birthday of a sainted religious figure) I visited that same evening in Khartoum, where tent-like booths were erected for various religious and workers' organizations around a square, and there were lights and loud music. I was taken to sit in the "river-workers" tent where, as a guest, I was given groundnuts to eat and sweet hibiscus tea to drink. Then, we went on to a similar but much bigger event in Omdurman, and, finally, we attended a yet bigger event in Khartoum on the way back, where a Dinka jump dance was taking place with sticks: the tall, thin performers rising and falling like graceful white cranes.

On 7 January, I had lunch with MOB and, among others, the Sudanese ambassador to London, followed by dinner with the Hodgkins, the Bedris, and the minister of the interior who talked anxiously about the "national interest" and his fear of a "southern succession." The next morning, news came that troops had closed the university and all the students had been sent home, thus ending any prospect of giving my seminar. It was the same story at the new University of Gezira at Wad Medani to which MOB drove me on 9 January, making quite sure that he had enough petrol for the nearly two-hundred-mile round trip. The long straight road took us out through the suburbs, past the occasional factory (one run by the Chinese to make textiles) and the occasional farm. We arrived to find the vice chancellor and his staff having tea together while preparing to close down. Yet another small demonstration was going on nearby with riot police chasing the kids across a field, throwing two tear gas grenades to make them disperse. The shops in the town were already closed. Lunch at the local club proved to be a somewhat gloomy affair with the very disconsolate vice chancellor drinking nearly half a bottle of whiskey to drown his sorrows. Others, including two left-wing Turkish academics who had been forced to flee from Boğaziçi University after the 1980 military coup, seemed much more relaxed at the prospect of a break from teaching. MOB and I drove back to Khartoum in a dark storm of dust.

Now that the main purpose of my visit was at an end, MOB and I decided I might as well go back to the United Kingdom a bit early, although I did this with something of a bad conscience. Given the rush of others to leave the troubled situation, it was also difficult to get on the BEA flight and, in the end, I boarded an Air France Airbus. This took me, on a cloudless morning, across the Nubian Desert and then down the Nile over a sparkling blue Lake Nasser on the Sudanese/Egyptian border, past Abu Simbel (which I could just make out from the tourist boats at its entrance), Luxor, Nasser City (a suburb of Cairo), and Alexandria, and over the Mediterranean to Charles De Gaulle where I changed planes for London. An Indian student who was traveling with me recalled seeing schoolboys demonstrating against a previous rise in sugar prices in 1975. This took place at least once more in 2012.

Part III. The Fertile Crescent

Jordan

I visited pre-1967 Jordan on two occasions, both times flying into Qalandia Airport near Jerusalem and then being taken around the major tourist attractions by car. Things then changed dramatically as a result of the Israeli capture of the whole of the old city in the June War. Afterward, Amman became the center of touristic activity with more or less statutory trips to Petra and the Wadi Rum in the south and the extensive remains of the Greco-Roman city of Jerash, just to the north.

December 1967

I flew down to Amman from Lebanon just before Christmas, arriving at the new Queen Alia Airport while members of the ruling family were there meeting another flight. It was my first visit to the city. I stayed with the UN resident representative, who arranged for me to meet various ministers including the one dealing with labor affairs such as work on Jordan's first official pension law. I remember being amazed by the informality of it all, the minister himself in an office that you reached immediately from the hallway—no secretary to protect him—often conducting his business in front of three or four friends and colleagues, his phone constantly ringing. It got me thinking about office layout and whether what I was witnessing was a product of the Ottoman period, or the British—or, perhaps, both.

91

(Right & Below) The old Jerusalem Airport at Qalandia, Jordan before the Israeli invasion of June 1967.

Amman was still a small, sleepy place in those days, well off the beaten tourist track to Jerusalem to the west, with whatever business and tourism there had been before 1967 yet to recover from the impact of the war. Few cars were on the streets and, if I remember correctly, only one "Spanish" night club, containing just a handful of clients on the evening I was taken there and with a minimal floor show provided by what may actually have been real Spanish dancers. It was a very dull place in the early part of the evening, although it might have livened up later, toward midnight, after we had left.

The highlight of my visit was an informal meeting with Crown Prince Hassan who had been a student of mine in Oxford. He had taken his final exams during the June War and then flown back to his battered country with great difficulty via Pakistan a week or so later. He was a short, stocky, broad-shouldered young man who had been up at Christ Church College leading, as far as I could observe from the few times I came across him at one of the local restaurants, the usual life of university royals those days. I supposed he lived privately with a few courtiers—including someone like Edward VIII's "academic secretary," who may well have helped him write his weekly essays—and spent most of his weekends in London. Yet he came into my Middle East economic history lectures alone, asking interesting questions about such matters as the cultivation of silk in Lebanon and—more tangential to the course matter itself—the behavior of various Middle Eastern rulers like Mohammad Ali of Egypt.

I prepared for my visit with some care, wearing a suit and tie and obtaining permission to use the United Nation's official car to go to the downtown Raghadan Palace, built in 1926. Trying to ape what I thought would have been the behavior of Prince Philip (of Britain), I walked up the steps to the front entrance and knocked. No answer. I knocked again. One of the Bedouin guards standing to the side of the steps below me giggled, then put his rifle barrel down in the soft earth, something no soldier ever ought to do because of the damage to the rifling, and very obviously relieved himself behind a thick rhododendron bush. Finally, I heard the sound of a toilet being flushed, and the prince's aide, an Egyptian called Bilbeisi, opened the door and led me to a large reception room with bench-like seats along the wall.

Prince Hassan came in almost immediately, we shook hands, and then sat down. I asked him how he had gotten back to Amman from Oxford and then what had happened to the palace during the powerful Israeli air attack during the June War when, to make a rather obvious point, a pilot had fired a rocket through the front window of the very room in which we were sitting. We also talked about an article on the future economic development of Jordan that the prince had written while at Oxford and that had eventually been published in the *Middle East Journal* in 1968 under the name of Hassan Bin-Talal. The aim of Jordanian development policy, as the prince and I and most foreign experts believed, was to get to a point at which the country was self-sufficient enough not to rely on the huge amounts of outside aid that had sustained it since its inception in the 1920s. Given the country's limited natural resources—a little agriculture and potash from the Dead Sea—this was a huge task even before the June War had taken away its main asset, the religious tourism centered on Jerusalem and Bethlehem. Now, as the prince and I surveyed Jordan's present prospects, it seemed even more of a dream than ever. What we could not know was the way the economy would soon be so hugely strengthened by the large amounts of Arab aid it received as a frontline state in the struggle with Israel after the Arab leaders' Khartoum Summit of 1969, while creating new dependencies of quite a different kind.

The prince was then widely talked of as the kingdom's one intellectual, as well as the probable successor to his brother, Hussein. He certainly read a lot of books and thought deeply and imaginatively about his country's place in the world. His ideas, as I listened to them over the years, were expressed in a unique personal language full of words and notions that, though they sounded impressive, I was not always sure I could properly understand—for example, Jordan's role as a kind of "terra media" in the Arab world.

It was clear, as he once told me, he regarded Jordan as one of the world's "best-kept secrets," an impression he was soon to do his best to rectify by hosting conferences, reaching out to people of other faiths, and generally acting as Jordan's premier cultural ambassador. I remember an evening some twenty or so years later when watching the evening news on Jordan's one channel with Oxford colleagues, we saw pictures of him opening four conferences within a single day, including the one we ourselves were attending.

I should add that as Prince Hassan was the only Middle Eastern royal whom I got to know personally, apart from an unhappy Saudi student in the early 1980s, it gave me great pleasure to maintain our acquaintance over the years. The acquaintance, of course, also gave me license to ask naïve questions that I did not have the opportunity to ask anyone else. How did he feel, for instance, when loyal Jordanians flung themselves on the ground in front of him and tried to kiss his feet? He wished they would not do it, he replied, but there was not much he could do to prevent it!

April 1968

I returned to Jordan with my wife, Ursula, four months later, in April 1968, on a much more touristic visit. This trip took us down to Petra in the Land Rover of Gualtiero Fulcheri, the UN resident representative, through fields where the rich green of the spring wheat in the north soon gave way to a more threadbare green and then to yellow as we reached the southern desert. We then had coffee in the new Ma'an rest house and then up through low hills to Petra. The sky grew darker, and it began to rain as we reached the new rest house built against some Nabbatean tombs. There we hired horses and a guide and clip-clopped slowly to the narrow entrance, or the Siq, which looked much more forbidding in the gloom than five years before. The sudden view of the red-pillared face of the rock-cut temple known as the "Treasury" was much more spectacular. We did not linger at the end of the wide-open space surrounded by the famous "rose-red" cliffs because of the deafening noise being made by some men using the rocks for target practice. Abandoning our horses to our guide, we walked back out through the Siq as quickly as we could, to get down to Aqaba before light fell.

On the way through the Siq, surrounded by black-grey mountains, we encountered a police post at which two thickly-bearded American hitchhikers had been temporarily detained on the grounds—odd to think of now—that anyone not clean-shaven must be a Jewish Israeli. No doubt the police were particularly jumpy in the aftermath of the June War, and because the Israeli border ran along the mountains just to the west of the Wadi Rum.

In Aqaba we had beer and fish at a restaurant by the beach looking at the lights of the adjacent Israeli town of Eilat twinkling across the dark sea. We slept at one of the new beachside hotels and swam the next morning in the warm shallow waters not far from where the fishermen pulled up their boats. The weather had now cleared, and on our return journey we had a wonderful view of the first stretch of the magnificent Wadi Rum, a wide finger of flat desert between high cathedral-like reddish rocks—the sun seeming to hit each with a different color and intensity—which then narrowed as it ran down toward the Saudi border. It had become something of a tourist attraction after its use in the film *Lawrence of Arabia* where Peter O'Toole as Lawrence first meets the famous tribal leader Sharif Ali, played by Omar Sharif. I was later to learn that David Lean, the film's director, had the sand floor of the Wadi especially swept for the occasion to clear it of its usual detritus of camel droppings and bits and pieces of food wrappings thrown away by their drivers.

We drank bitter coffee at the desert police post near the entrance, the off-duty troopers lounging on straw mats made by prisoners at the Amman jail. We continued down the Wadi, past some of the black tents of the Bedouin, to see the spring gushing out of the rocks by a small clump of olive trees where the real Lawrence had stopped for a rendezvous with one of the sons of the Sharif of Mecca. And back again through a drizzle of rain, wet enough to add a little green to the desert's dry grass, as well as to encourage the dramatic appearance of huge white mushrooms.

We met the young Americans again after we returned to our Aqaba hotel. We found that they had spent the whole morning at the police station, being questioned while having their belongings searched and the journal of one of them read by the headman, who tore out two pages in which the author had written about having seen "a lot of army." In the evening, we went to a huge dinner of fish and rice, followed by fruit and coffee, at the house of a friend of Gualtiero, a young man called Radwan who worked in a bank but whose piratical-looking father was a fisherman. Little children came to the door to peer in, cats squawked outside, while our host told us of the problems faced by the local fishing industry when moving into the Saudi waters just a few miles to the southeast and from the depletion of fishing stocks due to the illegal use of dynamite to stun anything below the surface of the water. The latter was demonstrated in a dramatic way when the father waved his hand to reveal several missing fingers, blown away when one of the sticks of dynamite he was using blew up before he could throw it. It was no surprise then that we found great difficulty in buying some fish to take back to Amman before we left the next morning. When we did find some, most of the pile scattered on the floor showed obvious signs of the effect of dynamite around their ears.

On our way back we made a diversion to the old hillside city of Karak, crammed into its Crusader walls, where we walked through the vaulted halls of the narrow steps to see the magnificent view of the Dead Sea below and to the west. Then on to Madaba to see the famous mosaic floor and its map of sixth-century Palestine with its towns, rivers, even animals, but, as we noticed, the few human figures scratched out—probably after the Arab conquest. The day ended with a wonderful meal of fish eaten with salad, potatoes, cheese, and white wine.

Our final visit was to the Greco-Roman city of Jerash the next morning. On the way, we passed its large nearby refugee camp. Many of its thirty thousand residents had only recently been driven out of earlier camps in the Israeli-occupied West Bank in June 1967. They now lived in garish blue and white holiday-looking beach tents delivered by an American aid agency.

1970: Black September in Amman

Just as the youth of the Middle East became radicalized by the crushing defeat of the June War, so too the youth of Europe became radicalized by "*Les événements*" in Paris in May 1968. These seemed, for a moment, to promise the start of a new revolutionary wave across Europe, as in 1848. In Oxford this took the form of a challenge to authority both in terms of teaching as well as college and university government, whereby students demanded greater participation. Characteristically, the unrest manifested in sit-ins, demonstrations, and the wholesale use of a new import from the United States: the "teach-in." When these failed to make much of an impact on domestic politics, there was a return to more intellectual forms of activism. Any number of new journals appeared, devoted to the critique of this or that "bourgeois intellectual practice," and thousands of reading groups formed that were devoted to the classic works of Hegel, Marx, and their disciples in the Frankfurt group, like Theodor Adorno and Herbert Marcuse, supplemented by more psychological and feminist treatises of Marx-inspired writers like R. D. Laing, Simone de Beauvoir, and Juliet Mitchell. "Texts," as most such works were now called after Michel Foucault, were read, reread, and often discussed almost line by line until they yielded new tools and new meanings. Needless to say, this was all something of a challenge to a teacher like myself of increasingly left-wing leanings, who was expected to share in all this revolutionary activity, and whose expertise, such as it was, could easily be made irrelevant by students confident in their own right to interpret any text. Then there was the Middle East component. A bewildering array of new radical groups began to emerge to challenge the old Arab order: Yassar Arafat's Fatah and also such groups as the Popular Front for the Liberation of Palestine (PFLP), the Popular Democratic Front for the Liberation of Palestine (PDFLP), and the Popular Front for the Liberation of the Occupied Arab Gulf (PFLOAG), and so on. Each had a military arm and was connected in some way or another to Maoist or Trotskyist groups in Europe, which in turn were connected to a shadowy organization called "The Fourth International." To adapt Marx's famous phrase: we were all being challenged not only to understand the world we lived in but also to change it.

My own introduction to the radical Middle Eastern student politics of the period came during a sabbatical year. I was spending this time between Oxford and London when I met Fred Halliday, a former Oxford student who had gone off to what was then South Yemen and then Dhofar to observe the guerilla movement against the Sultan of Oman. I also met three of his comrades: Fawaz Trabulsi and Hasna Reda from Lebanon and Walid Kazziha from Syria. All were engaged in political activity among the students at the School of Oriental and African Studies (SOAS) in London and the London School of Economics (LSE). These encounters led to an invitation to attend two congresses organized by the Fatah-administered General Union of Palestine Students. The first was in Amman in September 1970 at the Second World Conference on Palestine, and the second was in Kuwait the following January.

As neither the young Palestinian organizers nor their London-based Arab colleagues had any real sense of where support might come from, they wisely cast their net as widely as possible. They invited people from across the political spectrum, from Young Liberals and the International Socialists to the Movement for Colonial Freedom, the International Marxist Group, and the Communist Party of Great Britain (Marxist-Leninist), along with a few journalists and teachers like myself. None, as far as I could work out on our slow flight from London to Paris, Athens, and Amman to attend the first congress knew any Arabic, and few had been anywhere near the Middle East before. Nor did anyone apart from myself seem to realize the dangers ahead, although there were already widespread reports of fighting between various Palestinian militias and the troops of King Hussain's Jordanian army.

So it was with some anxiety that I sat in the back of the bus outside the airport as dusk fell, waiting for the Irish contingent to find their luggage. All things considered, it was no great surprise when two shots rang out above us as we made the slow drive into the town, causing most of those aboard to try to fling themselves on the floor. For general reasons of stubbornness, I remained sitting upright on the back seat and protected, or so I hoped, by a jumble of suitcases. Nevertheless, I did get more nervous as we passed lines of burning tires and then took some more time to get to our Palestinian-run downtown hotel, the Alcazar, across from the old Roman amphitheater. As was being made abundantly clear, the young members of the local organizing committee, though incredibly nice and helpful, were far out of their depth when trying to manage a complex program in what was becoming an extremely dangerous city. After all, Arab League mediators were coming and going, ceasefires were broken almost as soon as they were negotiated, and no one was at all sure what was going to happen next.

There were more delegates at the hotel from many more countries—including Yugoslavia, Denmark, Malta, and Egypt—as well as some Russian journalists who actually spoke Arabic and the Palestinian economist Yusuf Sayigh, whom I had previously met at the American University of Beirut. He was now dressed in a military-looking safari jacket and trying, uncomfortably, to sound like a Marxist revolutionary, although one who had only recently started speaking the language. Fawaz Trabulsi was also there, although as much to meet some real revolutionary comrades from South Yemen as to attend the actual conference.

I had dinner with some of the foreign attendees before going off to share a room with Fawaz, who much impressed me by staying fast asleep during what proved to be a noisy night. A regular exchange of automatic weapons, sometimes accompanied by the dull thud of mortars, between the two sides entrenched in refugee camps and army posts on the hills above was enough to waken all the dogs, it seemed, but not my combat-experienced companion. Not that we were in any real danger; the purpose of the exchange was only to make each side's presence felt and to force their enemies to keep their heads down. But it was enough to create a sense of considerable unease about what might be coming next.

After breakfast a bus arrived—late, of course—to take us to the conference hall in an Islamic school somewhere near the First Roundabout. The seats were hard, and the speeches of solidarity went on and on, although often not without some interest. My diary mentions one from a Jewish-American girl and another by an American from the south who belonged to the League of Revolutionary Black Workers (LRBW). We headed back to the hotel for lunch, and off again in a taxi to the heavily guarded headquarters of the Popular Front, which had pictures of the comrades killed in action on the wall. A very gung-ho speech from the local commander convinced me, wrongly as it turned out, that they stood to win hands-down in any confrontation with the Jordanian army, particularly since they were confident that, once they gave the signal, there would be mass defections by many soldiers of Palestinian origin.

The day ended back at the hotel watching a Fatah film and having a group discussion of the Rogers Plan, which Nixon's secretary of state had just put forward. The plan seemed quite a reasonable attempt at a solution for the Arab-Israeli conflict, but to most of those present it was not only an obvious piece of imperialist chicanery but also a patent sellout to Israeli demands. So I kept my thoughts to myself, especially since some of them jokingly pretended that it must be my plan because my name was on it.

The next day, 4 September, was much the same in structure but more lively in content. We were introduced to some armed Palestinians who said that they had been captured and then "tortured" for five days by Israeli troops while fleeing from the Battle of Karameh disguised as peasants after their ammunition had run out. This was followed by a performance of a "Kalashnikov Debke," danced by men in a circle, and an obvious if somewhat ungainly celebration of the significance of the gun both as a symbol of empowerment and of liberation. At some stage we were also taken off to give blood in a small field hospital run by the Palestinian Red Crescent Society. It occurred to me after I had been put to lie down on a narrow bed to recover that this was the most practical gift we could give, one worth much more than all our words of solidarity once the real fighting began. As I was later to conclude, we would actually have been much more useful if we were a delegation of doctors.

Wonder of wonders that I slept through most of the night, although many people at breakfast described how the firing had gone on almost all night. Perhaps it was just as well that I had not yet discovered that there was a Fatah firing position on the next roof and a similar Jordanian army one on top of the town hall opposite. Some of the day I spent at the conference I talked to a very intense young woman who was part of the US delegation. She had already been in Jordan a month, visiting refugee camps and taking part in what sounded like daily discussions about the "situation"—what to do next, etc.—during which her delegation had expelled one of their number for being a "bourgeois journalist first, a revolutionary second."

I also escaped from the conference to the almost empty Intercontinental Hotel where I had lunch with the UN resident representative, a writer for *Time* magazine called Edward Hughes, who was writing a book then, and Paul Martin, the Middle East correspondent of the *London Times*. I think that this was also the day when it was possible to buy a copy of *Le Monde* with an article by the famous French journalist Eric Rouleau, complete with a map of Amman with pictures of tiny explosions to indicate the main flash-points. It seemed to me a wonderful thing to be able to fly in, ring a few key people—perhaps even the king—and then write a comprehensible account of what was actually going on. Now I am not so sure. Who was to say whether the information was true or not, particularly in such a tense and volatile situation? All you could sensibly do was to try to work it out for yourself, as Edward and Paul did when they took a taxi down to the center of town to see whether that day's ceasefire was still holding. It was not. The streets were full of Jordanian commandos with guns, and there were occasional bursts of gunfire, causing Paul at one stage to yell, "Christ, they have started again!"

This was probably enough to persuade me not to go out again from the hotel after our evening meal, fearful of being shot on my last evening. Perhaps it was just as well: Ros, the woman with whom I was flying back to London the next day, had been out all night, stranded at a Palestinian commando headquarters on the other side of the city because of all the firing. We met up the next morning for a final scramble around Amman to make sure that we had all the documents necessary to leave, including our precious passports. Then we headed out on a back road that twisted through the hills to the east of Amman to avoid the shooting near the airport. I remember feeling both sorry for the tall uniformed Arab Legion sergeant who checked our suitcases, imagining that he was soon to be killed by fighting with a victorious PLO and its local allies, but also annoyed that he removed most of the Fatah posters and other material I had collected at the conference. Our plane finally took off at 11:45 and flew us to Istanbul and then Frankfurt, where we stayed the night in a hotel near the main station. Somewhere along the way we got the news of the dramatic Palestinian hijackings that resulted in four planes being flown to an abandoned airfield in the desert near Amman. It was the official beginning of the infamous "Black September."

Back in Oxford, I wrote down some impressions of my furious five days in Jordan. I noted that I had not been physically frightened in Amman except during the rather hair-raising expedition to give blood. But I had been aware of running risks, especially when being driven around the city at night. This sense had intensified when it became clear that there was little hope that any negotiated cease-fire would work and that a period of much more intense fighting was only days away. I also noted that the idea of "revolution" was no longer a slogan but something—the beginnings of which—I had experienced firsthand. I also recorded some changes in my thoughts about the political role of women, which I now saw as indispensible in the nation building process, and about my greater identification with the Palestinian cause.

I wrote all this because of the transformation that armed struggle produced when militants were able to take their destiny in their own hands. My position as an observer was clearly beginning to change too. It was more difficult to remain in the middle when a life-or-death battle was taking place all around me. A young woman in the US delegation told me that next time she and her comrades went to Jordan they would want to fight. Though not ready for that myself, I had come to feel that, when I returned to the United Kingdom, I must present the Palestinian side of the case as best I could.

December 1981

I returned to Amman's Intercontinental Hotel just over ten years later and wondered, not for the first time, "What am I doing here?" So much had changed. Then, the hotel had been almost deserted. Now it was full of guests, and I had dinner by candlelight listening to the discreet playing of a cocktail pianist and drinking some local wine under the old Latroun label. Mentioning that I had been there during Black September drew an uneasy response, reflecting, I supposed, a general desire to forget all about it.

I was there to try to organize a joint program of academic exchange between St Antony's Middle East Centre (of which I was then the director) and the Jordanian universities. I believed partnership in the study of the region should be the foundation of our work, and for a short period in the 1980s, we were actually able to put this into practice. For one thing, there was a great deal of goodwill on both sides, which was buttressed by a growing number of personal relationships, including the one between Prince Hassan and myself, as well as by the presence at the University of Jordan of several Oxford-educated teachers. For another, there was also the possibility of a certain amount of Jordanian finance as a result of the regime's obvious desire to create new universities with international connections, like the one at Yarmouk near Irbid in the north, whose first president, Adnan Badran, I had just met in the VIP lounge at the airport. Given the country's lack of natural resources, the king and his advisers had identified Jordan's main export as its well-educated men and women.

While I was there, I spent time at each university. I began in Amman where I was shown around the new facilities at Amman University and then driven to the royal palace for negotiations with the crown prince and representatives of both Amman and Yarmouk universities, including Adnan Badran. Offers of money were made, and we agreed on the outlines of joint seminars to be held in Jordan and Oxford the next year (1982), which I drafted. Next, I paid a visit to the Yarmouk University liaison office in Amman followed by a drive north to Irbid via a stop at Ajlun Castle—built to check the Crusader advance east of the Jordan—with its wonderful view across the valley and up to the hills around Jerusalem on the far side. The university was still a large construction site, but I remember marveling at the courage that the implementation of such huge projects required and the energy and imagination that were going to be needed to make it a success. Finally, I headed back to Amman through the gathering gloom, and had dinner, this time at the new Sheraton, before climbing thankfully into bed to take my mind off the day by watching a program about Studs Terkel on television.

Nobody, of course, could have predicted that only five years later, Adnan Badran would be unceremoniously sacked from his post by King Hussein for failing to prevent some anti-regime demonstrations by Muslim Brother-affiliated students in Irbid in 1986. I remember telling him how unjust I thought this was when I met him again a few years later. I added, somewhat more pompously, that in any properly run country the founders of new universities should have statues put up in commemoration of their achievements, rather than suffer public obloquy. But he had chosen to make no fuss, a lesson to me of one of the first rules of Arab, and perhaps any, politics—if you say nothing that prevents you from staying in the game, your turn will come again, allowing you to get the upper hand over those who helped to pull you down.

March 1983

Perhaps it was only to be expected that little of the initial program took place in quite the form that had been initially agreed on. However, I did return to Jordan early in 1983 for a workshop on "Jordan in the Arab Oil

Economy," originally planned to be held in Oxford the previous year. With me were Robert Mabro, an oil economist, and two other Oxford economists, Andrew Baring and David Soskice, who had a general interest in development.

Crown Prince Hassan opened the workshop, and, according to my diary, he arrived a "royal" twenty minutes late. The two university presidents, and then I, followed him. I made a short speech about Oxford/Jordanian cooperation for which I was later to receive a princely rebuke for having the temerity to mention the names of those two arch-imperialists with Oxford connections: D.G. Hogarth and T.E. Lawrence. Still, it gave us something to laugh about later as we lolled about in one of our hotel rooms drinking whiskey and hooting at shots of ourselves on television, me sitting prim and proper at the podium during the opening ceremony and Robert Mabro very obviously asleep in the front row. Altogether, we had two days of papers before the Oxford contingent was taken off on the usual tour of the south (Petra) and the north. Although, on this occasion, we did not return directly from Irbid but instead went on a long swing round along the Jordanian side of the great wide Jordan valley. The sun was gleaming on the plastic greenhouses where the Israelis were practicing intensive agriculture—mostly fruit, flowers, and vegetables—on the far side of the river.

December 1984 and November-December 1987

I returned to Jordan briefly in December 1984 on my way to Kuwait, staying in the new Anba Hotel, which was testimony to the great building boom that was going on at that time. This time, it was for a joint Oxford/Jordanian Royal Scientific Society conference I had organized on economic integration and on Jordanian/European Economic Community relations. To do this, I had been able to assemble a small delegation of Oxford-based friends: Robert Mabro of the Oxford Institute of Energy Studies, Loukas Tsoukalis to talk on the European Economic Community (EEC) and Middle Eastern economic relations, Cyril Lin on Asia/Pacific economic integration, and Ibrahim G. Ibrahim from the Organization of Arab Petroleum Exporting States in Kuwait. One of Robert's students, Mohamed El-Erian, who later became one of the leading investment bankers in the world, was also part of the delegation. As I wrote in a letter to one of our Jordanian hosts, Dr. M. Smadi, I saw "little point in outsiders like ourselves coming to Jordan to tell you things you already know about your own country. It is much better to produce papers which, we hope, will be of more general interest to Jordanian economists."

103

For once, there was no Crown Prince Hassan to grace our proceedings, but this was made up for by the presence of both university presidents: Adnan Badran, who gave a paper about the need for more research, and Abdelsalam al-Majali, with whom Robert Mabro and I had a private lunch. My opening speech was incorrectly transcribed in the local newspaper, *Al-rai*. My paper, delivered on the second day, was titled "The History of Arab Attempts at Economic Integration." Then, on the third day, those of our delegation who had not been to Jordan previously were taken on the usual tour, leaving me to visit the British embassy and the British Council before having lunch with a well-connected businessman, Raouf Abujaber. He was full of good gossip about local business practices, including some veiled allegations that I had not heard before about the need to hand over some portion of the middle-men profits on large contracts to the royal palace. Raouf also kept me entertained with information about any number of other peculiar local features such as the fact that, according to him, Jordan led the world per capita in both traffic accidents and students in higher education: fifty-six percent in each category.

The whole visit seemed to be a great success, with contacts made and a general air of optimism about what might be obtained in the future. It had also required a tremendous amount of organization, management, and personal enthusiasm on my part, input that I had hoped, forlornly as it turned out, to be institutionalized with the help of well wishers on both sides. But this was not to be. Either it was not really in anybody's interest to make the efforts needed to continue the exchange or there were silent, opposing forces, not to speak of a huge amount of inertia. It was a lesson of sorts, but not, I believe, one of the hopelessness of such a project, but more that I had failed to understand the problems involved and the fact that when it came to signing protocols of cooperation between European and Arab universities, it was only the public signing itself that mattered, not the follow-through.

Lebanon

1975

I returned to Lebanon on a number of occasions though only for the briefest of visits. Nevertheless, three stand out for their connection with the so-called civil war. The first was in the spring of 1975 when I went to stay with my friends Rashid and Mona Khalidi in Beirut only days before the assassination attempt on the Maronite leader Pierre Gemayel—which marked the first phase of the war. I cannot remember much more than the small size of their student flat, the sense of impending trouble produced by bursts of gunfire in the night, and the great relief I felt at getting to the airport. The situation seemed so different from what it had been when I left in 1968 that it hardly seemed like a homecoming at all.

1979

The occasion for what seemed like my real return was a seminar put on by Rashid Khalidi and others at the American University of Beirut in 1979: "Identity and Identity Formation." This was part of an effort to take advantage of a lull in the fighting to reassert the university's position of prominence—what AUB professor of history Samir Seikaly called, rather grandly, "the foremost agency for the spread of modern education and over-all enlightenment across the region."[1] Given the painful circumstances of the time, including the wanton destruction of one of the university's main buildings, College Hall, by outside forces, it was an occasion for a number of foreign academics—Michael Hudson, Robert Springborg, and others—to demonstrate our solidarity with those who had tried to keep the university going during these difficult times.

I flew out to Beirut together with a London-based friend, Abbas Kelidar, on an almost empty plane. He told me that his wife, a woman with family in Beirut, had begged him not to go, and he seemed visibly scared—with good reason as it turned out. We were met by a former Oxford student, Mohamed Mattar, now a local lawyer, at the nearly empty airport and driven to the huge Carlton Hotel, which stood high above the Corniche by the lighthouse. The French Middle East expert Dominique Chevalier and I seemed to be the only guests. I had the most wonderful view of the Mediterranean from my bedroom, which I looked at with some trepidation, having been told to stay away from windows as they were sometimes deliberately shattered by passing Israeli planes. I had a brief sleep, wrote out my lecture—with what I hoped was the catchy title "The Middle Eastern National Economy: Imagined, Constructed"—and ended the day with drinks on the terrace with Mohamed while we watched the bright yellow sun do its usual spectacular, and well-remembered, precipitous drop into the blazing sea. It was probably then that Mohamed told me of the contract he had drawn up between the hotel and Walid Jumblatt's Druze militia in which the latter were required to bring a certain number of armored cars in the early hours of the morning

---

1 Samir M. Seikaly, ed., *Configuring Identity in the Modern Middle East* (Beirut: American University of Beirut Press, 2009), vii.

to gather the rich takings from the hotel's well-patronized casino, gambling being an activity that flourishes in wartime.

The next day I took a taxi with Chevalier to the start of the seminar, had lunch in the faculty club, drinks with the university president—who lived alone in splendid isolation on the campus—and then finally had more drinks with Walid Kazziha at Beirut's closest attempt at an English pub: the Duke of Wellington, with a painting of the "Iron Duke" and all. Then more of the same the next day: the seminar in the morning, lunch in the city with Walid Kazziha, drinks with Elie Salem (the dean of the university before serving briefly as the country's foreign minister), and, finally, a visit with my former Shemlan friends Erica and Peter Dodd, now living down in Beirut as Shemlan was more or less on the fault line between the civil war's two embattled sides.

The Dodds kindly offered to drive me home. Dusk was falling, always a worrying time. Along the way, we met a small patrol of *Murabitun* (a Sunni militia) and then were waved through a roadblock manned (if that is the right word) by some teenage supporters of the strongly right-wing Syrian-backed Syrian National Party (SNP) lugging rocket-propelled grenade launchers—dangerous only, so it seemed to me, if they accidentally dropped one of them and it went off. As if to emphasize the point, I heard outbursts of firing in the night, another reminder that the civil war was still far from over.

AUB remained "almost too beautiful," as I wrote in my diary; the streets outside its main gate were superficially unchanged and more or less as I remembered them, but as I looked more carefully, I began to see that many of the shops were shuttered and that there were obviously fewer people about. New pictures of the most recent "martyrs" were also pasted over old ones on the walls and shabbily uniformed Syrian soldiers manned a few of the checkpoints. Then, as I talked to more old friends who lived in the city during the first years of the war, I began to get more of a sense of the strain under which they had been living—indicated, for example, by the almost universal acid stomach reflux, treated with the same antacid medicine.

There was yet more gunfire during my third night at the Carlton Hotel, but peace returned during the last day of the seminar. The final session was followed by lunch with Khaldun Husri, the son of the famous Arab nationalist writer and educator Sati' al-Husri, a tour of the city with Mohamed Mattar, and last drinks overlooking the famous Pigeon Rock near my hotel. All in all, I found it tremendously reassuring that the Beirut I knew, and the life my friends lived there, remained largely so recognizable and unchanged in spite of the traumas of war. And that this was enough, selfish though it may seem, to allow me to reestablish that special link with the Middle East after having been away in spirit for so long.

1997

Nearly two more decades elapsed before I returned to Beirut in 1997. These had been years of intermittent fighting and, more dangerous for foreigners, kidnappings for ransom by militant Shi'i groups hidden in the southern suburbs near the airport. These victims included some French academics, a subject I knew quite a lot about from Carol Hakim, who, before she came to Oxford as a student in the early 1990s, had covered these awful events for the French newspaper *Le Monde*, becoming a heavy chain-smoker in the process. Carol Hakim met me at the airport and then took me on a tour in her own car along the Corniche, past the shell of the old St. George Hotel, and around the new Solidaire Square where I observed that the prime minister, Rafik Hariri, had added at least one new floor to his official residence, the old Ottoman Serail building. Finally, back to west Beirut where my hotel was via a new development at the southern end of Hamra Street. Here, the prime minister had created an enclave for himself, heavily guarded by men in a fleet of black Nissan Range Rovers. Compared with the old days, Hamra, once the main drag, now looked distinctly dowdy. Other streets, like Verdun with its line of fancy boutiques, seemed a great deal glitzier. Parts of the old Christian quarter in the east of the city, which I had rarely visited before, also appeared to be thriving: many of the quarter's pleasant nineteenth-century buildings with their arched windows now turned into smart restaurants, few of which, we discovered, served food of any kind before about eleven at night.

The symposium I had come to attend was full of old friends. Many, like me, had come simply to help get the university going again after its long travail during which academic contacts with the outside were lost, the library depleted, and some vital subjects like economics simply not taught at all. This, too, was obviously the cause of some discomfort between those who had left and those who stayed; the latter were very defensive about how little they had managed to keep up with the latest developments in their fields and aware of how hard it was going to be to catch up, given the fact that they had lost the knack of applying for fellowships and research grants. Nevertheless, there was also considerable optimism in the air based on the billionaire Rafik Hariri's grand plans to return Beirut to its place as the main business capital of the Middle East. But this too proved to have its downside; it involved buying out the thousands of poor Shi'i squatters who had migrated into the empty homes in the east of the city with money stemming from dodgy insurance claims, as I was told by a man from a British insurance company whom I sat next to on the plane out.

March 2004

My last real visit to Beirut was to a workshop held in the name of Edward Said, who had died the year before. In spite of the inevitable sadness of the occasion, it was memorable for two main reasons. One was the company, all old friends of Edward, each of whom not only had their own memories of him but also told stories of the special way he seemed to have managed to have time for all of them. Often this was through regular middle-of-the-night telephone calls when, as he freely admitted, he was often awake for long periods, being one of those rare individuals who only seemed to need four or five hours of sleep. Although I had not met him face to face on more than a few occasions, this was enough to reveal his special gift for friendship, manifest in a delight in conversation, tempered in just a few instances by the need to share, or at least to have the decency not to mention, the names of those whom he regarded, sometimes misguidedly, as his political and intellectual enemies.

The second reason was that I took the occasion to pursue what had become a hobbyhorse of mine — the absence of any kind of Lebanese economic history in the post–civil war AUB course offerings — by giving a few classes on the subject myself. I believe strongly that college students in particular should know something of the economic history of their own country, and this makes even more sense in Lebanon where the distribution of state resources, including welfare, education, and employment, is still decided along sectarian lines. Not to speak of the historical moments, for example, during the latter stages of the civil war, when rival warlords got their hands on certain revenues like the income obtained from taxing foreign trade.

Iraq and Syria

I never gave myself the chance to see as much of either Syria or Iraq as I did of Egypt and Lebanon. In part, this was because I had fewer friends and connections in these countries; in part, it was because the Ba'thist dictatorships that ruled both countries from the late 1960s onward made academic exchange difficult. In the case of Iraq, for example, I remember being warned by my friend Fred Halliday, who in 1982 had paid a brief visit there, arranged by a former Iraqi student of his, that in such a state, everything you did or said was monitored closely by agents of the regime. And, as if to confirm this, an angry Oxford colleague, Mustafa Badawi, reported that when he was invited to attend the annual poetry festival in the late 1980s, he found an Iraqi military uniform laid out on his bed, which the organizers obviously expected him to wear.

Things were not quite as bad in Syria, where tourism continued to be encouraged. Therefore, the fact that I never got to Aleppo in the north, for example, was completely stupid. One time I insisted on wanting to travel from Beirut to Aleppo by train and then embarrassingly failed to find Beirut's railway station, which was so hidden away by the 1970s that even taxi drivers seemed not to know where it was. At other times I was defeated either by the lack of the proper visa or by simple bureaucratic errors. Nevertheless, the few brief visits I was able to make to Damascus remain not only especially memorable but also significant for increasing my understanding of Middle East political history and the architectural changes that took place in the major cities of the region in the twentieth century. As I was quick to learn, with the help of two of the greatest European journalists who covered the area, Patrick Seale and Eric Rouleau, the view of the world from Damascus is very different than that from Cairo, Beirut or Baghdad. Furthermore, Damascus presents clear evidence of the process by which the city burst out of its walls after the First World War to create new suburbs like al-Jisr and al-Salhiyya. It was also clear in the 1970s how the first tall modern hotels arrived to create a new and more jagged skyline no longer dominated by the minarets and towers of the centuries-old mosques and palaces.

Iraq, *1968*

So it was that I only visited Iraq once. During the flood season of April 1968, I flew to Baghdad from Beirut in that peculiar period of political hiatus between the Arab defeat of June 1967 and the final Ba'th Party coup in July 1968. The lackluster regime of Abdul-Rahman Aref had become so weak from its failure to do anything to fight the Israelis in the June War that its days were clearly numbered. I landed as dark was beginning to fall and, after a certain amount of the bargaining at which I was now becoming more adept, found a taxi driver who would take me into town for half an Iraqi dinar. He drove me through the deepening dusk, taking a bridge across the Tigris and passing a series of British-made red double-decker buses as they trundled through the deep puddles on Saadun Street, before ending up at the almost empty Ambassador Hotel.

Then followed one of those magical overnight Middle Eastern transformations when I awoke and pulled open the blinds to a view of the wide river shimmering in the gathering heat. The day was spent talking to development experts at the local UN office, having lunch with the resident representative, Omar Adeel, a Sudanese, and attending an evening party given by his deputy at his house in Officers' City, rented illegally, so he told me, from the real military man who owned it. My diary mentions that I spent some time talking to a man from the ministry of oil and that we all ate a meal out on the lawn. The next day was much the same: a morning spent reading reports at the UN office, lunch in a modern tree-filled suburb with an American architect, Ellen Jawdat, who was married to an Iraqi, and dinner with Mr. Adeel in a large, riverside club, its spacious rooms almost completely deserted. Fortunately, as it turned out, I also managed to do my own shopping in the old walled city with the help of Ellen's driver, treading gingerly along its muddy paths and choosing two bright red rugs almost at random, as well as two Bedouin blankets. Both were more or less the standard choice of all European travelers at this particular point in time.

I was less fortunate when it came to the weather; the rain began to come down in earnest as I set out on my prearranged tour of the ancient land south of Baghdad. The streets were full of puddles so deep that some cars had stalled so badly that they had been abandoned. My guide was a young Kurdish Iraqi with a Persian father from the UN office. He told me that after his military service he had worked for the British at the Habbaniyah Airbase. Although he spoke Kurdish, he could neither read not write it due to the absence of Kurdish schools in Baghdad. Needless to say, he was a strong supporter of the idea of an independent Kurdish state.

We drove first to Hilla through sandy-brown waterlogged fields and then on toward the holy city of Karbala on the Euphrates where the Prophet Mohammad's grandson, Ali, had been defeated and martyred. This was to enter a world I had only seen in the illustrations in books like Edward Lane's early nineteenth-century classic *The Manners and Customs of the Modern Egyptians* (1836), from the robed security police who came to check us out, to the lean brown faces of the white-turbaned mullahs, and the open shop fronts, some displaying what seemed like a hideous array of scraggly pieces of meat, occasionally presided over by a man in a Western-style suit.

Then we pushed on to another holy city, Najaf, across a flat sandy desert on which the occasional herd of camels could be seen leaning forward into the rain. We continued past a huge graveyard and into a system of circular streets that led, as in Karbala, to the central mosque. Here, we saw a funeral ending; the coffin was placed on top of a taxi and then driven off, followed by a line of cars. Just opposite the great front door, an old man lay on the pavement next to a few scattered possessions waiting patiently to die. In the street was a policeman on a red bicycle. There could be no question, my guide explained, of stepping inside the mosque as a non-Muslim. The thought itself was enough to give me a small frisson of excitement: for the first time in the Middle East, if I put a foot wrong, I might easily die.

On our way out we drove along streets of narrow shops and then through the muddy bazaar with its leaky roof. The smell in the meat section was almost more than I could stomach. More rain came down as we re-crossed the Euphrates, with cars drifting out of the drizzle with coffins on their roofs. Then, suddenly, we came to a stop in a huge puddle with a punctured wheel. In an instant, a boy appeared at the window saying that he would change the wheel for fifty fils—a fraction of an Iraq dinar. Other men appeared to lift up the car with the driver and me in it. In another ten minutes we were on our way.

Our last stop was at Babylon where, after a bad lunch in the dreary government rest house, we made a brief tour of the darkened museum with its shadowy drawings of what the city might have looked like four thousand years before. Outside were a few pillars supporting a ceremonial causeway that led toward what remained of the Ziggurat, the famous Tower of Babel, in the mist beyond. I was learning fast: although at flood time much of the electricity and almost all the phones went out, life still had to go on. It was also a crash course in the basics of Iraqi agriculture, a memorable lesson in how the Tigris and the Euphrates, fed by the melting winter snows in the Turkish mountains not far to the north, could flood at just the wrong time of year as far as the standing crops of winter wheat and barley were concerned. This was all so different from the quiet and peaceful Nile that, regular as clockwork, flooded Egypt in late August and September, after the spring cereals had been harvested and at just the right time to water the even more vital cotton crop in the early stages of growth.

Back at my Baghdad hotel, the phones were not working but the television was. I spent my last night watching a glossy-mustached male and self-satisfied-looking female reading the news in what seemed to me portentous and over-sincere voices, beset by large flies that tried their best to alight on their shiny black hair despite their surreptitious efforts to swat them away with their hands. And after that, murky pictures of a military sports event with the winners receiving cups and medals from large, round, bespectacled senior officers. Clearly I was witnessing the proud but very early days of Iraqi public television, with only one channel and, even by the standards of those days, the most primitive black and white equipment.

Omar Adeel dropped me off at the airport the next morning. He told me that he had been called to an emergency cabinet meeting at 1:30 a.m. to discuss the danger posed by a great wave that had swept down the Euphrates an hour earlier, threatening Karbala and the surrounding fields of standing barley. The army had been called out to try to limit the damage. I went quickly through the formalities of checking in, sat for a while near a party of Russians and Germans waiting for an Aeroflot flight, and finally took off for Beirut, up and through the clouds and away from Iraq's sodden land. Looking down, I saw that the sun had brought out a wide variety of browns in the desert, with occasional small green squares in the valleys where the water had been trapped to plant spring cereals. The colors changed endlessly, from a spectrum of yellow to red and then to black. The small patches of bright white houses as we passed over Syria looked to me like so many maggots suddenly exposed by the morning sun. And so I was back in Shemlan just after lunch, the end of a journey that, forty years before, would have taken at least a day, bumping slowly along from Baghdad to Beirut in one of the Nairn Transport Company's famous desert buses.

Short though my trip had been, it yielded a great deal of useful information for the future. For one thing, by flying over part of it, I had gained a general idea about the topography of the famous "fertile crescent." The Iraqi side was watered by large and unruly rivers, the Syrian by smaller ones as well as by winter rain, and the two areas were separated by a desert that had acted as a land bridge between them, allowing easy passage for caravans both east–west and north–south. For another, I could now make interesting and useful comparisons between the two great river valley civilizations, Egypt and Iraq: the one irrigated by a river with a controllable flood—the dam at Aswan—the other requiring an expensive series of (in 1968) unfinished dams, barrages, and "escape" channels to prevent annual disaster. Finally, my brief visit to the old quarter of Baghdad had provided an unforgettable whiff of a garrison city on the contested boundary of the eastern Arab and Ottoman world with an always-uncertain relationship to the powerful world of Persian Shi'ism beyond.

Syria

My few visits to Damascus seem to flow together in my mind—my memory is not much aided by the rather sparse entries in the one diary I kept intermittently between 1971 and 1980. I have written elsewhere in this memoir of the day or so I spent there in 1971 on the way back from a conference in Kuwait. I know I returned for a slightly longer visit in the mid-1970s,

Hejaz Railway—Building the station at Muazzem, 829 km from Damascus, 981 meters above sea level, 1908. (Imperial War Museum)

staying at the old, Mandate-period Orientale Hotel and making my way around the usual tourist sites of those days: the great Umayyad Mosque, the huge covered marketplace, the market gardens of the Ghouta along the Barada River, and the magnificent eighteenth-century Azm Palace. Here, far more than in Cairo, you could get a sense of continuous urban life going back over thirteen hundred years, of life lived seriously with great attention to quiet comfort and serious learning with none of the exuberance I had found in Egypt. The public rooms of the palace, for instance, were decorated with brightly colored tiles and cooled by splashing fountains, providing a place where you could sit quietly only a few feet away from the busy street outside. The large open courtyard of the Umayyad Mosque was used variously as a meeting place, a space to conduct small items of business or just to sit quietly in the winter sun—or, as I was later to work out, a place of recruitment for the type of militant groups of young men who took part in some of the bloody urban conflicts of the late 1970s. It seems, at that stage, the Ba'thist regime lacked the manpower or, perhaps, even the desire to monitor what went on in mosques, leaving the ground free for activists to keep an eye on pious young men before approaching them to attend a Qur'an study group that might quickly turn into something else.

Damascus is also a wonderful city for observing the restraint of late Otto-man architecture: its square, almost barrack-like schools and public build-ings, the simple Abdul-Hamid clock tower at the center of one of the main squares, and my particular favorite, the station where passengers and pil-grims had embarked on the old narrow-gauge Hejaz Railway. This train would take its slow-moving time—its top speed was perhaps no more than thirty miles an hour—to make its way south to Maan and Medina, with a spur over to Haifa on the Mediterranean coast. Looking something like an ornate palace from the front, with a beautifully ornate ceiling, the rear con-tained just four simple platforms under a stylish iron and glass roof.

Part IV. Northwest Africa

Libya, *1960*

My new wife, Ursula, and I spent our honeymoon in Libya in 1960, less than a decade after its independence from the international tutelage that had begun with the Italian defeat in World War II. My father was already quite familiar with the country and had worked closely with his friend Adrian Pelt, the United Nations representative, to provide the embryonic state with technical experts. It amused him to tell the story of one of his encounter with the king of Libya, in which he told him that he had a Welsh uncle with

Roger Owen in town square of Sirte, Libya, on his honeymoon in 1960.

the same name, Idris, to which the king is said to have replied, "We Arabs get around."

I had also begun to familiarize myself with the small amount of literature on the new country for my first post-graduation job, a commission from Chatham House to update one of their slimmer publications, *Libya: An Economic and Political Survey*. It was this, I think, that must have prompted me to suggest that we combine the second stage of our honeymoon with some academic research. I do not remember any objection, although it must have seemed somewhat peculiar. It also turned out to be something of an inspired idea as we had the whole place more or less to ourselves, from Brega in the east to Tripoli in the west. There was minimal tourism at the time, and we found the marvelous beaches and their accompanying Greek and Roman ruins—Leptis Magna, Sabratha, Cyrene—almost completely empty.

Tripoli Airport, like all Italian colonial airports, was some twenty-five miles inland and toward the Nafusa Mountains. Our first glimpse of the country, therefore, was of part of the route later traveled at high speed by the combination of Berber fighters and Western special forces that swooped down to "liberate" the capital from the Qaddafi regime in August 2011. We stayed in an empty flat lent to us by the UN resident representative, met the local UN experts, and in my case, went to the new Central Bank. There I found the country's only two graduate economists sitting somewhat disconsolately in their hot office reading A.J. Brown's classic work on the interwar depression, *The Great Inflation* (1955). One of them, Ali Attiga, later became the first head of the Organization of Arab Petroleum Exporting Countries (OAPEC).

Ursula and I were also driven to see the huge square red hole in the ground in the desert at Gharyan where the famous troglodytes lived in caves dug into terraces around the side. These ancient people were of uncertain origin and were also fierce in their desire not to be spied upon by any tourist they caught looking down. Unfortunately for them, they also lived close to another major tourist site: the remains of an Italian barracks that contained the crude relief map of coastal North Africa in the shape of a naked woman sprawled on her side. Known as the "Lady of Gharyan," this was drawn by a volunteer ambulance driver in the British army in 1943 with her many indentations marked with humorous place names like "Wadi Ya Know" and "Wadi Ya See."

It was at this stage too that I took up the offer of an American oil man whom I met at an evening party to fly to an oil rig deep into the Cyrenaican desert where oil had been found two years before, the first indication of Libya's huge oil riches to come. Not that there was much to see, and as the daytime temperature was something like 110°F in the boiling sun, with very little shade, I was happy to return in another plane as quickly as possible. Still, it made me feel that the work I was putting into the revision of the Chatham House "survey" now had a valuable extra dimension. I felt that the visit allowed me to speculate firsthand on the changes that oil would bring to what was then one of the world's poorest countries. Libya at the time survived on international handouts, the rent paid for its military bases, and the money earned from the export of scrap metal left over from the war as well as of its desert-tough esparto grass, then a primary ingredient in the manufacture of US dollar bills.

We were provided with a car to drive us to an agricultural field station run by the United Nation's Food and Agriculture Organization on the fertile Barce plain in the hills just east of Benghazi. We stopped on the way to buy the almost compulsory black and white Misrata rug, and then to spend the night in a rather primitive Italian hotel in Sirte. Supper was pasta and bread, and the lavatory had no more than a hole in the bathroom floor. Next morning we drove along the straight desert road that took us through the Italian triumphal arch that marked the boundary between the two former provinces of Tripoli and Cyrenaica, then up the steep and twisty road to the Jebal Akhdar (or Green Mountain). Many of the hairpin bends sported a crashed truck, left there as a warning about the danger of failing breaks.

The field station stood at the center of a range of fields and orchards created for the first Italian agricultural settlers who had arrived there soon after the region's bloody occupation in the early 1930s, a project that had lasted little more than a decade. Our hosts were an extremely hospitable Palestinian farming expert and his wife who provided their rare visitors not only with wonderful food but also rooms equipped with books and records—including the first songs Ursula and I had ever heard by Harry Belafonte. They were also wonderfully forgiving when, after borrowing one of their Land Rovers to drive down the extremely steep incline to the sea coast, I foolishly neglected to refill the radiator for the return trip, causing it to boil over and us to have to stop several times to allow it to cool down.

Altogether it was a memorable trip. It stood me in very good stead when, just over fifty years later, the popular revolt against the Qaddafi regime began in the east, producing a sudden demand for historical and military expertise. For, although the country was obviously hugely changed by its oil wealth, its basic geography remained the same, with the one coastal road still the only way for the rebels to get from Benghazi to Tripoli—and so subject to easy bombardment from the air. There also was a new set of obstacles on this road: the greatly expanded cities like Misrata, which sat across their route, full of opportunities for ambushes and for attacks from the rear. By the same token, the fact that there were no major cities between the mountains and Tripoli made it obvious that this was the way to get at Mu'ammar al-Qaddafi and his family, once it was realized that they could not be overthrown by the people of the city itself.

Morocco, *1972*

In the spring of 1972, at a painful moment in my personal life, I decided to take advantage of an invitation from my American friends, Bob and B.J. Fernea, to visit them in Marrakech in the south of Morocco where Bob was doing urban ethnographic fieldwork. I flew out from London via Gibraltar and then south across the long red plain that runs between the Atlantic and the Atlas Mountains—still with their winter snow gleaming in the sun—to a small airport just outside what was still largely a walled city.

The Ferneas and their children lived in an old house with a courtyard on one side and a busy street on the other. As I was quick to discover, theirs was a typical and entirely satisfactory arrangement for urban living. Their home had different degrees of privacy and public view, from the inside of the house and the roof where one could look out but not be seen to becoming part of the flow of people passing by on the street outside. I noticed, too, that it was much quieter than it would have been in Cairo, with fewer radios and honking horns, and hardly any noise at all after about nine in the evening. Altogether, it spoke of a much less ostentatious way of life, everything seemingly turned inward, with little sign from outside as to the wealth of those within.

Nearby was the main covered market and the open space known as the Jemaa el-Fna Square where all kinds of local entertainments were performed, as well as a variety of medical services from tooth pulling to the sale of salves and tonics. Although all of this—particularly the acrobats—was of obvious interest to tourists, I quickly realized that much of the rest of the activity went on with little reference to foreigners, given the fact that it was conducted in the local dialect that even native speakers of Arabic from elsewhere found difficult to comprehend. This meant, among many other things, that I could wander about on my own, almost unnoticed, and without anyone trying to sell me anything, a rare situation in most of the Arab countries I had visited before then.

I returned to Jemaa el-Fna Square again and again simply to observe the colorful and noisy scene while trying to make lists of all the things happening so I could write them down in my diary later. Here was a man examining a woman's tooth, there another apparently trying to relieve a boy's earache. Also on view were preachers, storytellers, folk-medicine men, magicians, comedians, dancers, gamblers, and men selling amulets and good luck charms. Other activities were more difficult to make sense of, like the two men showing off what seemed to be tapeworms held up in large glass jars and another giving what I thought was probably a physiology lesson through a microphone. These were accompanied by music from the insistent drummers, the small pops from the air guns in an outdoors shooting gallery, and the smells coming from the food stalls and the spice sellers. I was witness to a huge slice of local life, barely comprehensible to me, and with many other invisible transactions going on, the purpose of which I only read about in books later, like the verbal advertising of many services in a town where all written signs were subject to a tax.

My other form of investigating the town's economic activities consisted of walks with Bob Fernea through the covered market and on to see the tanneries and other smelly or noisome activities in their usual place outside the walls. Bob had been in the town long enough to have discovered much about some of the basic business practices. For example, the rug sellers had a way of calling out the price they had offered a passing tourist to their colleagues further down the central passage using a numerical code that only they could understand. He had also worked out some of the factors common to almost all price negotiations, such as the fact that the shop's owner was likely to offer a slightly better price than his sons, who were anxious not to make mistakes. But he was yet to find a fully satisfactory explanation for the apparent lack of competition between sellers of more or less identical shawls, although he suspected that it had something to do with the manipulation of the price to suit each individual customer.

As we headed out of one of the gates, we saw men with bare legs standing in square pits of chemical fluid cleaning the leather skins of any remaining flesh and gristle, a nasty, smelly, and sometimes dangerous task for which they were paid in *keef* (the local marijuana) as well as money. We also watched the potters at their wheels before returning home. It seemed to me that Marrakech contained a much wider variety of crafts than I had witnessed in Cairo as well as a much higher standard of leatherwork, almost all of it carried out by hand with the help of the ubiquitous sewing machine. Indeed, the only factory within the ramparts of the walled town was a tanning enterprise that used electric-powered machinery to clean and dry the skins.

One of Marrakech's other special features was its internationally funded hospital for badly treated donkeys. A local Englishman, Bryce Nairn, who was dismayed at the way the local donkeys were often both savagely beaten and forced to wear a fierce metal bit clamped over their lacerated tongues, had established this clinic in the 1920s. Nairn, whom I was taken to meet, was born in Morocco in the early 1900s, sent back to England by his parents in 1905—carried on a palanquin to a port on the coast he told me—and then returned in 1920s as a trained vet.

The Ferneas were also kind enough to take me on expeditions further afield, up to the top of the nearby Atlas range. These mountains rise sheer to some twelve thousand feet or so above the plane, though it was still hot enough on top for my face to become uncomfortably burned. We also went to the old trading port of Mogador (Essaouira) on the coast with its dark, colonnaded streets built to keep the merchants and their goods cool from the summer sun. But far and away the most memorable expedition was the two-day trip we took to the equally ancient city of Fez, memorable equally for what we saw and the way it started: with me heavily under the influence of some raw *keef*. Bob had sprinkled the stuff on my morning omelet, annoyed by the fact that, being a nonsmoker, I was unable to inhale the stuff properly the night before. He had told me nothing of this, of course. Sitting in the car, I struggled as best I could to prevent him from having the pleasure of discovering the full extent of what was going on in my head, while B.J. and him had their own conversation in the front as we whizzed along at some seventy to eighty miles per hour on the straight, tree-lined road that took us northward across the plain. No giggling, although I very much wanted to, no groaning, and no appeal for an aspirin.

It was the first of only two experiences of this kind. The *keef* pushed the inside of my head up higher and higher from one level to the next, while another part of my mind remained able to check up on the process by constantly asking itself questions about what was taking place. Colors remained the same. So too did my sense of smell. My mouth tasted dry and awful. But try as I might, I could not fix my racing mind on anything external, like my wife or my baby daughter, as free associations flickered by and the voice inside began to divide into several different ones. The most insistent of these acted as an observer whose comments were so quick that they sometimes appeared to precede the feelings they were called upon to analyze. It was like being both inside and outside my own story—writing it, experiencing it, commenting on it—all at the same time.

When we finally arrived and my head began to calm down, Fez proved to be an entirely different place than Marrakech: more Mediterranean, as opposed to Marrakech's Africanness, more austerely Islamic in style and feel, and also more colonial, with the division between the new modern city and the old medina much more clear cut. As we looked down from the balcony of our hotel onto the clear divide between new and old, we saw a checkerboard of square grey houses often with blackened top stories; the rushes used to shield the narrow streets from sun often caught fire in the sun. There was also much less noise apart for the tinny sound of hammering, the hoarse cries of "*balak*" from donkey men, and the chanting from the Quranic schools.

Then Bob and I ventured to the labyrinth of narrow alleys below. This was a dark world of great human density, with sudden glimpses of the insides of great mosques or of the elaborate doors that provided an occasional flash of color on the otherwise undecorated façades of the houses of the great merchants. Even the few open gardens seemed deliberately drab, while I noticed few of the public fountains that grace the eye in Cairo.

Altogether, the city seemed an alien, unwelcoming, and so somewhat dangerous place, with an atmosphere totally different from that of Marrakech, with Bob's search for more *keef* a furtive affair of whispers and quick exchanges. And I was not in the least surprised when, at lunch the next day with a couple from the United States Information Service, the wife informed us that there was an undeclared cholera epidemic in the old quarters of the city, though it would not reach alarming levels until the winter. All testimony, or so it seemed to me, to Albert Hourani's observation of some years before that each of the great cities of the Arab Muslim world had its own special character—if you were suddenly plunked down anywhere you would know immediately what city you were in.

Our return journey to Marrakech was much less exciting. We took a route closer to the Atlas Mountains across an emerald green plain dotted with crumbling *ksars* (big houses) of the well-to-do landlords that looked like the ruins of so many ancient Greek palaces. The walls of the courtyards of other, lesser, dwellings were covered by what looked like long hats of yellow straw and grass to provide cover for their animals. Then across a stretch of red-earthed country empty but for the black tents of the nomads and, along the road itself, clumps of men waiting for trucks to take them home from their day's work. Finally, there was the dramatic approach to Marrakech, with a strong wind raising clouds of red dust while bright flashes of lightening lit up the southern sky.

Tunisia, *2010*

My only proper visit to Tunisia was in 2010 as the lecturer on a large sailing ship chartered by the Harvard Alumni Association to conduct a party of some hundred passengers from Sicily to Tunisia and then on to Minorca and Malaga in Spain. This took me back to the various Mediterranean voyages I had undertaken in the 1950s and 1960s and the strong feeling I had at the time that Mediterranean port cities were best approached from the sea, and, if possible, on a boat with sails. It also seemed obvious that one of my lectures should be about someone who had written wonderfully about this same sea: the poet Samuel Coleridge, author of *The Rime of the Ancient Mariner*, a survivor of all that the Mediterranean could manage by way both of storms and calm on his way to Malta in 1799 to take up his new post as secretary to the new British governor of the island.

Another lecture had to be about Zine El Abidine Ben Ali, the dictator of Tunisia who had just announced his proposal to stand for yet another term as president, a move that would, in effect, make him president for life. For various fairly obvious reasons, he still had a very good reputation among Europeans and Americans as a man who presided over a country of wonderful beaches, fine hotels, and the most progressive personal status law in the Arab world. I had already begun work on my book *The Rise and Fall of Arab Presidents for Life*, and so one look of his smug self-satisfied features and his rather too black bouffant hairstyle suggested a sinister attempt to appear not only much younger but also much more benevolent than he really was. I took it upon myself to ask my fellow cruisers to search for signs of his megalomania when they went ashore, looking particularly for variations of his official portrait, which were everywhere to be seen, and the use of the omnipresent offices of his single party, the Rassemblement Constitutionel

Democratique (RCD) to act as the equivalent of temples for the worship of his power and his munificence.

We called first at Sousse on the fertile plain south of Tunis where we took a bus to the great al-Uqba mosque at Kairouan. For centuries this had been one of the main centers of Islamic learning, and its large courtyard with a covered area at the far end supported by Roman columns made it one of the most powerful early influences on subsequent mosque architecture. Then on to El Djem with its huge Roman amphitheater, with seats for some thirty-five thousand people, so well preserved that you could sit there, as I did, imagining the gladiators and the animals fighting, before climbing down to see the very cages and the places where they waited in the wings below.

Our next port was La Goullette in the Gulf of Tunis. The port's wide views of the city included the area along the water known as the Bardo, which contained a linked set of public buildings including the palace, offices, and government buildings that constituted the core of the Ben Ali family's power. Other signs of the family's wealth were kept well hidden away. It was only much later that I learned that our bus drive to the old Roman city of Dougga had taken us past a huge complex of offices hidden behind a long wall that constituted the headquarters of Sakher El Materi, Ben Ali's son-in-law and rumored to be his chosen successor. His many monopolies—ranging from telecommunications to auto-distribution to cruises—were both a huge source of wealth and whispered criticism, before they were all confiscated after the 2011 revolution. What we did see were red and white flamingos rising from a pale blue lake and then large fields being plowed for winter cereals. We also saw many RCD offices covered in signs both in praise of Ben Ali and containing exhortations by him, for example, *"Khayyarna al-Awad,"* which I took to mean, "We have made the choice of hard work." This propaganda was barely offset by just a few traces of what I took to be anti–Ben Ali graffiti; such comments as "FI Fighters" were hastily painted overnight on official road signs, and were fated to be just as quickly erased by the next passing police patrol. When I asked our young local guides about them, they pretended not to know what I meant—even more evidence of the state of fear in which they and their fellow countrymen lived and from which tourists, like us, were supposed to remain completely unaware.

Algeria, *2013*

My fourth Harvard alumni cruise in the spring of 2013 provided what was probably going to be my last opportunity to visit Algeria. Starting in neighboring Tangier, the boat then visited four Algerian port cities in succession before finishing up in Palermo, ancestral home of Kings Roger I and II of twelfth-century Norman Sicily. Now much confined in my walking by my weak left leg, I had to experience events on shore at a distance or, after I returned home, by watching movies set in the famous Algerian Kasbah, which rises steeply from the harbor of the old city. This circumstance provided the essential drama of at least two French films of that name, in which a notorious French jewel thief, Pepe le Moko, who is safe inside its narrow alleyways, is lured out by his love for a beautiful foreign tourist on a cruise like mine.

My other Algerian experience came from talking to the four male Algerian guides who slept on our ship every night and who befriended my nephew, Hugh, who was looking after me. They told me something of what it was to be a young man growing up in their rich but secretive and badly managed country. While obviously as patriotic as anyone could be, all knew that they were unlikely ever to get a job that paid them well enough to get married, or even rent an apartment. Instead, they dreamed of winning what they called the Canadian Lottery, which allowed a select few to obtain work across the Atlantic now that France and other parts of Europe were more or less closed to them by anti-immigration legislation.

Part V. The Gulf States

For most of those who teach and write about modern Middle Eastern politics, Egypt is usually their model. The Gulf was, and remains, something distinct. Hence, in my own case, my early visits there were the result much more of the accident of invitation than by design. These first trips were complemented by two Harvard alumni cruises in 1997 and 2000 in which I got to see most of the major ports—Bahrain, Abu Dhabi, Dubai, and Muscat—arriving there as travelers of bygone days had always arrived: from the sea. Not, of course, that time had simply stood still. Bahrain had become a major US naval base after the British decided to pull out from the Gulf in the early 1970s, and the site of growing popular resistance against its Sunni rulers. This unrest was only half hidden by the obvious attempts to rub out the blue anti-regime signs on the white walls of the small houses hidden among its huge forest of date palms. Meanwhile, Dubai had converted itself from a hub of the *dhow* (traditional sailboat), with traffic to and from Iran and India, to a major center for the repair and refurbishment of ships in its huge new dry dock. It also benefitted from the decline of the Arabian Peninsula's old hub Aden, whose enormous historical role as a port of call for international shipping had come to an abrupt end. The closure of the Suez Canal from 1967 to 1975 first began affecting traffic to Aden, then the war between North and South Yemen in the early 1990s had left its airport strewn with wrecked Russian MiGs and its port services catering to a dwindling number of cruise ships.

Indeed, constant change was the name of the game in the Gulf; nothing ever seemed to stay the same. New buildings kept appearing in place of old, and what had once been a hotel-lined corniche along the waters of the Gulf often disappeared entirely, to be replaced by another with even larger hotels stuck out on landfill and looking completely different. As a result, most towns turned into twenty-four-hours-a-day, brightly illuminated construction sites, with trucks rumbling through at all hours carrying stone and rubble from the few small hills to make new living space. I was later to observe the aftermath of all this hectic activity. In retrospect, it seemed a little as though I was seeing another Boston Back Bay being built, when the site of the famous Revolutionary War Battle of Bunker Hill was leveled in the late nineteenth century to facilitate the creation of the wholly new residential area just across the Charles River.

The logic for all this, as I managed to analyze it over time, consisted of three separate but interrelated factors. First, the Kuwaitis, loathed surrendering their earnings from oil during and after World War II to their British protectors, and so invented good reasons for it to be spent at home. They created a welfare state, requiring the construction of hundreds of new hospitals and schools, as well as houses for the largely immigrant workforce that was required to staff them. This practice then spread to their Gulf neighbors once they too had access to royalties from oil and gas. Second, a competition developed between the separate Gulf states in terms of a string of distinct and always larger projects: an airport here, a dry dock there, all the way up to the world's tallest building, the world's largest mall. Third, most of them also began to compete for various types of tourists: some shoppers attracted by duty-free bargains or enticed to stop over on their way through the Gulf from East to West and back, while others, as I found for myself in early 2013, simply there for the sun and dune bashing.

Kuwait, *1971*

I first visited Kuwait early in 1971 at the invitation of the General Union of Palestine Students, the same organizers, and much the same participants, that had come together in Amman just before the Black September fighting the year before. The conference itself proved to be a somewhat surreal affair, given the tight reign upon it imposed by the Kuwaiti government as well as the fact that there was little disposition among the Palestinian students themselves either to criticize what had gone wrong or to suggest what their movement should do next. I remember being interviewed in a rather primitive Kuwaiti television studio about the event and being told, in no uncertain terms, that I was not allowed to say anything critical of King Hussein, whose forces had driven the Palestinians out of the Jordanian capital just a few months before. I also remember the obvious unease of Tariq Ali—then a fierce International Marxist Group revolutionary firebrand—provoked by the young Palestinians' failure to engage in any type of post-defeat auto-critique or policy revision. This failure incited him to stand up and denounce one of the speakers, who had made a particularly adulatory reference to Yasser Arafat, as an example of the dangers of an unthinking reliance on Arafat's one-man leadership as opposed to Ho Chi Minh's much more collective style.

All this gave us little time to explore Kuwait, apart from a characteristic expedition into the desert organized by Fred Halliday and some local Kuwaiti radicals. The purpose of this trip was to show us how, for all the vaunted success of Kuwait's cradle-to-grave welfare state, there were still tent-living members of the local Bedouin community who were unable to take advantage of the free schools and free hospital services due to the lack of transportation necessary for regular access.

Later, on the way back to London via Damascus, my friend Bob Sutcliffe and I met up with some young radicals from the Popular Front for the Liberation of Palestine (PFLP) who took us to visit their discreet local headquarters. In another room, we caught a glimpse of the PFLP's militant leader, Nayif Hawatmeh. He was generally regarded in the West as one of the world's most dangerous men, but perhaps, even then, he was beginning the process of rethinking Palestinian strategy that led him, only a year later, to become the first leader to propose a two-state solution, a position most other Palestinians regarded as tantamount to a heretical recognition of the existence of the state of Israel.

I had a much longer visit to Kuwait a little over thirteen years later, in 1984, when I went there to collect information for a report that I had been asked to write for London's Minority Rights Group on the condition of labor migrants in the Gulf. I was fortunate not only to have had a place to stay in a building belonging to an Oxford friend, Hashim Behbehani, but I also had other friends who knew the whereabouts of some of the information I needed about the precariousness of migrant life there.

As it turned out, this was a particularly bad time for the little city-state. Business confidence was crippled by the 1982 crash of the unofficial stock market: the Souk al-Manakh, actually a large garage where, in a frenzy of speculation, huge numbers of shares were bought and sold at inflated prices using postdated checks. This left the lobbies and lounges of the newly built international hotels—the Hilton, the Hyatt Regency, the Marriott, and the Sheraton—almost empty. The shock was palpable and its origins and its effect the subject of much intense speculation and comment. Some of the progressives I met—Khaldoun Naqib and others—pushed for greater public accountability from the ruling al-Sabah family; others, like Hashim, maintained that the event marked the end of that moment in local history when what he called the "oil generation" had seen and done everything, leaving them with no further challenge and, so, a life without any particular meaning.

I must say that I felt very much the same. Kuwait's role as an innovator in the use of its oil wealth—the establishment of a welfare state, the Kuwaiti development fund for investment in the rest of the Arab Middle East—seemed over. Much more creativity and excitement seemed to be found in some of the states further down the Gulf. Even those old friends from Oxford like Khaldoun Naqib, whom I met teaching at the university seemed somewhat defeated. They were turning their interest to trends in the wider Arab world, where they may have been the first to identify a new species of dictatorial government that they may have been the first to style "authoritarian."

Nevertheless, life for the well-to-do still went on in its old way in the famous diwans, rooms in private houses where huge meals of fish and rice were still served by the host to guests sitting or lying on the floor. At the Behbehanis, the food was followed by coffee and conversation carried on above the blare of ubiquitous television sets. These, too, were the site of political deals, as well as a source of recruitment for those standing for parliament for constituencies so small that most of the electorate was not only known personally to the candidate but could also be invited to a meal in one large tent. As for my impressions of the city, I used my diary to sum up it up with weary brevity: "blue skies, big cars, lighted light towers, men without women, empty restaurants in palatial hotels, aggressive driving at roundabouts, empty streets."

As for my research into the lives of the non-Kuwaiti labor migrants, I was able to observe some of them not only at work but also, more visibly, on their one day off. There were then Indian women to be seen in the square by the Sheraton, Filipino maids by the cathedral, various sub-continentals playing cricket on two dusty pitches, Afghans kicking a football, Koreans in an enclosed compound washing their clothes, and others playing tennis.

Many, however, were also unseen; I was shown some of their labor contracts, and I knew that they were required to work seven days a week without any day of rest. Even more shocking, all had had their passports taken away from them by their employers, lest they try to leave the country without fulfilling their obligations. Additionally, they often entered into these arrangements by signing an Arabic document put in front of them that they could neither read nor properly understand. It was a kind of servitude that only made sense in terms of the extreme poverty in their place of birth, and, in the case of the women, from the fact that there was simply no work at all for them back home. Hence, and this was another chastening discovery, well-meaning attempts by their local consular authorities to protect them from, for example, rape by their employers were usually resisted; without their wages, their families would have nothing to eat and their children no means to buy the textbooks and other materials needed for school.

The United Arab Emirates (UAE), *1976*

I was first invited to visit the UAE in February 1976 to give a well-paid talk to its fledgling crop of diplomats, a much sought-after boondoggle at that time for relatively impecunious Oxford academics like myself. Along with the pay—a large sum of local currency handed over with some embarrassment in a small brown envelope—it also provided an opportunity to visit the Emirates. This included its one and only university: the United Arab Emirates University at al-Ain, strategically-placed at some distance from the coast to prevent its students, and perhaps more importantly, its largely Egyptian faculty, from making any kind of political trouble in the main towns. Perhaps, too, to allow the local authorities to keep an eye on what was going in the nearby Buraimi Oasis, thought to sit atop a major oil field and so subject in the 1950s to rival claims of ownership by the governments of the Emirates, Saudi Arabia, and Oman, backed by their different great power supporters, Britain and the United States. This dispute was finally settled by arbitration in 1972. As it turned out, the university did seem to be full of disgruntled professors who resented having to teach in such a primitive place with nothing at all to do in the evenings. As for the world-famous oasis, it was just that: a small grove of palm trees around a well, with no sign of the oil wealth beneath, and only a small military checkpoint on the road in.

Back on the coast, I spent a small part of a day being driven the whole length of the UAE, from Abu Dhabi to the green "mountain" above Ras al-Khaimah and back. The road was almost empty, the main danger coming

127

from camels and from the occasional motorcycle cop hiding behind one of the vast roadside billboards, waiting to ticket anyone going more than seventy miles per hour. It was also quite hot and so something of a pleasure not only to stop for lunch in a hotel but also to enjoy a postprandial snooze in a room that had been hired especially for the purpose by my thoughtful hosts. Otherwise, the tiny city-states with famous names flashed by, so small that we were in and out of Sharjah, Ajman, and Umm al-Quwain in little more than the blink of an eye. Some of these were still so poor that they received their main income from the manufacture and sale of colorful but strangely shaped postage stamps. Altogether, I am glad to have seen the Gulf as it was then, in the sleepy decades between the decline of the pearling industry and the distribution of great wealth from oil. Then, Abu Dhabi and Sharjah seemed only to come alive when a British Overseas Airways—after 1974, a British Air plane—arrived at dusk, when Land Rovers raced out to meet it, and the passengers disbursed slowly in the evening heat to the various rest houses and waterside villas scattered about.

Gulf Cruise, *1997*

My second wife, Margaret, and I returned to Dubai for the start of a Harvard Alumni Association cruise in 1997. We stayed overnight in the newly built Hyatt Regency Hotel with its characteristic revolving restaurant and then joined our boat at Jebel Ali, the world's largest man-made harbor, with sixty-seven berths and a nearby Free Trade Zone with over a hundred companies already installed. The cruise itself involved a day tour to Abu Dhabi along a grass-lined road—the grass imported, we were told, from California—protected by an anti-camel fence. Indeed, almost everything seemed to have been imported, including natural gas from Sharjah. What also seemed extraordinary and unusual was the ruler's obvious delight in new buildings; structures built only ten or fifteen years before were being pulled down to make way for a nest of twelve-story towers, all the same height but each exhibiting a different color and design.

Tourism was still in its infancy, but everyone seemed to be giving it a try. In one place we saw an ostrich farm, in another the preparations for a camel race, the tiny jockeys—then imported from Sudan—attached to the backs of their tall mounts by Velcro pads in the seat of their pants. We also witnessed some of what were to become a staple of the Gulf's attempt to create its own history: the first museums, the one in Doha housed in the ruler's former palace and full of all manner of arms and armor. Even Saudi Arabia appeared to be trying to get into the business in its own cautious way, allowing us to be one of the first foreign cruise ships to dock at Jeddah. The passengers were allowed to wander about the main square of that beautiful stone-built city more or less un-chaperoned; the one concession demanded of us was that the women should cover themselves from head to foot in black abayas. It was a learning experience indeed, of what it was like to be a Saudi woman out in public, or a Saudi man who had to identify his wife, so I was told after I had completely failed to identify my own, by her shoes or her handbag.

Dubai-Sharjah, *2000*

I did not return to the Emirates until I was invited to Sharjah for a ceremony to commemorate the opening of the first part of the new Sharjah University in 2000. The Qasimi rulers had taken it upon themselves to promote the cause of local higher education, two of them having obtained their PhDs from Exeter University in the United Kingdom. They had written their dissertations on the destruction of the old port city in the early nineteenth century by the British on the grounds of it being a haven for what they called "pirates"—simple defenders of their own commerce in their eyes. They had then gone on to write many books and articles in the same vein. In return, they had become wealthy donors to the new Centre for Gulf Studies at Exeter, several of whose members were also present on this occasion. They sat not far from me under the huge rotunda, which was so large that it seemed at least to rival the central dome of St Paul's Cathedral in London.

The New Universities of the Gulf

In spite of their tiny indigenous populations of literate citizens, the rulers of the small city-states of the Gulf began to build new university campuses, partly, it is said, for reasons of prestige, and to be able to cater to a demand that girls not have to go abroad for their education. They probably also wanted to be able to control what was taught in class and read in libraries, although this was strenuously denied by all concerned. In some cases, existing universities were simply expanded, in others, new ones were financed and built either in association with American universities, for example the New York University campus in Abu Dhabi, or along the lines of the American University of Beirut, which provided the model for the American University of Sharjah.

Like many of my friends in Middle East studies, I was initially skeptical of this whole process, doubting that promises of free speech, easily given by each ruler, would actually be adhered to. Nevertheless, at the time of writing these memoirs (2013–14), and as far as I know, this does not seem to have been a problem. According to those whom I have spoken to, who also teach at NYU Abu Dhabi, it is more likely that the whole process has encouraged a form of self-censorship that has yet to surface in any kind of blatant way. What is obvious is the competition among the Gulf universities themselves for what remained only a small pool of local and foreign students, augmented in at least one case, by the interference of the local security services, which warranted the cancellation of a conference I was invited to attend in Sharjah—about which more below.

The most interesting academic event I attended was one in Abu Dhabi in 2005 with my new partner, Ruth. Although sponsored by the local university, it was actually organized by an international group of local and foreign students—the World Educational Forum—as a celebration of global civil society and featured presentations by luminaries like Muhammad Yunus, the Bangladeshi inventor of the concept of microcredit. Other participants included the Spanish opera star Placido Domingo, who sang for us on a makeshift stage out in the desert. He told me the next day that he found the event very peculiar; without any walls to act as a baffle he could neither hear himself nor the voice of the woman he was singing a duet with. My own small contribution was to give a brief talk to the assembled students in a hall outside Abu Dhabi's new seven-star hotel, the Emirates Palace, an edifice so large that guests were transported about on the kind of motorized carts used in airports. Ruth and I were housed in a nearby Hilton hotel with a friendly bar that served alcohol to foreigners. From here we walked the small distance to the conference along a corniche hung with banners that welcomed us and the other "guests."

My second visit to a Gulf university, the American University of Sharjah, in 2013, was much more dramatic. The event itself was cancelled while I was on the plane from London as the result of the detention and then deportation of one of the invitees from the London School of Economics. The precise reason was unknown to us at the time, but we speculated that it had something to do with his willingness to criticize the ruling family of Bahrain. This left me, and a few of the other participants who had arrived before the news was out, to mill around in the same Hyatt Regency Hotel that I had stayed in at the beginning of one of the Harvard alumni cruises a decade or so before. Round and round went the revolving restaurant, taking three hours to show the new Dubai Tower (then the tallest building in the world), the desert, the waters of the Gulf, and back again, a memorable sight at sunset. Fortunately, there were interesting colleagues to talk to. We also went on a short excursion with our hosts from the American University to a would-be French restaurant called the Madeleine, which had a wonderful view but food that Proust would certainly have found very ordinary; most of the ingredients were imported, frozen, from far away.

Malls and Museums

As if by an iron law, the Gulf museums became larger and larger over the years: their concern with artifacts and folklore tricked out with the help of experts from places like the British Museum in London. Of special interest to me was the effort to stress local history's popular pre-oil origins — the main activity of the local working class appeared to be either building dhows on the beach or diving for pearls offshore. The malls were similar; they began as covered markets and ended up, as in Dubai, with what is said to be the world's largest, with miles of brand name shops along brightly lit, air-conditioned passages, interspersed with places to sit, eat, and enjoy various attractions such as skiing or swimming in a cage with sharks.

* * * * *

Visiting, as I hope I have been able to express, has many functions for those who want to maintain an interest in countries at some distance from where they live: a way of keeping in touch, of noticing important developments, of exchanging ideas, and, perhaps above all, of maintaining a dialogue with local friends and colleagues unable, for so many reasons, to travel freely themselves.

4   INTERPRETING THE MIDDLE EAST

When I first went to Cairo in 1962 to conduct research for an Oxford DPhil, I had no academic training in anything except a little British and international political history and some basic economic theory. This was very much a sign of the times. There was at that time no equivalent of the American comprehensive exams designed for PhD students and no field of Middle East studies, and so nothing had prepared me for research into nineteenth-century Egypt, let alone the wider Middle East. My only true exposure to the field was a set of lectures by Albert Hourani on Middle East history. These focused on the growing sense of an Islamic civilizational malaise produced by an expanding and ever-more powerful Europe, followed by the break up of the Ottoman Empire into separate, and politically unstable, Arab entities after World War I. Moreover, as I was soon to discover, there were, as of yet, very few specialized books on my subject, apart from Helen Rivlin's 1961 *The Agricultural Policy of Muhammad Ali in Egypt*. Additionally, access to the Egyptian state archives was limited and their use constrained by the absence of a proper catalog.

Much like the previous generation of Middle East scholars such as Albert Hourani, I was forced to make my research methods up as I went along, talking to people, visiting whatever archives and libraries I could find, and relying very much on friends to point me in the right direction. In this way I finally obtained enough information to write a thesis—that then became a book—on the impact of the production and exportation of long-staple cotton on Egypt's nineteenth-century economic development. Then, from 1964 onward, I gave university lectures on various aspects of the Middle East's economic history.

Some years later, on my return from Lebanon at the end of the 1960s, I started to add a political history component as well. The basis of this was a rather crude notion of political economy that revolved, in Judith Tucker's words, around three main themes: "the growth of the state, the penetration

132

of capitalism into the region, and the cultural impact of the West."[1] Central to this approach was a theme not enormously different from the one I had learned from Hourani, of a process of defensive Middle Eastern modernization set in train by a series of financial reforms and military overhaul in response to the threat posed by European encroachments beginning with the Napoleonic invasions of Egypt and Syria in 1798 and 1799. This approach, crude though it now seems, also provided a jumping-off point from which to develop a critique of Orientalism in terms of its failure to address the major historical forces at work in this process, compounded by its exaggeration of the "backwardness" of the Ottoman Empire and its Arab provinces in the eighteenth century.

Just as important was the assistance I received from discussions with a small group of friends and colleagues I met in the early 1970s later to become known as the "Hull Group." This group then broadened out into a series of annual mini-conferences held at the University of Hull by men and women engaged in much the same task of revisionism from much the same social science perspective. For the most part, we relied on a form of Marxist political economy modified by readings from Max Weber, which we employed both to critique and then—in line with what we thought of as the essence of early nineteenth-century Germanic critical practice—to form the basis of a more satisfactory alternative. This involved drawing on approaches heavily influenced by former French Marxists like Jacques Berque and Maxime Rodinson, and French structuralists like Michel Foucault, with their focus on the exercise of political power by the modern state and its use to build new and increasingly durable forms of authoritarian regimes of the Nasserist type. It was in this same vein that I wrote "Studying Islamic History" in 1973, my first critique of Orientalism in a review of the *Cambridge History of Islam* published in the just-established *Journal of Interdisciplinary History*. My next critique was of the first volume of Hamilton Gibb and Harold Bowen's *Islamic Society and the West in the Review of Middle East Studies*, published in 1975 by a good friend of the Hull Group, David Wolton, the owner of Ithaca Press.

My second set of influences stemmed from my membership in the Near and Middle East Committee of the American Social Science Research Council, which I was asked to join in 1985 on the recommendation of P. J. Vatikiotis. Quite how this came about I still do not know, but it must have had something to do with the council's decision to abandon its previous

---

1 Judith E. Tucker. "Taming the West: Trends in the Writing of the Modern Social History of the Anglophone Academia," in *Theory, Politics and the Arab World*, ed. Hisham Sharabi, (New York: Routledge, 1990), 201.

joint project on political "behaviorism" in favor of the new field of area studies, and so searched for regional experts whose own work was of an interdisciplinary kind. In a very short period of time, I was followed on to the committee by others connected with the Hull Group: Talal Asad, Sami Zubaida, Huri Islamoglu, and Timothy Mitchell. With them came an intellectual agenda that focused on the examination of the relationship between the "state"—best defined in Mitchell's term as an "effect" of policies designed to stress its cohesion and its ability to act separately from the social relations embedded in it—and society, a topic that was fast becoming the central concern of area studies in general. This interest was led, as usual, by those concerned with Latin America but was soon given an extra boost by a revived interest in the notion of "civil society" promoted by the peaceful Eastern European revolts against Soviet domination that triggered the fall of the Berlin Wall in 1989.

Thinking about this process of intellectual apprenticeship now, as I look back on it toward the end of my career, it seems most useful to divide the question of how I came to believe, and so to write and lecture about the Middle East as I did, into two closely interrelated sections: becoming an economic historian of Egypt and then of the Middle East, and then becoming a teacher, a writer, and then a pundit on twentieth-century Middle Eastern political history.

Becoming an Economic Historian of the Middle East

When deciding what subject to read at Oxford University I chose Philosophy, Politics, and Economics (PPE), although my main "A Level" subject at my British boarding school had been history. For one thing, the Oxford history syllabus not only stopped at 1914 but also required undergraduates to learn Anglo-Saxon—a waste of time, so it seemed to me then, for anyone interested primarily in the modern world. An additional reason may have been my observation that history, as taught in England in the 1950s, was almost completely without any overt theoretical concerns except in two more or less self-enclosed areas. One of these was the fierce dispute between Hugh Trevor Roper and R.H. Tawney over the so-called "Rise of the Gentry," with its suggestion that the explanation for England's seventeenth-century civil war may have had as much to do with social change as with ideological and religious factors. The second was the remains of a rather tired dispute over the nature of imperialism. This second debate did not really spring back into life again until the 1961 publication of Ronal Robinson's and John (Jack) Gallagher's *Africa and the Victorians* with its direct challenge to Marxist or other economic explanations for imperial expansion. I also could have thought that a smattering of economics might be useful for the career I then imagined: in government, or working for some type of international development organization.

It turned out to be a fateful choice, although I only prepared for two economic papers in my final Oxford exams: "Principles of Economics" and "Economic Organization." I was already well aware of the limitations imposed by my shortcomings in mathematics and I was never able to master calculus or undertake proper regressions. Nonetheless, this exposure was still enough to allow me to spark my interest and become engaged in development economics, like my father, as well as to form much of my thinking about the major forces shaping world history. It was important, too, because most academic historians then thought—and many still do—that talking and writing about economic matters, even ones so simple as those involving national income, indifference curves, the multiplier effect, etc., was a much more arcane activity than it actually seemed to me to be, clearly giving those who were familiar with its technical language some kind of an edge. So it was that when Chatham House asked me to revise their political and economic survey of Libya in 1959–60, I immediately said yes. And that when I came to apply for a scholarship to do graduate work at St Antony's College, beginning in 1960, I suggested a topic involving a comparison of the impact on national development between two economically significant export sectors—that dominated by cotton in Egypt and oil in Iraq—a notion that I had come across in the work of Jonathan Levin.

Once launched into the research, first in Oxford, then in Cairo, I made two very significant personal discoveries. One was that I was, by temperament, more of a historian than an economist, preferring to study cotton in the nineteenth century rather than the twentieth. The second was that, by so doing, and by extending the notion of economic "development" back into Egyptian history, I was much more likely to write something original, something that of all the people in the world, only I, as a foreigner, and one or two elderly Egyptians, was likely to know anything very much about.

It followed, too, that I began to be forced to think about the different methodologies employed by economists and historians, including their approach to such basic questions as what constitutes an explanation and what constitutes meaning. There is a good example of this in one of my diaries for early 1964 when, after a period of reading in the New York Public Library and the National Archives in Washington DC, I tried to sketch out the basics of a series of lectures to be entitled "Mohammad Ali: A Problem in

135

Economic History" in which the key questions to be addressed were posed as "what happened?" and "why?"

In this formulation, and in the absence of almost any direct evidence as to what Egypt's ruler himself had been thinking, the sparse information to be found from the accounts of travelers and other foreign visitors was supposed to yield two things. The first was a form of explanation deriving from context and chronology: one event or decision was assumed to have caused another. The second was evidence of the operation of a particular form of administrative logic—the desire for a modern army to defend Egypt from external invasion led to the introduction of a new cash crop (long-staple cotton) necessary to provide money from taxes and monopolies and to fund various ancillary needs like military hospitals, technical education, and, above all, the creation of a large cadre of native Egyptian technical experts.

As my study also required access to the figures needed to measure growth and progress, I soon came across a basic distinction between economic historians with regard to these indispensible tools of their trade: those for whom any number was good enough and who paid little attention to how it had been calculated, and those who, like me, were more concerned with where the same figures had come from and so how reliable they might be. Bent Hansen, then the leading economist working on Egyptian economic history, seemed to me to provide a perfect example of someone well within the first camp. He created national income statistics based on a few available figures that he then used as proxies for the much larger aggregates needed to talk about changes in basic sectorial indices relating to production and consumption. I also found this trait in the work on Japanese growth by the US historian Henry Rosovsky. Whereas I, though forced to use whatever figures I could find relating to the volume and value of Egypt's annual cotton harvest, did my best to test one set against another, was always conscious of their origin and on the alert for those who, even in the post-World War II period, simply made them up. Even though few persons were able to be as open about it as those responsible for Ethiopia's first five-year plan in the mid-1960s, in which they disarmingly explained that it had been drawn up: "Without the necessary statistics but with the help of Almighty God!"

More questions arose when I moved from studying the history of Egyptian cotton to teaching, and then writing about, the larger economic history of Egypt, Turkey, and the countries of the Fertile Crescent. For the most part I was concerned with measuring, as well as describing, their different growth paths. But, as such work also requires a certain amount of international comparison, I was also forced to use what data I could to evaluate their development in terms of both the region itself and of other non-Euro-

136

pean countries in India, Africa, and Latin America. I always tried to indicate the lack of precision in what I was doing to my listeners and readers, most of them anxious for some greater degree of statistical certainty than I was willing to provide.

The result of the research conducted according to these principles and understandings was first my PhD thesis, which was then adapted as a book for Oxford University Press. Over a decade later, in 1981, I also produced *The Middle East in the World Economy: 1800–1914* (1981), a work of synthesis based mostly on printed sources designed to provide a general account of the regional economy up to 1850, followed by a country-by-country analysis of the remaining decades before 1914. Although not intended specifically as a textbook, that is what it became, mainly because students found its emphasis on different country experiences more comprehensible than the more general treatment of themes to be found in other rival works, notably Charles Issawi's 1966 *An Economic History of the Middle East and North Africa, 1800-1914*, with its division into chapters on agriculture, manufacturing, trade, and so on.

My last endeavor at this type of work was an attempt to continue the story through the next century: my 1998 *A History of the Middle East Economies in the Twentieth Century*, which covered the period from 1918 to about 1990 and which was co-authored with a friend, Sevket Pamuk, who wrote the sections about Turkey while I wrote those about the Arab states. It was a subject of considerable personal annoyance that plans for a second edition that would have brought its story up to the beginning of the twenty-first century were stymied by a disagreement with its commercial publisher.

Becoming a Student of Middle East Politics

It is one thing to visit a country or a region, or even to live there for a while, and quite another to find structured ways of understanding the ways of its people, as well as its modern political and social history. In Israel and Jordan in the 1950s, Egypt and Lebanon in the 1960s, and then the wider Middle East from the 1970s onward, I was very much at the mercy of whoever I met, what books I could find, and what access I had to local news and to those who wrote and reported on it. All this I added to some rough and ready general historical context stemming from notes I had taken on Albert Hourani's general Middle East history lectures. These emphasized the beginnings of a "modern" period at around 1800 in which the key figures were Mohammad Ali, the so-called "founder" of modern Egypt, and the "reforming" sultans in Istanbul, who initiated a process of centralization known as "defensive modernization" designed to protect their domains both from each other and an expanding Europe. This led to a process of over-borrowing from Western bankers in the 1870s and then to a brief period of enthusiasm for constitutions and elected assemblies following Egypt's bankruptcy in 1875. This period ended in the exercise of what today would be called a neoliberal influence by Britain, France, and the other creditor powers over the Egyptian and Ottoman governments: enforced policies of low tariffs, low taxes, and sound finance. As a result, more aggressively nationalist and anti-imperialist governments replaced the Egyptian and Ottoman ones from the 1930s onward.

As for the contemporary world of Middle East politics, I was very much influenced by my time in Egypt from 1962 to 1963. I tended to assume that the basic model was a "revolutionary" one in which the old, pre-independence political order was overthrown by revolutionary forces led, in most cases, by the military, for instance, Egypt in 1952, Iraq in 1958, Sudan from 1958 onward, Libya in 1969, and Syria in the early 1970s after a long series of coups by a Ba'th Party-backed military government. According to this scheme of things, military-backed power was used first to introduce programs to achieve greater social justice, such as reform of the system of (unequal) land tenure. About a decade later, the same power would be used to promote schemes of general economic and social development, usually embodied in terms of Soviet-style five-year plans with their stress on the promotion of rapid industrialization, seen as the sine qua non of a Western-type modern society.

It was particularly exciting to be living in Cairo in 1962 and 1963. It was difficult not to be caught up in the general enthusiasm for the Nasserite project, whether in terms of its concern with big plans and big projects or of what appeared to be its larger goals of development: the redistribution of income and of justice for all. Some things were impossible to miss, such as the construction of the Aswan High Dam, the regime's blue ribbon showcase. This was lauded at the cinema—there was always a compulsory showing of a short documentary, *The History of the High Dam*—and endlessly praised in many cafes and public spaces in the form of Abdel Halim Hafez's chant exalting the dam's victory against colonialism. Others, like the often-unsatisfactory consequences of the expansion of the universities to admit tens of thousand more students, were only just beginning to make their presence felt in our talks with professorial friends and colleagues.

Most memorable of all were the huge demonstrations that greeted the announcement of a union between Egypt, Syria, Iraq, and Yemen in April 1963—the only time I had seen the regime allow such a manifestation of popular enthusiasm along Cairo's narrow streets. From the windows of the second floor of the American University I could observe a long procession of (mostly young) men waving national flags, now with four stars rather than the usual two to represent Egypt and Yemen. Their chanting was orchestrated by a youth at its head sitting backward on the shoulders of two burley supports. Much to my shocked surprise, some in the procession then broke away to enter the university, going from classroom to classroom, including mine, to urge the students to come out into the square to join them. It was a momentarily frightening invasion, enough for the university to close down for the day and for our students, most of whom came from local minorities with little taste for the Nasser regime, to hurry straight home.

My wife and I had left Egypt by the time it became clear that there would be no union after all, so we missed any sense of the public reaction, whether pro-Nasser for standing up for Egyptian interests or a feeling of schadenfreude at the obvious discomfort of the leading Ba'thist in the Syrian delegation. This last was revealed for all to see when the Nasser regime published an edited version of the secret transcript of the unity talks a few months later. But there was obviously more to it than that, something that became clear to me on reading Malcolm Kerr's superb *The Arab Cold War* (1966). Kerr offered a clear-eyed analysis of the politics involved as the nervous representatives of two relatively weak new Ba'thist regimes made their pilgrimage to Cairo to seek the legitimacy that derived simply from talking to Nasser and so to appear to be sharing his dream of a united Arab world under his leadership.

Sadly, I do not have any record of the first series of lectures I gave in Oxford after my return there in the summer of 1964. Nevertheless, I do remember banging them out, double-spaced with two fingers on my ancient typewriter the night before, eighteen pages providing enough words to fill up some fifty minutes of time. I can also remember the room I lectured in and just one member of the class, Crown Prince Hassan of Jordan, whose reasonable interest in the actions of rulers like Mohammad Ali I have already recorded.

Altogether it was something of an anxious experience, but no different, I imagine, from many academics' early years of teaching, reading assigned books and articles only a day or so before each new class. Given the fact that being a graduate student might be thought of as roughly similar to that of an apprentice in a medieval guild, I had learned enough at this stage to know how to make my own academic *chef d'oeuvre* in the form of a written thesis but not how to "sell" it to other people. Nor was I capable of imagining how it might fit into the context of other such works, let alone how to judge where it might find a place in terms of the collective wisdom and lifetime experience of my fellow guild members as a whole.

Becoming a Political Historian of the Middle East

While living in Cairo in 1962–63, and probably even before, I took a general interest in Egyptian politics, reading what books I could find and talking to Egyptians about their own experiences. I was also somewhat aware of the problems involved in finding out anything about such a secretive regime, with conducting academic research on the Nasser period being virtually impossible. These difficulties were made worse by the fact that the few Egyptian students who came to the United Kingdom—including Nasser's own daughter Huda, whom I got to know when she came to Oxford for a year in the early 1970s—were forced to choose subjects at some remove from politics. The few exceptions to this rule were some of the small MA theses written by students at the American University that drew on personal information provided by their own families, almost automatically members of the business and professional elite.

This state of affairs continued through my almost-annual visits from 1965 onward. I was able to obtain only the most general sense of the economic "crisis" that began with the failure to introduce a second five-year plan in the mid-1960s, and the political "crisis" triggered by Egypt's crushing defeat in 1967. These were dark days indeed, in which visits to Egypt seemed like visiting some kind of prison: visas were needed to get in or out, foreign currency was fiercely controlled, and very few foreign newspapers were freely on sale. Meanwhile, Israeli forces were just across the Suez Canal, and Israeli planes seemed able to fly over the country more or less at will. Retrospectively, it seems that some new blueprint was required on the political, economic, and military fronts. Its outlines took some time to emerge, first becoming visible with Nasser's Helwan speech of February 1968, suggesting the need for a vaguely defined economic and political opening up (the much-discussed *infitah*). This became clearer after Abdel Nasser's untimely death, when Sadat began to prepare Egypt for another war.

The year 1967 was also a pivotal one in modern Arab history, much better viewed, in my opinion, from Lebanon, where I was spending the academic year. Egypt's Arabism always seemed to me something of a stretch, only a small part of the ordinary Egyptian's identity despite Nasser's insistence to the contrary. Arabism involved great burdens as well, as evinced by the nature of the costly military support that Egypt provided to the Republicans in Yemen in the 1960s and to the Syrians and Palestinians in the disastrous

June War of 1967. But in Beirut, watching the obvious public enthusiasm that greeted the rise of the Palestine guerillas after the Battle of Karameh in March 1968, I got a clear sense of the many strong links between the peoples of the eastern Arab world. It was not just about the constant flow of traffic across what were still regarded as artificial borders, exemplified by the drivers of the "service" taxis offering rides to Damascus, Aleppo, and Amman from Burj Square, but also the obvious existence of family and emotional connections often going back to the years before the break up of the Ottoman Empire after World War I. As a result, what happened in Palestine, Jordan, and elsewhere often mattered personally, and viscerally, however much the actual presence of political refugees might be irksome to the Beirutis on a daily basis or regarded as threatening to Lebanon's fragile sectarian balance.

It took me longer to realize the way in which the Arab world was viewed in somewhat different ways in each Arab capital and by each different Arab regime. This insight was of enormous importance for an outsider like me trying, as best he could, to learn to think about the world from a Middle Eastern point of view. I was fortunate to have had a number of good guides, notably the two journalists Eric Rouleau (*Le Monde*) and Patrick Seale (*The Observer*). Their reporting from Syria provided what I began to think of as the "view from Damascus:" an instinctive, un-reflexive attitude toward the surrounding cities and states that combined comradeship with caution, particularly when responding to the overtures of the country's more powerful Arab neighbors, Egypt and Iraq.

Hence, when it came to converting this raw experience into an undergraduate course of weekly tutorials, accompanied, in the late 1970s, by a set of lectures on the political, as opposed to just the economic history, of the Middle East, my central focus was on the process of state building within a somewhat uncertain postcolonial political order. It was an order that was shortly thereafter threatened by the shock of the 1967 defeat, after which more durable, coup-proof regimes made their appearance in the core countries of my analysis: Egypt, Syria, Iraq, and, on the few occasions when I mentioned North Africa, Algeria.

I cannot now remember when I first used the word "authoritarian" to describe such regimes, though it was probably some time in the mid-1970s. Clement Henry Moore, whose work (with Samuel Huntington) on single-party regimes I was becoming aware of, more or less at the same time that Clement spent some months in Oxford in 1974, introduced me to the notion. However, I do know that I began by presenting it in a reasonably benign way, obsessed as I was by the central importance of state building, and so taking little note of the reliance on the use of force to secure compliance. It was not until the appearance of Kanan Makiya's pseudonymous *Republic of Fear* (which I read in manuscript form a year or two before its publication in 1986) that I felt the need to try to factor in the role of fear, torture, and political repression in day-to-day political management. Of course, the true significance of such methods remains controversial to the present day. This is evident, for instance, in the unease produced by Joseph Sassoon's 2012 *Saddam Hussein's Ba'th Party*, with its more balanced notion of a system of well-calibrated rewards as well as punishments, which is paralleled by continuing efforts to justify the 2003 British and US occupation of Iraq in terms of Saddam Hussein being a "genocidal tyrant."[2]

In these circumstances, I did not feel confident enough to try to publish much on the Middle East's political scene in the 1970s and early 1980s, with only three exceptions. One of these was a 1976 tentative sketch of the political economy of Lebanon, the second was a 1977 critical review of Michael Hudson's *Arab Politics* (1977), and the third was a more general criticism of contemporary writing about the role of the army in Middle Eastern politics in 1978. Looking back on it now, it seems to me that, in my defense of economic history's centrality to a Marxist notion of political economy, I had developed an antipathy to reliance on anything that smacked of a political "science." I had a strongly held belief that there could be no actual "science" of politics with its own rules and, therefore, an ability to make hard and fast predictions. My reading of Gabriel Almond and James Coleman's 1969 *The Politics of the Developing Areas*, then the standard work on the subject, further strengthened this belief. The volume claimed that, over time, the study of politics could well be reduced to statistics; this seemed to me then, as now, a perfectly ridiculous claim. What I was less aware of, until Theda Skocpol's hugely influential *Bringing the State Back In* (1985) drew my attention to it, was the way in which Almond and Coleman, as well as most of their contributors, sought to examine the political process with little reference to the central role of state power—a shortcoming they also shared with most Marxist and Marx-influenced theorists at that time. However, it took me some time to become fully aware both of the significance of this lacuna and the enormous problems that the study of this omnipresent but strangely intangible entity, the state, actually involved.

My search for a credible alternative methodology began fortuitously in the 1970s, involving a form of systematic critical analysis of the works about the modern Middle East in association with some of the founding

2 Jeff Jacoby, "On Balance, the Iraqi War Was Worth It," *Boston Globe*, (20 March 2013): A11.

members of the Hull Group, notably Talal Asad. We based our critique on its polemical character, its essential Eurocentric approach, and its supposed lack of "objectivity." We argued that such an approach would inevitably lead to these studies' total rejection on the basis of being so flawed as to be of no proper use. In its place we proposed a set of principles upon which our own, new approach was to be based, most notably on the idea that we were not interested in the production of new models for their own sake but, rather, a more careful and critical discussion of existing texts in search of "precise evidence of their strengths and weaknesses."

Reading this more than thirty years later I cannot remember how, if at all, this related to the arguments developed in Edward Said's *Orientalism*, which was published some years later in 1978. Certainly, I was already familiar with Said's work, having met him in Oxford some years before, after which he asked me to read various drafts of parts of the manuscript. My memory now is that I welcomed the appearance of *Orientalism*. After all, it did what Talal Asad and I, and the others of our group, no longer wished to do: continue our general attack on the phenomenon of Orientalism as both intellectually flawed and a valuable ideological tool for easy use by supporters of both imperialism and Zionism. Nevertheless, whether we had Edward directly in mind when we argued for critical engagement with the texts he himself condemned I cannot properly remember, but we most probably did not.

The point is an important one, however. Whatever the immediate facts of the matter, Edward was definitely regarded as an ally in the heavily politicized and highly ideological war we were fighting against Orientalism and Orientalist assumptions in general. I have now come to believe that this war unfortunately became highly personalized. Its two most high-level rival combatants, Edward and Bernard Lewis, were perceived as dividing the field into two rival camps. This indeed reflected the temper of the highly charged times following the Arab defeat in the 1967 War. But, in the longer run, I now see it as having had an unnecessarily deleterious effect on our intellectual and teaching life, taking up far too much of our and our students' time in rehearsing a quarrel of only minor methodological significance.

My own personal contribution to the Hull Group's new journal, the *Review of Middle East Studies*, was a critique of the existing treatments of the role of the army in Middle East politics by writers in the US political science tradition as well as two Egyptian Marxists—Anouar Abdel-Malek (writing as Mahmoud Hussein) and Samir Amin (writing as Hassan Riad). These last two had produced influential works involving the political role of their country's military from what I believed to be a vague and unhelpfully general point of view. Against this, my own approach was heavily influenced by a recently published chapter by the political sociologist Robin Luckham, "The Military, Militarism, and Dependence in the Third World: A Theoretical Sketch."[3] Luckham's piece encouraged me to conduct my analysis of Middle East armies along four interrelated dimensions: the particular character of armies as organizations and the relations between armies and state and society, with both aspects then placed within their larger international and historical context. Looking back on this at a great distance in time, the confidence with which I was able to take on such a subject must have come as much from the fact that I, unlike almost all of my comrades, had been a soldier myself, as from the iconoclasm we all felt at being able to expose theoretically naïve attempts at political analysis.

The same growing confidence can also be found in my only other attempt at political analysis at this period: my contribution to a collection I edited called *Essays on the Crisis in Lebanon*. This book had its inception in a small seminar I organized at Oxford in December 1975 at which I presented some thoughts on the political economy of Lebanon based on ideas that I had been developing since my residence in that country some few years earlier. It owed a great deal to my fellow essayists, notably Albert Hourani and Percy Kemp (writing as Tewfik Khalaf), as well as to other members of our Hull Group like Michael Johnson, but the book also demonstrated my development as a historian in that it concentrated on identifying the historical logic set in motion by the French attempt to divide their Syrian mandate into a number of smaller states. One of these, Lebanon, consisted of a mixed population of Maronite Christians and Sunni and Shiʻi Muslims, each with its own particular combination of residence, occupation, and external alliances, and each with a set of communal leaders uneasily united in maintaining their own in-built economic and social power. Could the "contradictions" inherent in the Lebanese political economy have established a certain zigzag path that led, via a series of accommodations and breakdowns of trust, to the almost complete collapse of the system in 1975? It was this central concern with trying to identify the way in which a certain historical logic could stem from an initial set of preconditions that represented a significant theoretical advance from my more structured examination of the role of Middle Eastern armies.

Somewhere along the way, most probably in the late 1970s, I got interested in the attempts to create managed political systems in Arab countries

---

3 "The Military, Militarism and Dependence in the Third World: A Theoretical Sketch," in C.N. Enloe and U. Semin-Panzer, *The Military the Police and Domestic Order* (London: Richardson Institute for Conflict and Peace Research, 1976).

like Egypt and Tunisia in which the single government party created other parties so as to give the pretense of contested elections. Although this form of playacting was, at least initially, designed for US and international consumption, it seemed to have the seeds of developing into something more constructive. At the very least, it provided some of the actors with the political skills they would need to develop new economic and social programs designed to appeal to the new constituencies that were being formed in the process of rapid urbanization and other forms of social change. And this, in turn, also led me to look at previous moments of multiparty electoral democracy, as in Egypt in the 1920s, in search of clues to the difficulties such experiments entailed. For example, the Egyptian case led to frequent changes in the electoral laws in search of particular advantage, whether in terms of limiting the electorate, changing constituency boundaries, or amending the new constitution.[4] But certainly the most important lesson I learned from this small study was the difficulty of establishing a working democracy in a fundamentally peasant country where, particularly before the introduction of the secret ballot, "one man/one vote" almost inevitably meant most people were dragooned into voting for the landlords who employed them.

Two of the most fascinating attempts to create managed party systems were in Egypt and Turkey, a country that I first became interested in after the military coup of 1980. In Egypt, President Anwar Sadat and his advisers simply created an appearance of opposition by arbitrarily creating two new parties, one on the right and one on the left, under rules designed to prevent either of them from appealing to any kind of subnational constituencies, whether based on religion, ideology, or simply regional identity. A similar system was devised in Turkey and later in many parts of the Arab world, certainly based on the Egyptian example. Another interesting aspect was the constant attempt to find ways of combating the apathy that prevented people from even going to the polls when they knew in advance what the results were likely to be. Looking at the Egyptian initiative, it seemed to me that I could recognize the guiding genius of Usama el-Baz, a close adviser to the new president, Hosni Mubarak, who assumed power after Sadat's assassination in 1981. It was he, I supposed, who found ways of making the 1984 election more interesting by allowing the once-banned Wafd Party to offer candidates, and in 1987, by permitting independent candidates to run, a practice previously banned on the grounds

---

4 See, for example, my "Socio-economic Change and Political Mobilization—The Case of Egypt" in *Democracy without Democrats? The Renewal of Politics in the Muslim World*, ed. Ghassan Salame (London: I. B. Tauris, 1994).

that this might lead to the election of candidates unknown to the security apparatus.

By finding a way to marry my interest in the underlying structures of any national political economy to an examination of the main forces for significant changes therein, I possessed the tools I needed to widen my economic history concerns to include an attempt to teach, and then to write, political history in its own right. This process ended up with my 1992 book, *State, Power and Politics in the Making of the Modern Middle East*, which I contracted, much too hastily, to write for a new series devised by an editor at the publishing house then known as Routledge & Kegan Paul. This work could never have been completed in the way that it was without a long period of reading, thinking, and above all, trying out my ideas in front of students. As I had learned from two of my senior mentors, Albert Hourani and Elizabeth Neame, the Oxford system of three annual eight-week teaching terms provided a wonderfully useful framework for organizing one's thoughts into the same number of eight chapter-size bites. This could then be supplemented by the opportunities provided for testing both reading material and new ideas in the more intimate discussions that took place in individual tutorials and small classes. In my case, those that were devised to meet the needs of students who had elected to take courses in the then very new subject of the politics of developing countries were particularly useful. Other teaching opportunities were provided by the introduction of a new research degree, the Oxford Bachelor of Letters (BLitt)—then changed to the Master of Letters (MLitt) in 1974—which required a thesis but no mandatory coursework. The latter immediately provided me with four students to supervise—two of whom chose subjects in Middle East political history—and a steady intake of one or two a year thereafter.

Given the fact that Oxford contained so few teachers in Middle East studies, I was soon able to widen my horizons by having to accept students who were working on countries or subjects about which I knew little or nothing at all: for instance, the Sudanese efforts to absorb Eritrean and Somali refugees in the 1970s or the development of the coal industry in Morocco. In ideal circumstances, it seemed to me, such students should not have been admitted to Oxford in the first place, considering there was no one there with the knowledge to look after them properly. Yet they were already in residence, and there was nothing better to do than to try to ensure that they received as good advice from as many quarters as possible, supplemented by the often-rich resources to be found in the university's various centers (for example, the Department of Refugee Studies) and many specialist libraries.

To begin with, this was almost as much a learning process for me as it was for them, given my general ignorance about many of their topics, but then, over time, I began to realize that I had a more basic role to play. I discovered that Oxford DPhil theses worked best if each had its own appropriate shape and structure, something that an interested outsider could often more easily discover than the student him or herself. I also offered help in shaping a set of particular arguments that gave the whole notion of a "thesis"—or perhaps better a "hypothesis"—its raison d'être. Other types of advisory input included guidance concerning bibliography, citations, and the always tricky matter of the correct way of transliterating names and words from Arabic and Persian into English, a routine practice that Middle Eastern students who habitually worked from the sound of a word, and not the sight of its Arabic characters, seemed to find particularly difficult.

Notable among those of my advisees who took me furthest into new areas of knowledge, as well as some initial understanding of the many problems involved in separating facts from strongly held opinions, were those working on Israel/Palestine. Fortunately for me, I was never called upon to supervise anyone working directly on the political history itself, something about which I knew little and was therefore quite happy to leave to colleagues like Albert Hourani and Elizabeth Neame, who, via their experience of the early stages of the conflict, were both much more personally invested. This left me free to concentrate on the few students who were working on the economic history of Mandatory Palestine before 1948. This subject, although containing an ideological component—for example, the supposed existence of something called a separate "Jewish" economy in the 1930s—could more usually be approached using the normal tools of one's trade, as in the case, say, of the growth and export of Palestinian oranges, the country's most valuable nineteenth-century cash crop.

Nevertheless, it was impossible not to have opinions about the rights and wrongs of the way in which the independent state of Israel came into being, and, therefore, to try to substantiate them, or at least to try to test them, by discovering the rare books that attempted the virtually impossible task of being truly objective. By and large, the ones I found the most straightforward and least ideological were the ones written closest to 1948, such as John Marlowe's 1959 *The Seat of Pilate*. They tended to place what had happened in Palestine firmly within its late colonial context; most of the later writing on the conflict, whether pro-Palestinian or pro-Israeli, seemed to view the brief British presence as almost wholly subordinate to what seemed to me their larger concern, that of converting the fight for the same land into a timeless struggle between good and evil. As a Briton, and particularly one who had witnessed anticolonial nationalism firsthand in Cyprus, this seemed a strange way of letting the British, and their ham-handed attempts to mediate between Palestinian Arabs and Jews, almost completely off the hook. When for me, as for many other British analysts of our empire like David Fieldhouse, Palestine ranked with the partition of India as one of the bloodiest and most unforgivable of all imperial disasters.

Nevertheless, from a purely academic point of view, the quasi-colonial aspect of the Mandate provided an obvious way to study the economic history of the period. It came as somewhat of a surprise when, after publishing my contribution to a volume on Palestine, *Economic Development in Mandatory Palestine 1918–1948* (1988), I found myself being praised for making what seemed to me such an obvious point. It also led on to thoughts about the way in which, in retrospect, both pro-Palestinian Arab and pro-Zionist historians used a partial selection of the evidence to try to convince their readers that British colonial policy favored one side rather than the other. The subject is a complex one, and I was much helped by the arguments contained in the doctoral thesis of my student Barbara Smith which allowed me to come to the conclusion that, while British policy and practice certainly assisted the Zionists greatly in the 1920s, the results were rather more balanced from then on. I also concluded that they mattered much less, at least until the Partition Agreement of November 1947, than certain major external factors such as Hitler's policies toward the German Jews, the outbreak of the Second World War, the impact of the Holocaust, the lack of preparation on the Palestinian side, and the general imbalance between what was an essentially European population of incoming Zionists as opposed to an essentially non-European population of resident Palestinian Arabs, exacerbated by the grave shortcomings of their leaders, exemplified by the wartime behavior of the pro-German Mufti of Jerusalem.

Work by other graduate students with whom I was close in Oxford, such as Gabriel Cohen and Ilan Pappé, also demonstrated that, though the British made an initial effort to divide the public assets of the mandatory government equally between the Palestinians and the Zionists up to about February 1948, their troops were then ordered to head straight for the port cities on the coast, leaving the local forces to fight it out among themselves. Their work also indicated that one of the main reasons why no Palestinian government could establish itself from 1948 to 1949 was that it was not in the interests of any of the main outside powers involved—the Americans, the British, the Israelis, the Egyptians, or the Jordanians—that there should be one, especially if dominated by the Mufti himself. As for the refugees, although it was obvious that many of them were simply pressured to leave by the Israelis, the more important point is that their return was prevented by the Israeli unwillingness, demonstrated at the Lausanne conference of 1949, to readmit more than about a quarter of the total, soon followed by a blanket refusal to allow more than a handful to return at all.

Given the highly ideological nature of the conflict, its economic history held out some promise of a fact-driven approach, with judgment only coming later. And this is still what I try to teach my students—facts first, meaning second—rather than, as with almost every new book, the presentation of facts being immediately put at the service of some prior ideology in such a way that you can tell almost from the initial paragraph which side it is going to be on. Still, it remains a difficult, although I would hope, not an entirely impossible task, to see structure and process determining actions rather than individual conscious intent, just as Gershon Shafir pointed out in his 1989 *Land, Labor and the Origins of the Israeli-Palestinian Conflict: 1882-1914*, one of the first books I helped to commission for the Cambridge University Press's "Cambridge Middle East Library."

A Detour into Political Biography

One large subject that did not easily fit into my highly structured approach to the political economy of either the development of the economic systems or the abstract processes of state building in the Middle East was the role of individual political leaders. Most people of my generation had consigned the notion of the importance of "Great Men" to the historical dustbin, or so we earnestly believed. Even Marx's famous observation that "Men make their own history, but they do not make it as they please," was taken to mean "men" in the plural and provided no particular license to distinguish one president, one general, very much from another. While we may have made some brief use of the Weberian notion of "charisma," particularly in the case of Abdel Nasser, it was its "routinization" into a set of new institutions that concerned us more.

So it was a rather momentous moment for me when, soon after I had joined the Harvard history department in 1993 and felt free to try a new and different type of historical writing, I started looking around for a figure connected with Egypt whose public life stood at the core of some stage in the history of that country. Ideally, I felt, this should have been Abdel Nasser who then, as now, lacked a full biography dealing with his impact on Egypt's domestic policy. But, as hardly any of his private papers were available to work on, I turned instead to one of his powerful predecessors: the Briton Sir Evelyn Baring, later Lord Cromer. I had written a little before about his time in Egypt between 1883 and 1907, and his imperial apprenticeship in India, a country I had long wanted an opportunity to visit.

After a short period of concentrating just on Baring's public life as revealed in his official papers in the British government archives, located first in Chancery Lane in London and then in Kew Gardens, I was soon pulled somewhat unwillingly toward the personal by two powerful currents. One was the attraction of having to follow your biographical subject around, which was brilliantly on display in Richard Holmes' compelling 1985 *Footsteps: Adventures of a Romantic Biographer*. This move took me back to Cairo and then on to Calcutta where Baring had served in the 1870s and again in the early 1880s, as well as to the Raj's summer capital, Simla, high up in the foothills of the Himalayas.

The other event that pulled me into Baring's personal life was the moment when I gained access to some of his private papers in the Knightsbridge flat of Lady Esme Cromer. I was immediately handed a file of letters announcing the surprising existence of an illegitimate daughter born during his time in Corfu in the late 1850s as a member of the British garrison there. With my curiosity now thoroughly aroused, there could be no question of attempting anything short of a complete "life"—an impossible task, of course, but, nevertheless, an exciting goal.

"What is a life?" I asked myself, a question posed by so many through the ages and answered in so many different ways. And what is involved in writing the life of someone other than oneself? I bought some books about what was rather grandiosely called the "biographer's craft," but found my best guide in other biographies. One of these was Baring's own fragmentary *Autobiographical Notes*, which he wrote as he approached retirement and in which he gives his life a particular shape, he says, in order that his sons might "know what manner of man" he was after he was gone. Yet it remained something of a chastening and often bewildering process. For one thing, it did not take me long to realize, as a would-be social scientist, how limited and bare my descriptive vocabulary was, and, in particular, how few adjectives I seemed to have at my disposal to provide a sense of how things felt and how they looked. For another, and at a somewhat deeper level, I had to wrestle with the inherited assumptions of a man living in a different age and belonging to a different social class from myself. Yet, in some ways, strangely and possibly misleadingly, Baring was familiar in terms of his desires, his peccadillos, his adolescent love of dressing up, his pride, and his work ethic. Then there was the shocking gap between his obvious love of his first wife and his lust for her English maid while his wife lay bedridden and exhausted by childbirth in Simla in 1882. All this encouraged me, the

150

biographer, to become part detective, part amateur psychologist, part a kind of eavesdropper, always hoping to catch his subject alone and off his guard, always hoping to have achieved enough familiarity as to anticipate what he might have been going to do next. I was so happy to feel that I had almost reached the stage at which I could imagine how he would have answered questions from that popular Victorian parlor game when you were asked: "who was your favorite author?" or "what was your favorite color?"

Judging him and evaluating the impact of his life was more difficult. I did not particularly like Baring as a person and knew that I would not at all have been comfortable to have met him in his prime. There were times, however, when I felt quite close to him in terms of the particular anxieties that affected him, like approaching important milestones in his life or worried about his children's health and prospects. I was also aware, of course, of his tremendous impact on the lives of millions of people in both India and Egypt, where he pursued policies of low taxation and the creation of new public works—railways, bridges, dams, and canals—to increase agricultural productivity. Some of these, like those that provided extra water for the country's fields, had serious unintended consequences in the shape of waterlogging and, in the case of Egypt, a dramatic if only temporary fall in cotton yields. In this sense his career was little different from that of the "development czars" of the mid-twentieth century whose huge projects in places like Punjab or Nigeria sometimes had disastrous consequences for those who lived off the land. And, perhaps most of all, I was conscious of his reliance on armies of occupation to keep him, and the local regimes subservient to him, in power, a policy which led directly to what was almost his last act in Egypt: the harsh exemplary punishments meted out to some of the people living in the Egyptian village of Denshawai who had the temerity to chase away British military pigeon shooters in 1906.

Yet, in the end, I chose to focus on his role in what could be called the "making" of modern Egypt, shepherding it from a province of the Ottoman Empire to a quasi-independent political entity with its own system of government and its own administrative, legal, and statistical profile. In a large sense, this was self-consciously perverse of me. For many young Egyptians, Cromer was the man they most loved to hate, a symbol for all their country's humiliations at foreign hands. But, nevertheless, he was still someone they had to come to terms with as the real ruler of their country for nearly twenty-five years.

In spite of the freedom that Harvard provides professors to teach almost any course they want, I never taught the life and work of Evelyn Baring (Lord Cromer) as a self-contained unit, worried that it would not attract much of either an undergraduate or a graduate, audience—at a time when the size of my enrollments mattered to me. Nevertheless, I did take advantage of the same flexibility to put on a graduate reading course in an attempt to get my students to listen to individual Middle Eastern voices—admittedly only in translation. This was an effort to get away from the fact that these same voices were usually interpreted for them by the media and academic middlemen and so only heard in especially chosen fragments. As a rule, I started with Taha Hussein's *The Future of Culture in Egypt* (translated in 1954), as an example of the period of hopeful and creative thinking in the period just after Egypt gained full independence. I followed this with other examples characteristic of the revolutionary period and the many expressions of cultural grief after the 1967 Arab defeat. It was, in some ways, a rather depressing experience, listening to the way Middle Eastern intellectuals passed so quickly from optimism to despair. Several of those students went on to live in the Middle East, sometimes in embassies and consulates, and they later told me that they found the course a useful guide to the dominant trends in local thought. Now, some years later, I also see it as representing such a significant moment in Arab intellectual and educational life that knowledge of it is necessary to understand the full effect of the existential transformation produced by the Arab uprisings of 2011, seen by many as catapulting the Arab world back into the mainstream of world history.

From Structural Analysis in *State, Power and Politics* to the Personalized Politics of *Arab Presidents for Life*

In retrospect, it was only a short jump from writing a biography of Lord Cromer to composing what turned out to be highly individualized portraits of the seven Arab republican presidents, several of whom showed every sign of trying to establish family dynasties before they were overthrown in the 2011 Arab uprisings. Observing the situation before Zine El-Abidine Ben Ali, Hosni Mubarak, and Mu'ammar al-Qaddafi were deposed, this seemed to me a process that began in the 1980s in Syria when the Assad family was made the guarantor of the permanent security of the Alawi notables and their Sunni business partners. Other dictators then copied this move, urged on by their crony-capitalist compatriots who were anxious, above all, to maintain their monopolies and other privileges intact without the need for a potentially costly renegotiation with their successors. The result, in my analysis, was the growth of a monarchical style of rule, with palaces, wives as first ladies, and sons as crown princes in waiting. This could only be charted by finding personal information that was often very difficult to come by, given the general secrecy that surrounded their living arrangements, friendships, lifestyles, family circumstances, ages, and health, as well as the general system of corrupt practices within which they were all enmeshed.

What followed was a form of collective research I had not undertaken before, with information concerning different aspects of presidential life— anecdotes, photographs, descriptions of work habits, scraps of news—often provided by students, Middle Eastern friends in the know, and others. They attached particular importance to the stories told by anyone who had actually met the presidents themselves or observed them at very close quarters. Certain insights that friends provided were also important, notably when it came to trying to understand presidential behavior from a more psychological perspective. For instance, Mu'ammar al-Qaddafi's strange antics at the beginning of the Benghazi uprising against him seemed best analyzed in terms of a form of narcissism in which he saw the world around him solely as the mirror image of his frenetic desire to believe in his own omnipotence.

I had actually thought that my research had ended when this exciting new phase began, but the fact that the uprisings broke out at the moment I had completed my manuscript in December 2010 gave me a brief opportunity both to revise some sections and to add to others in light of the huge amount of new information that the overthrow of the Egyptian, Tunisian, and Libyan heads of state suddenly threw up in the few months that remained before I had to submit it for publication. Key to my new thinking was the notion that those around Qaddafi, and probably the other presidents as well, took great care to present their masters with pictures of the world as they wanted, perhaps even needed, to see it, rather than as it actually was. While this was also to some extent the case of the advice received by the French, American, and other powerful presidents, they at least seemed generally to take some care to check it against a huge variety of readily available alternative sources.

Later still, I read Gil Eyal's wonderfully insightful *The Disenchantment of the Orient* (2006) and learned that Israeli military intelligence analysts concentrated most of their attention on the speeches of the Arab presidents. They believed, sometimes rightly, sometimes wrongly, that these were the best clues to presidential intentions when it came to matters of war and peace. Given the paucity of direct access to the inner circles of such regimes, this was probably the only realistic thing to do. Finding myself in more or less the same position, I, too, was forced to observe presidential behavior from afar, though I was asking a somewhat different set of questions than the Israeli analysts. I was more concerned with the presidents' attitudes to their own successions, the grooming of their sons to take over after them, their concern with their own aging, and so on.

Becoming a Political Pundit

For the first several decades of my academic life I tried to avoid speculating about why events were happening in the Middle East in the way they were and what would happen next. When telephoned by the BBC to answer some questions or in reply to someone in a public meeting, I would plead that as a historian I had great difficulty working out how and why things had happened in the past, and so I would be foolish to imagine that I had anything useful to say about the much more difficult task of anticipating the future. Nor was I prepared to speculate on matters about which I could not possibly have any inside knowledge. For me, this is summed up by a memory from the latter stages of the allied occupation of Kuwait in 1990. At the time, a BBC reporter asked me, "What are the members of the Iraqi Republic Guard thinking?" and I replied that speaking from a peaceful office in North Oxford some thousands of miles away I could not have the faintest idea.

Yet, over time, I found myself weakening, partly due to the pressure of instantaneous questions from men and women I knew in the media, partly due to the fact that I became associated with two institutions for which attempts to answer such questions were practically inescapable. One was an organization called Oxford Analytica, a high-level consultancy service whose founder, David Young, started a forum in 1984 called the "Daily Brief" in which various experts, mostly Oxford dons, sat around a table each morning to discuss each day's news and what we might write in explanation of it in the "Brief" itself.[5] In light of the pressure to produce written opinions that were then circulated anonymously among the firm's clients—some in government, some in business—it was virtually impossible to avoid considered speculation about what might happen next, particularly since, to my knowledge, getting things wrong never seemed to be held personally against you.

The second set of temptations derived from a meeting I had in Lebanon with Jamil Mroue, the re-founder of an Arabic daily called *al-Hayat*. Beginning in 1988, he asked me to submit a regular column for the paper's opinion page. These were written in English and then translated into Arabic, just as Edward Said's pieces were. Ever since, I have continued to turn out

5 See David Young, "The Oxford Analytica Story: Oxford in Brief," *The American Oxonian* LXXXIII (Winter 1996), 1.

my thousand-word opinions at the rate of at least once a month. I was left free to address any topic I wanted, although I submitted myself to a certain self-censorship when it came to contentious subjects about which I clearly knew less than most of the paper's readers, such as the various trends and tendencies within political Islam. Of all my public writings these are probably the ones that have given me the greatest satisfaction, knowing that I was reaching friends and other interested persons right across the Arab world. Nevertheless, it remains a somewhat pernicious process, with all the disadvantages of daily journalism when it comes to forming instant, and often ephemeral, opinions for which one is rarely held accountable—al-Hayat has no readers' letters—and almost always overtaken by the next day's, or the next week's, or the next month's news.

I must confess that, as I grew older, I found it easier and easier to rationalize my joining the ranks of the minor pundits and so sounding off from time to time about things that either mattered to me personally or that, in my role as a university teacher, I believed my students but also others ought to know. Fortunately, enough instances confirmed the value of such a stance to make me feel that I might be on the right track, particularly by local New England audiences after I left Oxford for Harvard in 1993. New Englanders, as I soon found out, were desperate to learn what was "really" going on in the Middle East, often fuelled by their bitter sense that no one in the local newspapers or on radio and television was telling them the whole truth.

Friends and others in the Middle East who read my columns sometimes thanked me in more or less the same spirit. It is, after all, vital that one has some way of testing one's opinions about the region in the region itself. Moreover, in my own case at least, part of this process of testing was to make sure that my picture of what's going on in, for instance, Egypt, is recognizable to those who live there.

That said, as I grow older and learn more about the infinite variety of human activity, human thinking, and human experience, I am made less uncomfortable by partial opinions, distortions, and half-truths, given the general difficulty that even the greatest novelists and others have in precisely pinning down this extraordinary complexity. And so, it finally came as no surprise to find myself agreeing wholeheartedly with an opinion I would never for a moment have thought that I might one day come to agree with: Nassim Nicholas Taleb's statement in his book *Antifragile Things That Gain from Disorder* (2012) that less of the world than we might like is "academizable, rationalizable, formalizable, theoretizable."

Bringing it All Together: State, Society, and Personalized
Government in an Interconnected World

How do I now regard the study of Middle Eastern political history, and
what is it that I try to teach those graduate students of mine who seem
destined to teach it? At root, I still see it as the story of an exercise in state
building in a world of other states and the particular context of imperialism,
colonialism, and the various global movements within the capitalist system
that followed, with particular emphasis on the elements of unequal power
that they still contain. Though I passed through a phase in the late 1980s
when I, like my colleagues in the SSRC's Middle East Committee, was obsessed with trying to define just what the "state" was, and how it interacted
with that other entity, "society," I am now content to observe, with Talal
Asad, that the word itself exists in too many different political vocabularies
to allow a single definition. I also agree with Timothy Mitchell that what
we call the "state" is best conceived of as largely a collection of different
groups, ideas, and entities that are most easily observed as acting as a single
unit when those who control it have some overall project, like economic
development, in mind.

Whether control over society can also be conceived in the same way
as a single project is another matter. There was a time when, looking at
the subject via the notion of bureaucratic authoritarianism, I thought that
it was, but now that the Arab uprisings have revealed how easily so-called
"authoritarian regimes" could be overthrown, I am much less sure. For one
thing, elements of what we used to think of as "civil society," such as trade
unions and other forms of associational life, proved much more resistant to
political management than was previously supposed. For another, even in a
thinly populated oil state like Libya, the ability of the Qaddafi state to reach
everyone with either resources or regular policing seems often to have been
surprisingly attenuated. All this is not to speak of the blinkered narcissism
of many rulers who were encouraged by their close advisers and other cronies to believe in the loyalty and affection of their people in such a way that
they were almost totally unable to respond effectively to the threats they
faced or the deep-rooted grievances that propelled them.

I now believe, with Sami Zubaida, in the importance of the "state" as
the creator and guarantor of the continued existence of something best described as a "political field." This field is best defined by the activities at its
center (usually the capital city), using the institutions suggested by another
Zubaidian notion: the "Jacobin state." The Jacobin state places its constitutional emphasis on the sovereignty of the people, its creation of national

emblems, and its ability to employ certain ideological, educational, and administrative methods to mobilize the population behind certain central tasks like defense and resource creation, and in support of certain central beliefs like the right to private property, regardless of whatever party or faction is temporarily at the helm.

Lastly, I believe in the importance of seeing what I have just been setting out as a dialectical process rather than as the imposition of a single blueprint, a struggle between two or more well-defined social or ideological groups, or even as some type of coherent interaction between local and global forces. It is here that the old French notion of the "conjuncture" is of great utility—a moment when the major forces at play, and the interplay between them, can be observed most distinctly. Such moments are particularly useful in the Middle Eastern case, given the secrecy that usually surrounds so many of the individual components, particularly those involving the policies of the regimes themselves. For instance, the outbreak of the Arab revolutions, and their root-and-branch attempts to create new political orders based on new constitutional structures with a built-in concern for political and personal liberties, in which the "people" in whose name these structures are being developed have to find their place via elections or some other form of representation.

For me, having been brought up in a country without a written constitution, observation of this same process elsewhere has been as puzzling as it has been fascinating, as was the attempt to combine a presidential form of government with a parliamentary one. At least initially, in each case, the prime minister and the head of state were set to work in an uneasy form of partnership, with the speaker of the assembly sometimes playing a significant role, as in Tunisia. Yet, for reasons I cannot quite understand, this replay of some central processes in the history of many of the world's republics, including the revolutionary attempt to give meaning to the whole notion of popular sovereignty, has not seemed as exciting as I think it should have been to my colleagues in the Harvard history department and elsewhere. But, perhaps, this is no more than just another example of the way that developments in the ex-colonial world are still not taken as seriously as they should.

Interior of Dudley Hall, original home of the Center for Middle Eastern Studies, Harvard University. (Harvard University Archives)

Roger Owen talking to Lady Cochrane in the Sursok Palace, 2011.

Roger Owen with Tarek Masoud and Malika Zeghal at John F. Kennedy Jr. Forum, Harvard Kennedy School, 2011. (Jon Chase/ Harvard University)

Roger Owen and Rami Khouri at John F. Kennedy Jr. Forum, Harvard Kennedy School, 2011. (Jon Chase/ Harvard University)

Roger Owen speaking at "Arab Spring in the Fall" event, Harvard University, 2012. (Scott Eisen/ Harvard University)

Roger and Edward Said relaxing during a break at a conference in the South of England.

Susan Miller, William A. Graham, Roger Owen, Thomas Mullins, and Roy P. Mottahedeh at Center for Middle Eastern Studies, Harvard University, mid-1990s. (CMES Archives)

Current home of the Center for Middle Eastern Studies, Harvard University. (CMES Archives)

Roger Owen, William Granara, and Roy P. Mottahedeh at Center for Middle Eastern Studies after conference on Iraq, 2016. (CMES Archives)

Roger Owen sitting with Dr. Muhamed H. Almaliky, MD MPA Fellow, Weatherhead Center for International Affairs at the Center for Middle Eastern Studies during a Symposium on Iraq, 2016. (CMES Archives)

5 TEACHING THE MIDDLE EAST

I began teaching at Oxford in 1964, a year before I had completed my thesis and obtained my DPhil. My official position was that of a faculty lecturer, which is a position of lower status, and so is less well paid, than a university lecturer. But the position was also indicative of how teaching was organized in those days: lectures were one of the major ways of transmitting knowledge, the other being small group tutorials. As for the "faculty" part of my title, I was placed within the economics subsection of the Faculty of Social Studies. At the time, this was a matter of no great importance as I rarely attended faculty meetings. Yet it became significant much later in the 1980s when, as a result of Margaret Thatcher's conservative political attack on the old university order, the system opened up a little. The faculties became sites for what seemed like an unseemly rivalry between those seeking to move up to the next academic rank, that of reader, and then, in a few instances, on to the once-unimaginable heights of becoming a professor; there were still only a very restricted number of professorial positions. The effect on Oxford, and no doubt other universities as well, was to introduce a system of competition for promotion that favored those who were good at lobbying and self-advertisement. This disrupted our cozy, uncompetitive world in which all those who were paid by the university and not by a college obtained more or less the same salary and conditions. Many lecturers like me were soon forced to the unhappy conclusion that we were unlikely ever to become professors if we stayed where we were.

Moreover, this also coincided with a period of growing academic movement and exchange, which meant that many of us became aware of the US system in which almost all our colleagues were professors. Few academics in the United States had any idea about where lecturers and readers in the United Kingdom fit into the larger academic scheme of things. We were usually honored with the courtesy title of "professor" whenever we traveled west, but this was not enough to satisfy our pride. Additionally, we realized that in Oxford we would have to retire in our mid- to late-sixties, whereas many US universities were beginning to remove the restriction that you had to leave even at the age of seventy. These factors proved to be one of the major causes for a widely commented-on "brain-drain," when some of my colleagues and I began to seek positions at US universities.

This was no trivial matter. On the one hand, there was our egalitarian Oxford world in which most teachers enjoyed the same status and roughly the same pay and prospects. On the other hand, it increasingly had obvious disadvantages, including in my case the fact that my academic salary did not provide sufficient income to maintain a mortgage and support a growing family. I was forced to seek extra paid work wherever it could be found, usually in writing for the Arabic newspapers. No wonder that some of us began to contemplate the possibility of finding better paid employment overseas, using whatever academic connections we possessed and applying for whatever positions were available.

I remember all this coming to a head during a family holiday in Scotland in the mid-1980s when, after much thought on a number of lonely cliff walks, I decided to apply for a post at Princeton, even though I knew that my chances were slim—as indeed they quickly proved to be. A few years later, I had a conversation with my friend Roy Mottahedeh in which I indicated my desire to come to Harvard at just about the same time that the new post of A.J. Meyers, Professor of Middle East History, was about to be advertised. It was clearly a fortuitous moment, although it was only after I had finally arrived in the United States with my family that I also realized how bored I had become with the same old Oxford round and how much I was in need of a new set of intellectual and other challenges.

The Oxford System of Lectures, Tutorials, and Seminars

The Oxford system of teaching I experienced as both student and then teacher relied, as it had done for several centuries, on the centrality of the weekly or biweekly lecture, which was supplemented by guided reading from one's tutor. This seemed to me to be a somewhat strange combination of forms of instruction. The lectures themselves were never compulsory, sometimes incomprehensible, and rarely, if ever, appeared in written form as a book, making the hastily scrawled notes an essential form of aide-memoire when revising for our final exams. What the lectures did though was provide an important opportunity to get to know the "stars" in our field, as well as something of the tricks of their trade. This often gave them a value that lasted long into our own teaching years.

For me, the series I remember the best were those given by the historian A.J.P. Taylor on the origins of both the First and the Second World Wars, and by the visiting American George F. Kennan, which contained a trenchant critique of the conduct of US diplomacy since the beginning of the twentieth century. Taylor's also consisted of something of a studied performance. He started at the unusually early hour (for Oxford) of nine in the morning in a big lecture hall in the Examination School, delivered without notes, and always preceded his talk with a "Good morning, gentlemen"—except for the one occasion on which he had obviously spied a young woman present, on which it became, "Good morning, lady and gentlemen."

Sadly, though, neither series had much relation to my core subjects: politics, philosophy, and economics. None of these lent themselves easily to the lecture form, being better taught in small group tutorials and discussions when these were available. So it was that J.L. Austin's biweekly demolition of A.J. Ayer's attempt to introduce Austrian notions of phenomenology to the British philosophical scene, or Isaiah Berlin's rapid-fire comments on the thought of certain Russian and other philosophers, passed entirely over my head. I did a little better with R.M. Hare's exposition of a philosophy of ethics that was dependent almost wholly on seeking to define the many usages of the word "good"—a promising notion that was spoiled by being almost entirely based on trivial examples like "what do I mean when I say that this marmalade is good?" When I returned to Oxford as a lecturer to find that I was expected to give something like thirty-two lectures a year, I had some sense of the form itself but little idea how to go about preparing the individual presentations in terms of structure, delivery, etc., not to speak of how much knowledge I could reasonably try to cram into any given fifty minutes. It was all a process of trial and error with no one to guide me and, in the absence of sustained lecture room discussion, little opportunity for useful feedback from my student-audience.

From an administrative point of view, my first task was simply to get a subject title included in each term's lecture list—something like "Introduction to the economic history of the Middle East, 1798–1914"—then book a room and turn up once a week for eight weeks, the length of each of Oxford's three terms. I read from a hastily prepared script, mostly typed out the night before, double spaced, on something like seventeen to eighteen pages; this would take me the fifty minutes to read if I went slowly. Sometimes, if I managed my allocation of time just right, there might also be space for one or two questions. No doubt, in my first years, listening to me must have been rather a boring experience. Particularly since, in those days, lecturers did not provided a syllabus and used few visual aids other than one or two key names chalked quickly on a blackboard. And, of course, none of my senior colleagues ever came to check up on what I was saying, let alone offer any sensible criticism. It was only when I got a post as visiting fellow in the UC Berkeley history department in the spring of 1982 that I was exposed to any other way of teaching. This too had its problems, of course. For instance, I needed to provide copies of class readings to the students, which were painfully churned out on an early version of the universal Xerox copy machine after making sure to white-over any of the particularly objectionable graffiti—for example, "what a boring old fart"—that I occasionally found written by a previous reader in the margin.

On the whole, lecture classes seemed to go better in the more informal setting of a small room rather than a large hall. The lecturer could sit rather than stand—perhaps even dispensing with the heavy black lecturer's gown that made us all look like portly crows—and there was greater opportunity to answer questions, which in turn invited further discussion. In particular, I remember the challenge of having students from the Middle East. Crown Prince Hassan of Jordan, for instance, like any aspiring ruler, was interested in the nuts and bolts of practical subjects like agricultural production. He sometimes asked detailed questions about the whens and wheres of, say, the introduction of the first Lebanese silk factories, which I was often hard-pressed to answer. From this I also learned the somewhat chastening lesson that it was much easier to create the impression that you knew what you were talking about when using the spoken word than trying to write about the same subject later in words, clear and cold, on the printed page of a book.

Then there was the question of how much economics I could assume my students might know when it came to such relatively simple subjects as vocabulary, as well as basic theory—such as the use of demand curves and the major principles of national income accounting. Fortunately, I had some prior practice with this from when I had given a series of classes on introductory economics to students at the Institute of National Planning in Cairo in the spring of 1963, teaching which relied almost exclusively on working through the relevant pages of Paul Samuelson's wonderful introduction *Economics* (1947), which I had used at Oxford a few years before.

Lectures were supplemented for undergraduates by one-on-one or one-on-two tutorials that generally involved the reading of a short essay of just a few pages, its discussion, and then an announcement of the chapters and articles for the following week's assignment. Given a reasonably interested and lively student, these were my favorite form of teaching because they allowed me to get to know the students, where they came from, and why they were concerned to know more about the Middle East. Such an approach became even more useful when I moved from teaching economic to political history in the 1970s and came in contact with a range of more mature students, often with some sort of Middle East background, like Caroline Hawley, Zeinab Badawi, and Owen Bennett-Jones, who then went on to make a name for themselves as correspondents working for the BBC World Service.

For graduate students, lectures were augmented by what were called "seminars." These seminars, as I came to understand over time, owed very little to their most rigorous German prototype with its orchestrated discussion of previously circulated research papers. At Oxford, these were mainly of two types. The first were teaching seminars where students read out their own papers to be discussed, usually in a somewhat desultory fashion, by the teacher and a few of their peers. The second were the more flashy general seminars, addressed by someone with a big name and dependent very much on whoever was in the chair to make the whole proceeding relevant and interesting. Like everything at Oxford in those days, there was also a great deal of informality about it all. As far as the teaching of the graduate students was concerned, I saw only rare signs of anyone spending much time mulling over which was the best method for instilling some overall notion of how knowledge and research skills could be taught in a structured, orderly way, without formal requirements or any general examination.

Nevertheless, over time, and as a result of greater knowledge of practices in the United States and elsewhere, the more formal practices of Oxford undergraduate teaching began to be extended to the graduate level. University officials started to pay greater attention to the use of a new degree course, an examined M.Phil, to provide a more systematic course of basic training. By the time I left to teach at Harvard in 1993, none of this had been taken very far.

The Harvard System

As I was quickly to discover, of all the US universities, Harvard as I experienced in 1993 was the most like Oxford, notably in its almost complete absence of printed academic rules regarding how and what to teach. Apart from the fact that there seemed a general pattern of fulfilling one's obligations by teaching one general undergraduate course and one graduate seminar, no one in either the history department or in the Center for Middle Eastern Studies seemed prepared to tell me exactly how I should go about this. Fortunately, I had my small experience of teaching at the University of

166

California, Berkeley and at the University of Texas at Austin to guide me so that I knew about the importance of handing out a fairly detailed syllabus on the first day of class both as a general guide and as a way of attracting students shopping around for how to meet their own course requirements. Fortunately, too, teaching still seemed to consist of a combination of formal lecturing—that is, standing up before a class for an hour or so twice a week—and weekly informal seminars lasting two or three hours. All of this was reasonably familiar. Then there was the need to hold regular office hours, to which, as I soon discovered, appeared graduate students anxious to become my TFs (teaching fellows), or what in other universities were often called TAs (teaching assistants).

I was also fortunate that there seemed plenty of time also to experiment, finding out what worked best by a kind of trial and error. After a few years, I settled into giving a regular introductory course, first for the core curriculum, then in the economic history of the Middle East. I also held a two-hour seminar on a variety of subjects—including Middle Eastern political writings and speeches in translation—and offered what at Harvard are called 3010s in which you prepare either a single graduate, or group of graduates, for the fields in which they will be examined orally as part of their general exams.

One of the many advantages of this system was the way it structured both my own working day and everyone else's expectations of me, but not to the extent that it prevented personal contact, first at office hours, then in inviting graduate students to lunch at the faculty club, or later, an early evening drink somewhere, as a way of getting to know them better. As many of the latter were also either expats or recently naturalized US citizens, the fact that we all perched somewhat uneasily between the Middle East and North America seemed to help communication; all of us were trying to help each other understand both ends of a complicated historical and political relationship.

Teaching Aids: The Personal Library

Teachers like me, both at Oxford and Harvard, habitually built up our own libraries over time. These particularly consisted of books and articles from the journals to which we personally subscribed together with boxes containing collections of the offprints of the articles and papers of colleagues and endless old brown files bulging with handwritten or badly typed notes. It was not until the 1980s and the appearance of the extremely expensive Amstrad, the first British personal computer with its own screen and keyboard, that we had a way to store files electronically. Even this took some time to master, as the machine itself was hardly user-friendly, a situation exacerbated by its notoriously opaque book of instructions. Only after a great deal of trial and error did my output begin to improve significantly in terms of quantity, allowing me to write more prolifically for *al-Hayat*, for example. Whether there was an associated decline in quality was anyone's guess. Although I do remember knowing that there was something very ludicrously wrong with the enthusiastic assertion made in a letter to one of the liberal British newspapers suggesting that, if a great novelist like Flaubert had been alive in our electronic times, he would have written twice as many good books.

Another advantage of the teacher's personal library was that it might contain books in other languages, in my case in French and some in Arabic, which I had bought while doing my research in Cairo. These could then be used in various ways, such as the extra authority they seemed to provide. They also served as a reminder to me—and my students—of the enormous intellectual effort put in to understand the economic history of Egypt by Egyptians writing theses for either French or Egyptian universities, many of which were quickly published in book form. One example was the flourishing school of local agricultural historians like Dr. A.A. al-Hitta, whom I met briefly in Cairo and whose 1950 book *History of Egyptian Agriculture in the Age of Mohammad Ali the Great* (*Tarikh al-Zira'a fi 'Asr Mohammad 'Ali al-Kabir*) had become the standard work on the subject. The existence of such works was an important discovery for me on a number of counts, not the least as a way of combating British and European assumptions about the poor quality of both Egyptian scholarship and the data to be found in the Egyptian archives.

As I watched my own private library expand from a couple of shelves as a graduate student to the floor-to-ceiling bookcases of my college study, I took this to be an essential part of the way a teacher made his way in the world of a relatively rooted academic setting, with the books generally being moved home after retirement, and then perhaps sold after his or her death. That the library also had a commercial value was not something that struck me as important until I began to be aware of professors who were either selling their books to their own universities after they retired or, more shocking to me, disposing of them to members of the scholarly book trade—persons I regarded at that age as somewhere between vultures and money-grubbing businessmen. New types of problems were always arising too: for example, the need to find the large sum of money necessary to ship and to insure Charles Issawi's working library back from Columbia

University to Cairo after he retired. As well as the happier solution provided for Professor Hamilton Gibb's Harvard collection after his stroke; his student Roy Mottahedeh was able to obtain the fifty thousand dollars the university required to set up a "Gibb Room" in part of the Widener Library system—a wonderful place in which to contemplate the intellectual life of a great scholar of a now bygone age.

Other Sources: The Article and the Conference Volume

Specialized academic journals like *Middle Eastern Studies* and the bulletins of both the British and North American Middle East Studies Associations provided a second source of information. Several entrepreneurial publishers identified a relatively easy way to obtain prestige for their houses as well as secure sales for their journals: they discovered that there were some two or three hundred libraries in the world that were prepared to subscribe to almost anything.

A third source of information was the growing popularity of conferences and the consequent demand for conference papers. For a great variety of reasons, the "conference" itself soon became a major feature of post-World War II academic life, providing prestige for the organizer and his or her institution, as well as, at the very least, some free travel and perhaps even a free holiday for the participants, something I was only too anxious to take advantage of myself. It was only when I had attended several dozen of such events that I began to ask myself questions about the point of paying tired academics to travel about the world to talk briefly to other tired academics about papers they had rarely read in advance under the chairmanship of yet more academic worthies who just happened to be around at the same time. Surely there must be a more efficient way of organizing academic exchange, I thought. But what?

In the end, the answer came to me after holding smaller and more intimate roundtables or workshops with a clearly defined central topic, with the chairmanship of each session kept tightly in my own hands or those of a co-organizer, and with publication a matter of something like a concentrated synopsis of the proceedings presented as a single journal article. As a model this reached its acme for me in February 2013 with a Harvard Center for Middle Eastern Studies "Arab Transitions Project" to study the Arab uprisings' effects in Egypt, Libya, and Tunisia after 2011. To this event I was able to invite such distinguished commenters and political actors as the Egyptian prime minister, Hazem Beblawi, and one of the foremost Tunisian economists, Mustafa Nabli, for one and a half days of intense, well-informed discussion.

Sabbaticals and Visiting Professorships

While the notion of a sabbatical every seven years has an inspiring Biblical origin—God striving mightily to make the world in six days and then resting on the seventh—in my experience it rarely turned out as inspiring in practice for a whole variety of reasons. In theory, at least in the Oxford tradition, it was supposed to be a time of what was called "recharging one's batteries" by catching up with readings. Yet it was more usually employed to clear one's desk of old work, to continue to see graduate students, or to get on with a long-neglected manuscript. Indeed, it was the rare scholar who had the willpower to do more. I can only remember one: Yehoshua Porath, of the Hebrew University in Jerusalem, who came to St Antony's College in the mid-1980s.

Also, in theory, one of best ways to use one's sabbatical properly was to leave town for somewhere else. But this too had its problems in terms of family life—wives working, children in schools, etc.—as well as the concerns of finding someone to rent one's house and the often-difficult negotiations required to obtain an attachment to another university, often in another country, with its own complex rules about libraries, research permissions, and the like. Ideally, although this was only possible for me on a single short sabbatical to Berkeley, California, in 1982, you exchanged both houses and cars with a family moving the other way.

Given such practical problems, it was not surprising that practices were modified over time. People began taking shorter sabbaticals, perhaps one Oxford term in every seven, which then came around more often. In my own case this led from my one-year sabbatical in London in 1970–71, to much shorter ones in the Middle East and the United States thereafter. These trips were more like "raids" on foreign archives than periods of sustained research. I then practiced the same policy when I arrived at Harvard. There, the practice was made more necessary for me by the fact that Harvard paid only half your salary on such occasions, making it necessary to obtain a grant or a fellowship to make up the rest. Being a foreign historian made this very difficult.

Perils of the Open Office Door: Weirdoes and Other Obsessives

Both of the two Middle East centers with which I have been most closely associated—Oxford and Harvard—were housed in what had once been Victorian family homes. Such an arrangement had both advantages and disadvantages: on the one hand, collegiality and companionship; on the other hand, bad sound proofing, uncertain heating, and most difficult of all, weak general security. As I was to learn very early on in my career—from a Rosicrucian who informed me that the secrets of the world could be found by studying the dimensions of Egypt's largest pyramid—almost anything to do with the Middle East, and particularly its religious history, can encourage an intensity that can spill over into overexcitement, or, occasionally, fanaticism. As a rule, this is best dealt with by having any open discussion well chaired by someone with some considerable academic authority. Perhaps surprisingly, this has usually proved to be enough. And while I can remember any number of tense exchanges and many instances of shouting, I do not remember one that got so sufficiently out of hand that the police had to be called.

This was not true, however, for those unsung heroines, our secretaries (when we had them) and receptionists, who were our first line of defense and were equipped with little more than their good sense and, for real emergencies, a "panic button" under their desks. Nor were they always able to intercept and divert the genuinely disturbed persons who, for one reason or another, had come to believe that your open door was a standing invitation for them to come in for a chat, a rant, or even to beg your assistance in some great scheme such as getting their share of the last Russian Tsar's family jewels. Happily, only in this last case was it necessary to call the university police.

6 THE CREATION OF THE FIELD: A PERSONAL VIEW

What we now know as international "area studies" had its origins in the Second World War and its consolidation as distinct fields of knowledge, via the establishment of separate British and US university area studies centers, in the initial decades of the Cold War. Much of the initiative came from a combination of governments, the American Council of Learned Societies—which had considerable experience in organizing scholarly expertise around an area or a cultural region—and the big US foundations like Ford and Rockefeller, which also provided much of the early funding.[1] In these particular circumstances, the development of area studies must be conceived of, at least initially, as a close partnership between government and the academy, although this relationship tended to become somewhat looser as it developed its own place within the academic world and its own set of intellectual practices.

Moreover, as has been pointed out by Nicholas Dirks, many of the early exponents of area studies, and most of the directors of its first centers, had been involved in some form of wartime political or military intelligence.[2] Just what this entailed is generally difficult to discover, of course, due to the fact that they rarely talked publicly about it, no doubt because they had all signed official secret acts. It could have involved running agents or collecting useful information on areas about to be conquered or coastlines about to be attacked for something like the US Country Guides for use by the military serving abroad or for the United Kingdom's naval equivalents. More to the point, we do know that many of them maintained continued access to

---

1 See, for example, Yves Dezalay and Bryant G. Garth, *The Internationalization of Palace Wars* (Chicago: University of Chicago Press, 2002), and Osamah F. Khalil, "At the Crossroads of Empire: The United States, the Middle East and the Politics of Knowledge" (PhD diss., University of California, Berkeley, 2011), etc.
2 Nicholas B. Dirks, "Spies, Scholarship, and Global Studies," *The Chronicle Review*, 17 August 2012, B4–5. Examples of scholars whose wartime work was hidden by the British Official Secrets Act would include Albert Hourani and Bernard Lewis.

wartime networks, such as those forged at the Special Operations Executive headquarters in Cairo, and that some of them used reports written at this time as the basis for their first scholarly books.[3] Dirks mentions work by John Fairbank, the first director of Harvard's Fairbank Center for Chinese Studies, established in 1956.[4] In the case of British Middle Eastern studies, one could cite two of Albert Hourani's wartime reports based on travel through the Fertile Crescent, which were published as *Syria and Lebanon* in 1946 and *Minorities in the Arab World* in 1947. These were soon to become the basis for structuring academic thought about the modern political history of the Middle East, much of which, as I will argue later, remains the conventional wisdom on the subject until the present day.

In the United States, a key role was played by Harvard's William Langer, who brought back to his university ways of organizing research already established by William J. Donovan in the Research and Analysis Branch of the State Department, then reborn as a key unit in the Office of Secret Services (or OSS—the forerunner of the CIA), which was created just before Pearl Harbor in 1941. These included two key features. One was an interdisciplinary character: joint work by historians, economists, political scientists, sociologists, anthropologists, geographers, and others. The other was the division of the world into separate areas such as Africa, Asia, and Latin America, the study of which was carried out by experts who possessed both the necessary languages and actual lived experience in the regions they reported on. Needless to say, their conclusions were heavily policy oriented. As Dirks notes, Langer had a notion of "useful knowledge:" information that was deployed to help develop the United States' relationships in parts of the world previously dominated by old European empires—the Russian as well as the British and the French—which were now assumed to have a common interest in the new imperatives of modernization and economic and political development.[5]

All this is relatively well known and has been written about a number of times. I would like to focus on the particular role of some of those I will call the "pioneers" of modern Middle Eastern studies as a separate academic discipline. I will also concentrate on their efforts at shaping this field into something of a coherent intellectual enterprise with its own technical language, canon of essential readings, sets of practices for training new stu-

---

3 Christine S. Nicholls, *The History of St Antony's College, 1950–2000* (Oxford: Macmillan, 2000), 115–19.
4 Dirks, "Spies."
5 Ibid.

dents, but without, as I shall argue, any great sense of its own history. This, in turn, involves an examination of the establishment of new programs of area studies located, for the most part, in specialized "centers." These centers were not only the physical plants but also the places where ideas and practices were formulated and tried out, where new courses were developed, and where directors networked with each other to identify gifted students, obtain resources, and define the new field in both its intellectual and practical aspects. In this sense, as in physics, fields are defined, not in terms of their putative boundaries, but by the powerful forces working outward from the center that energize and inform the space around them.

Nevertheless, there has never been a consensus about the related questions of what the field of Middle East studies actually consists of, or when, to use Timothy Mitchell's words, it "arrived" as an "organized field of expertise."[6] There is not even a common definition of what the "Middle East" itself consists of geographically, as even the most casual look at the situation with regard to the institutional members of the Middle East Studies Association of North America (MESA) will reveal. Some centers still use the relatively old term of "Near East" in their title and a few add "North Africa."

I should add that mine is a largely Anglo-American, English-language story, confined to center building in the United Kingdom and North America. There will be occasional extensions to other countries where leading students of the modern Middle East habitually wrote and spoke in English: Holland, Norway/Sweden, Israel, and to a lesser extent in the Arab countries, Turkey, and Iran. New fields need a common language, I would argue, at least in the early stages of their development, much as the expansion of modern chemistry used German as its lingua franca.

Lastly, mine is also something of an insider story, written from the point of view of someone who started his graduate work in Middle Eastern economic history at Albert Hourani's Middle East Centre at St Antony's College in 1960 and who then obtained one of the first government-sponsored posts in Middle East studies at Oxford in 1964. This was more or less the moment when modern Middle East studies began to be created in its present form, but, as I also argue, it was a moment that cannot be properly understood without knowing something of its prehistory in which, in both Britain and the United States, the key role was played by someone I met only once: the Orientalist scholar Sir Hamilton Gibb. His huge and varied influence can still be observed

---

6 Timothy Mitchell, "The Middle East in the Past and Future of Social Studies," in *The Politics of Knowledge: Area Studies and the Disciplines*, ed. David Stanton (Berkeley and Los Angeles: University of California Press, 2004), 74.

via his writings, the testimony of his former students, and more generally in the many traces he has left upon the conduct of the field, long after a stroke robbed him of most of his faculties in February 1964.

Gibb, a Scotsman born in Egypt, was one of the first people to identify the need to supplement "Orientalist" knowledge of Middle Eastern cultural and religious beliefs and practices with those of the social scientist. Having tried, and failed, to find ways of marrying the two approaches in post-war England, he turned his attention to the United States and finally moved there permanently in 1955 to become a professor of Arabic at Harvard. He believed that this prestigious university would not only be more welcoming to his ideas but could also be used as an example that other US universities would certainly follow.[7]

To end this section on a more pedantic note, the provision of dates is of the utmost importance when tracing influences—what happened before or after what, as well as what was published when—a task that requires learning not just the date of first publication but also in what form and by whom. One example, to which I will return below, is the big battle to prevent the publication of Fred Halliday's *Arabia Without Sultans*, which concerned London's widely popular Penguin Books, a fact obscured by its later republication by Random House in 1975.

Pioneers and the First Middle East Centers at Harvard and Oxford

In most cases, the first centers for Middle Eastern study were founded by a small group of academic entrepreneurs who, at least initially, had to battle the institutional inertia of their own universities before any new initiative could be allowed to take place. Most notable is the stranglehold exerted by long-established departments like those of Semitic or Oriental studies. Others, such as those at Durham University and the School of Oriental and African Studies in the United Kingdom, were the result of more teamwork and were somewhat less of a struggle. They were based on existing structures that were expanded and given new tasks as a result of government funding provided after the reports of the Scarborough Committee in 1948 and the Hayter Committee in 1961.

As I have already noted, the most influential and important of the original pioneers was Hamilton Gibb. While his motives are generally clear, his own role seems to have depended a great deal on his belief that, for reasons now difficult to fathom, he was not a historian of the type to anchor the new

---

7 George Makdisi, "Sir Hamilton Alexander Roskeen Gibb, January 2, 1895–October 22, 1971," *Journal of the American Society* 93/4 (Oct–Dec 1973), 491–93.

field. This understanding led him to seek out young academics, like Bernard Lewis at the School of Oriental Studies in London before the Second World War, and Albert Hourani just after it, who were prepared to work on "modern"—that is, nineteenth- and twentieth-century—Middle Eastern historical subjects.[8] This then involved devising novel systems for their personal training, including many of the basic practices still in use today: travel to the Middle East, immersion in the languages, and familiarity with whatever archives were then available. In Lewis's case, this led him to the Ottoman archives in Istanbul to which Gibb secured privileged access for his students through his diplomatic connections.[9] Alternatively, Hourani spent time in Cairo improving his language skills and reading Arabic texts, some of which, I surmise, formed the basis for his 1962 *Arabic Thought in the Liberal Age*.[10] One immediate result was Lewis's 1951 publication *Arabs in History*, which was facilitated by Gibb's personal appeal to the publisher, followed in 1958 by *The Emergence of Modern Turkey*.[11]

Another significant aspect of Gibb's larger project was an ambitious plan involving the writing of a series of books under the general title *Islamic Society and the West* (1957), beginning with his own introductory volume of the same name coauthored with the independent scholar of Turkey, Harold Bowen. The general intellectual schema involved was one derived from Arnold Toynbee's notion of historical progress being the result of a series of creative clashes between civilizations, defined as "networks of nation states." This perhaps explains the use of the word "society" in Gibb's title, as well as his general reliance on the notion of seeing the Middle East's modern history as, essentially, the story of the impact of West on East.[12] In this way, the purpose of Gibb and Bowen's work was to identify the key features of Middle Eastern economic, social, and political arrangements as they existed in the eighteenth century before the impact of Europe, beginning with the Napoleonic invasion of Egypt in 1798. This was to be followed by works commissioned from younger scholars on the Ottoman center, the Fertile Crescent, Egypt, and Iran, detailing the various responses to this impact in the nineteenth century.

---

8 Bernard Lewis, *Notes on a Century: Reflections of a Middle East Historian* (New York: Viking, 2012), 27–28. A reading of Lewis suggests that Gibb regarded history more in the German tradition as a science rather than in the Anglo-Saxon as one of the humanities.

9 Ibid., 33–34, 88–94; personal information from Albertine Jwaideh Lewis.

10 Personal information from Walid Khalidi.

11 Lewis, Notes, 83–86.

12 For example, Albert Hourani's review of *Islamic Society and the West* in *International Affairs*, 34, 201–12.

In the event, however, it seems that only one of these works was actually completed—Ann Lambton's *Landlord and Peasant in Persia* (1953)—with the rest being abandoned or put aside for one reason or another. Fortunately, however, all was not lost. In the case of Albertine Jwaideh's still-unpublished study of modern Iraq, invaluable chapters were published in a volume edited by Albert Hourani in 1963 and another by George Makdisi in 1965, while a third appeared as the Sixth Wadie Jwaideh Memorial Lecture at Indiana University on 30 October 2007.[13] Then, as far as Albert Hourani was concerned, his work on the introduction to his putative history of modern Syria was published separately in 1957, and still remains an essential part of the intellectual foundations of the study of the modern field.[14]

The moral is as old as it is relevant today: publishers like series, scholars sign contracts far too easily, and, anyway, the concept that animated the whole process in the first place becomes rapidly overcome by changes in the field itself. By and large, historians like Albert Hourani were quick to abandon the Toynbee/Gibb notion of the basic building blocks as interacting civilizational units, then running straight into all the problems posed by the post-World War I arrival of a vast array of new social history methodologies. Most notable, in their case, were the attractions of the more material, bottom-up type of historical writing that began to appear in the United Kingdom and France during the 1950s, methodologies that they thought valuable but did not always fully comprehend.

Be that as it may, the attempt to reposition traditional Oriental studies at the center of an emerging field consisting largely of historians and social scientists remained something of an uphill struggle. Getting individual academics, let alone whole departments, to agree to cross disciplinary boundaries is always a difficult task. Forced marriages, such as the one that led to the creation of a new discipline known as Philosophy, Politics, and Economics (PPE) or "modern greats" in Oxford in the 1920s, rarely work as their founders wished. Often they are defeated by what the warden of St Antony's, Ralf Dahrendorf, used to call the "Republic of College Tutors,"

13 See Albertine Jwaideh, "Midhat Pasha and the Land System of Lower Iraq," in Hourani, ed., *St Antony's Papers* 16, *Middle Eastern Affairs* 3 (London: Chatto and Windus, 1963); "The Saniya Lands of Sultan Abdul Hamid in Iraq," in George Makdisi (ed.) *Arabic and Islamic Studies in Honor of Hamilton A. R. Gibb* (Leiden: E.J. Brill, 1965); and "The Marsh Dwellers of Southern Iraq: Their Habitat, Origins, Society, and Economy," Wadie Jwaideh Memorial Lecture in Arabic and Islamic Studies, Indiana University, 30 October 2007.

14 Albert Hourani, "The Changing Face of the Fertile Crescent in the Eighteenth Century," *Studia Islamic* 8 (1957), 89–122. Reprinted with revisions in Hourani, *A Vision of History* (Beirut: Khayats, 1961).

who are unwilling to alter their own individual teaching and examining practices. In the case of PPE, this was exacerbated by the ways in which the discipline's separate components drew apart as a result of the Keynesian revolution and then the abrupt switch from neo-Kantian to ordinary language philosophy.

Very similar problems existed in the United States after Gibb moved to Harvard in 1955. He, too, encountered entrenched interests, particularly in the university's Department of Semitic Languages, whose name, after a great struggle, he finally managed to change to Near East Languages and Culture, or NELC. But this was offset by the possibilities open for overcoming initial opposition through the acquisition of new financial resources from government and the wealthy foundations then heavily engaged in the process of developing regional expertise for national political ends. Fortunately, he was well supported by many at the center of Harvard's administrative structure—notably President Nathan Pusey, the dean of the Faculty of Arts and Sciences, McGeorge Bundy, and William Langer, the Harvard Center's first director (1954–55). These were all "internationalists," determined that Americans should understand more of the outside world via the establishment of centers and programs devoted to the study of important regions of the Soviet, Eastern European, and former colonial worlds.[15]

Harvard, too, possessed a group of scholars already well practiced in the organization of multidisciplinary study groups, like the famous sociologist Talcott Parsons, whose Department of Social Relations was already a "landmark in interdisciplinary collaboration in the behavioral sciences."[16] This allowed things to move fast on the organization side, so that by the time of Gibb's arrival in 1955, the Middle East Center already possessed an office on Dunster Street alongside those of other area centers, two programs—an MA in Middle East regional studies and a joint PhD with a number of well-established departments like those of anthropology, economics, etc.,—and over forty Middle East–related courses listed in the 1954–55 university catalog.[17]

What Gibb brought was not only an enormous scholarly reputation but also, as Don Babai points out in his excellent history of the center, the human, managerial, and imaginative skills required to attract students, faculty,

---

15 Don Babai, ed., *Center for Middle Eastern Studies, Harvard University: Reflections on the Past, Visions of the Future* (Cambridge, MA: Harvard University Press), 2–6.
16 Wikileaks entry for "Talcott Parsons."
17 Zachary Lockman, *Contending Visions of the Middle East: The History and Politics of the Middle East* (Cambridge: Cambridge University Press, 2009); Babai, *Reflections*, 6–7.

academic visitors, and donors.[18] Meanwhile, Gibb was branching out, with a new and highly successful experimental course in Islamic institutions. Although he directed some of his first students to take courses with social scientists like Robert Bellah and Talcott Parsons, he seems to have been wise enough to encourage them to find their own specific topics within the general areas assigned to them, and then to allow them to be guided by whatever they were able to find, looking for, as Babai put it, "breadth" just as much as depth.[19] The result was a formidable list of theses and publications by students such as Hanna Batatu, Ira Lapidus, and Roy Mottahedeh.[20]

Gibb was wise, too, to leave much of the day-to-day administration, as well as much of the fundraising, to his tireless adjutant Albert Jules "A.J." Meyer. Meyer, though not much of an academic economist, and spurned by the Harvard economics department, was adept at using his Saudi connections to raise considerable sums of money for the center from the big international oil companies, particularly Aramco. A.J. was also much more socially adept than the shy and reticent Hamilton Gibb and provided the ever-open door and hospitality that his director lacked. The result was a further expansion of the functions of an area studies center in terms of reach and approachability as well as a constant addition of new activities — graduate recruitment, courses aimed at undergraduates, books and monographs published in association with Harvard University Press, etc.,—that served as a model, and a challenge, to create similar centers elsewhere.

One good example is that of the foundation of the Chicago center by one of Gibb's favorite pupils, William Polk. Polk had studied at Oxford and, when at Harvard, was expected by his professor to introduce what could be "translated" from the Oxford Oriental language program in terms of language instruction and related lectures.[21] But rather than staying in Cambridge as Gibb's chosen successor, Polk moved to Washington, DC, to work for the Kennedy administration in the early 1960s before moving back to academic life in Chicago with the aim, as he himself pointed out, of "creating a better organization" than the one he had helped to create at Harvard. There he found the university's unique system of committees of dis-

18 Babai, *Reflections*, 7–9.

19 Ibid., 9.

20 Hannah Batatu, *The Old Social Classes and the Revolutionary Movements of Iraq* (Princeton NJ: Princeton University Press, 1978); Ira Lapidus, *Muslim Cities in the Later Middle Ages* (Cambridge, MA: Harvard University Press, 1967); and, Roy Mottahedeh, *Loyalty and Leadership in Early Islamic Society* (Princeton NJ: Princeton University Press, 1980).

21 Personal information from William Polk.

parate scholars with shared interests greatly to his liking and set about the task of bringing together people with "at least some interest" in the Middle East, enticing them with offers of funds for travel and other activities that their home departments could not rival.[22] Unfortunately, Polk's search for big money to support new professorships in Turkish, Persian, and Islamic studies soon got him into trouble when the law school turned down money promised from King Faisal of Saudi Arabia, and then the whole university vetoed more millions of dollars to be given by the Shah of Persia. This was enough to cause him to "move aside" to establish the Adlai Stevenson Institute of International History, before going off to live in Cairo in 1973.

What was more difficult for Gibb, however, was finding senior scholars to teach and to undertake basic research on the modern Middle East; there were simply too few of them at this stage to go around. As Babai once again shrewdly points out, the whole Harvard enterprise was highly dependent on just one man, Gibb himself, whose debilitating stroke in February 1964 left the center leaderless for a number of years.[23] The lesson is an obvious one. The role of Gibb and the other early institutional builders and academic entrepreneurs was so highly personal and dependent on an almost unique combination of Middle East experience, vision, and diplomatic and intellectual skills that there was bound to be a gap before the system they created had been in existence long enough to train a set of successors.

One of the institutions that played a key role in the creation of area studies in the United Kingdom was St Antony's College, a graduate institution founded in Oxford with French money in 1950. Praised by Gibb for its academic daring, it focused almost exclusively on the world outside Western Europe, developing a "nucleus" of teachers, researchers, and students concerned first with Russia and Eastern Europe, then with the Far East, followed by a Middle East center in 1957 — the first such concentration, as Albert Hourani notes, to be officially designated as a "center."[24] Some of this had to do with the fact that, as Hourani also notes, members of Oxford's post-war academic leadership were determined to create ways for the soon-to-be independent states of the non-European world to be studied at the graduate level by persons already "formed" as historians and social scientists.[25] No doubt this was particularly true of those like

---

22 Personal information from William Polk.

23 Babai, *Reflections*, 11–13.

24 Albert Hourani, "The Middle East Centre: A Short History, 1957-1987" in *The Middle East Centre, 1957–2007: A Book of Record*, ed. Eugene Rogan, (Oxford: St Antony's College, 2007), 1–8.

25 Hourani, "The Middle East Centre," 1–2.

the former Oxford history tutor William Deakin, the first warden of St Antony's, who were just back from wartime service. In Deakin's case, his service was in Cairo and then with Tito's partisans in Yugoslavia. Weight, too, must also be given to Deakin's recognition that, for a relatively poor and under-endowed college, money for buildings, libraries, and research could be obtained for area studies from outside organizations, including the big international oil companies and foreign foundations like Ford, Rockefeller, and Gulbenkian.

The new center's first director was Frank Stoakes, a man with oil company connections who was also the coauthor of the 1958 book *Iraq* in the Benn "Nations of the Modern World" series, and the second was Albert Hourani, who was brought to Oxford by Hamilton Gibb as a lecturer. In many ways he was an inspired choice, possessing many of Gibb's own academic and entrepreneurial assets, but nonetheless directing the new center was often very hard going. Just as Hourani had been left to train himself in the study of the modern Middle East, he also had to work out how best to use the new center to promote and to sustain an interest in the region within the university, in the larger Oxford area, and, to some extent, in London communities. The university's existing departmental structure, with its emphasis on only the classical study of religion and language, was unable to provide much support.

The ideas behind many of the new center's core activities, for example the weekly seminar chaired by the director and open to all, must have come from Hourani's own observation of such practices in other centers both at St Antony's and outside. Held usually on a Friday afternoon, these attracted speakers, and often audience members, from London, in addition to the usual combination of students and old Middle East hands: retired diplomats, administrators, and others who had spent most of their working lives in places like Palestine, Sudan, and the Gulf. Other initiatives involved the establishment of a more personal style of direction than was usual at that time, in which visitors and students could be made to feel that, in some sense, they were actually entering the Middle East when they came in through the front door. There were posters and pictures, there was the regular hospitality of parties and receptions attended by a mix of British and Middle Eastern teachers and students, and there were the invitations to meet and to dine at home with the Houranis themselves. These dinner invitations were ritual procedures that began with guests being offered sherry in Albert's own book-lined study and then a meal cooked his wife, Odile.

Just as important were Albert's energetic and time-consuming forays into the university proper, using his considerable diplomatic skills and powers of persuasion to persuade the university administration to provide financial support for the library, the more traditional colleges to accept Middle Eastern appointments, and members of the university's Oriental Institute to provide a temporary home for Middle Eastern visitors. Much of the success of this difficult work depended, as it often does, on the creation and maintenance of informal personal alliances such as the ones he established with Professor Richard Walzer, an expert in the classical roots of Islamic learning, and Dr. Samuel Stern. These gentlemen came together to form something called the Middle East History Group, the members of which read and discussed important books as well as organized a series of successful interdisciplinary and internationally comparative conferences, beginning with one on the Islamic city in 1965. Not the least of Albert's virtues was his desire to learn more about the prehistory of his own field by getting to know the academic biographies of leading Orientalists trained in different parts of Europe, like Walzer, and of European visitors to Oxford like Jacques Berque and Maxime Rodinson from Paris.

Many of these activities depended on the power, prestige, and international reputation that came not only from personal authority but also from the money that came to Oxford as a result of the Hayter Committee—the 1961 report by a subcommittee appointed by the government's University Grants Committee on the "Development of Oriental, Slavonic, East European, and African Studies," usually known after the name of its chairman. As director of one of the three premier Middle East centers named by the committee, Hourani eventually, and after complex discussions with the university, college, and various interests, obtained the finances not only to create eight new posts in Middle East studies but also to finance research and travel.

As with all highly decentralized universities—Harvard is another—small initiatives are easy to take but large ones much less so, given the variety of vested interests involved. It is to Hourani's great credit that he managed to steer a way through this thicket, helped greatly by the support he got from William Deakin and his own college. Nevertheless, such victories are rarely without cost. In Albert's case it left a permanent residue of hurtful suspicion among some of his colleagues in the Oriental Institute and elsewhere, accentuated by a subtle—and sometimes not so subtle—form of English racism through which they chose to see him as some kind of wily Levantine trader, at best as "not quite one of us." The use of all such personalized power in relatively small communities runs the risk of being taken somewhat too personally by those it affects. This risk must surely have been greater, at least in the former colonial countries like the United Kingdom and France, when a director of the area studies field is, or was, perceived as not being sufficiently distanced from the area studied.

It is difficult to say whether Albert's Lebanese origins also played a role in creating and then maintaining the type of partnerships with Middle Eastern universities and research institutes that Gibb had identified as being central to the success of the new area studies project. Certainly, he was completely at home in Beirut, particularly the American University of Beirut, where he had taught briefly in the late 1930s, and at which his father had been a student. He was also invited, from time to time, to lecture at other Middle Eastern universities like those in Baghdad and Damascus, as well as spending two sabbatical years in the region in the troubled years of 1956 and 1967–78. Nevertheless, much the same was true of many other British and US scholars, particularly in the early years of Arab independence when universities were smaller, more elitist institutions than they were to become under growing state control.

Where Albert Hourani may have been more unusual is in the care he took to make visiting scholars from the Arab world feel at home. An example of a recipient of this hospitality is the Egyptian leftist intellectual Anouar Abdel-Malek, who came to Oxford to see him in the mid-1960s shortly after he had published his powerful article "L'Orientalism en crise," now seen as one of the first major interventions in the attack on many of the basic assumptions of old-fashioned Orientalism.[26] I remember Albert introducing me to Abdel-Malek on this occasion and learning something of both the respect and the intellectual excitement that informed their exchange.

Yet, like all the new area studies ventures, the ongoing success of the St Antony's Centre was more than a one-man show. In its early days, its vitality owed a great deal to Elizabeth Monroe, a British journalist and writer and the author of *Britain's Moment in the Middle East* (1963) who had met Albert in Cairo during the war and who brought back to Oxford with her a string of interesting Middle Eastern contacts. These included the Palestinian notable Musa Alami, the Philbys (St. John and Kim), Freya Stark, and any number of former ambassadors and colonial officials whose private papers she soon began to collect. Then, over time, a second generation of younger academics began to find a place within the center's administration, notably Derek Hopwood, Robert Mabro, and myself, all of whom acted as director at one time or another either while Albert was away or after his early retirement in 1971.

Some Other Influential Pioneers and One Notable Freelance

Like any other new area studies field, the establishment of modern Middle East studies was dependent on a particular type of academic entrepre-

26 Anouar Abdel- Malek, "L'Orientalism en crise," *Diogenes*, 44 (1963), 109–42.

neurship: persons able to carve out a space for it in their own, often hostile institutions, to create new programs, to find funds, and to recruit the expert teachers and researchers necessary to staff their new centers and make them lively places of learning. As a rule, they also knew each other quite well, visited each other's centers, and, whatever their own particular intellectual skills and interests, produced what were very much carbon copies of each other's basic modus operandi. As for their students, they quickly came to know who was who in the field, who was writing what, and perhaps just as significantly, the nature of the friendships and rivalries between their seniors. This would have occurred through the inevitable forms of academic gossip that go on in university and other professional settings, some probably true, some mere speculation—such as when it came to speculating about their real feelings either about each other or about such central issues as the nature of Islam, Arab nationalism, or the Arab-Israeli dispute.

In what follows I will use my own personal vantage point of Oxford, and later Harvard, to say a few words about some of the other early centers I got to know and to observe. Chief among these were the School of Oriental and African Studies in London (SOAS) and the University of Durham. At these schools, the study of the modern Middle East had been grafted more obviously onto an older concern with Orientalism and Semitic languages, sometimes via new appointments, sometimes by providing service courses for missionaries, soldiers, and aid workers posted to the region. Probably as a result, management of the centers in these two places was more a matter of team work, although accompanied with rather less collegiality than I had experienced in Oxford; lunch was the main social occasion, and most teachers retired to their homes outside the city in the late afternoon.

Turning to SOAS first, the historian who anchored the school's Middle Eastern intellectual activities, Bernard Lewis, was both an old-fashioned Orientalist as well as an influential historian of modern Turkey. Yet, like Albert Hourani, he also seems to have been conscious of his lack of knowledge of the social sciences, demanding simply that their practitioners base their work on documents in the appropriate Middle Eastern languages.[27] Fortunately, parts of London University contained people like the redoubtable oil economist Edith Penrose, who could step in to teach and advise SOAS graduates. Others, like P.J. Vatikiotis, had to be hired from outside for their teaching, Middle East connections, and most importantly in P.J.'s case, enthusiasm, energy, and entrepreneurial skills. The result, however,

27 For example, Lewis, *Notes*, 275.

was to give the SOAS team a somewhat conservative bias in which the Weberian notion of an essential passage from tradition to modernity was used to criticize the Arab world's revolutionary movements much more harshly than their more radical students were willing to allow. This difference of opinion gave rise to boycotts, sit-ins, and a general assault on academic authority during the more muted British version of the European student uprisings in 1968, something from which the centers for Middle East studies outside London were largely immune. Perhaps being in the nation's capital city had something to do with this. Perhaps the presence at SOAS of an unusual number of activist students from Syria, Lebanon, and elsewhere, who were generally much better versed in the works of Marx, Trotsky, and Hegel than their British counterparts, played a role.

What I think I believed at the time was that what were called "revolutions" were an essential part of both the anticolonial movement and, more generally, the forward movement of history. Moreover, nothing in my schooling in what was essentially the Whig view of history had prepared me for the notion that the conservative, antirevolutionary side had anything that could properly be called an intellectual defense. At school I was vaguely aware of a thinker called Michael Oakeshott at the London School of Economics whose work, as I later learned, had been a powerful influence on the worldview of Elie Kedourie, but it was not until later that I came across a number of teachers and writers whose own experience of pre-war extremism seemed to have led them to conservative political positions. At the same time, I began to have some sense of the work of great European thinkers like the philosopher Eric Voegelin whose writings served to underpin the belief in order—at almost all costs—that was so significant in the political thought of friends and colleagues like Vatikiotis.

I used to visit SOAS at regular intervals during my Oxford years, and soon got to feel quite at home in both its old quarters and then the new: the cramped older building, often smelling of food from the basement cafeteria, with its wonderful library staffed by some of the most beautiful female librarians I had ever seen, and then the somewhat less friendly new quarters, with its required entrance pass, windowless library, and long passages of, unusually as it seemed, empty offices. As for the Durham Centre for Middle Eastern and Islamic Studies, this was too far away from the Oxford/Cambridge/London access to allow regular contact, and for a long time I knew it only through its many publications and some of its students who came to Oxford for graduate work. Like the other two "Hayter" centers, it had its own great man: the geographer W.B. Fisher, described by one of his colleagues as a "dedicated expansionist with great entrepreneurial flair," who had served in the Middle East during the Second World War and then gone on to publish a much-used textbook, *The Middle East: A Physical, Social, and Regional Geography* (1950).[28] Like both Hourani and Lewis, he was convinced of the importance of the social sciences and made great efforts to train and recruit young scholars who could use such skills for research purposes. Like them, too, he seems to have been something of a one-man show, seeking advice but making all the major decisions on his own. But, unlike them, he was also interested in the promotion of immediately useful knowledge, obtaining any number of grants to advise Middle East governments about urbanization, arid land agriculture, social geography, and other related topics, particularly in Libya, Saudi Arabia, and the Gulf. No doubt this was another reason why I was only invited there once by a Durham-based friend to give a seminar, never met Fisher, and felt no need to use its rich archives until my interest in Lord Cromer led me to some material there concerning the management of the Sudan after the British conquest of 1898.

Lastly, some remarks about two of the other early pioneers: Gustave Von Grunebaum in the United States and Gabriel Baer in Israel. The former started his academic career as a professor of Arabic at the University of California, Los Angeles as very much a typical Orientalist of the Austrian school, albeit with a cultural approach to Islamic civilization. Von Grunebaum was given a new professorship in Near East history in 1957 and was made director of the university's Near East center. This gave him the opportunity to take on young scholars, often on one of his famous "recruiting" missions to Europe during summer vacations, and to attract noted scholars to come for short-term visits. Perhaps aware that getting academics to Los Angeles presented certain obvious problems in terms of both distance and general European and East Coast cultural prejudice against the "vulgar" goings on in California, he also created the Giorgio Levi Della Vida conference and award for work in Islamic studies, allowing the awardee to suggest the conference topic and the names of participants.

Gabriel Baer worked in the very different academic environment of a country emerging from its various confrontations with both its local Palestinian/Arab inhabitants and its Arab neighbors. It was also a country in which, as the result of the immigration of a large number of German-Jewish scholars, the hold of classical Orientalism was particularly strong. This was not only in terms of its particular practices—knowledge of all four major Middle Eastern languages, veneration of texts, etc.,—but also in its

---

28 John I. Clarke, "A 50 Year Retrospective: Durham and the Geography Department Fifty Years Ago in 1955" (unpublished paper, Durham University).

ideological underpinning: a worldview stressing the undying hostility of an Arab-Muslim world whose own actions had done so much to provoke.

Baer migrated to Palestine in 1933, learned Arabic, and was educated in Haifa and, for a short period during the Second World War, at the American University of Beirut. There is also evidence of him visiting Cairo during the war where, being on the political Left, he may have become acquainted with various progressive thinkers as well as senior members of the local Egyptian trade unions. After 1948, he did his own military service in Israel during which time he seemed to have acted as an adviser to the Israeli prime minister, David Ben-Gurion, on Arab affairs.[29] It may also have been that he was one of those responsible for the basic organization of the joint Israeli academic/intelligence activity toward the Arab world. This structure divided research into two main sections—one on Arab armies and another on each country's political and social structures, with particular attention paid to the biographies of its heads of state.[30] Meanwhile, his own academic work consisted of researching and then writing a PhD on landownership in Egypt at the Hebrew University from 1950 to 1957, supervised by Albert Bonne, the author of *State and Economics in the Middle East* (1948), after which he was appointed a lecturer with special reference to the "History of the Middle East in the Modern Era."[31]

Baer went to become one of the founders of the Israeli Oriental Society and the founder of the English-language journal *Asian and African Studies*. He was also active in advancing the study of the modern Middle East at the new University of Haifa. More generally, he was instrumental in recruiting graduate students and then training them in the tools they needed to write academic studies on the history of the region under both the Ottomans and the Western powers: the British and the French. As for his own interests, these moved from an initial focus on agrarian relations and Egyptian social history—in which he did important early work on peasants, rural/urban relations, and guilds—to one in which he concentrated on work on local endowments (*waqf*) and other religious documents, including the many court records captured by the Israelis in the 1967 war. For this task, we might suppose, he believed that an Israeli cut off from day-to-day contact with the Arab world

---

29 Personal information from Yoram Meital.

30 Gil Eyal, *The Disenchantment of the Orient: Expertise in Arab Affairs and the Israeli State* (Redwood City: Stanford University Press, 2007), chapter 6.

31 Published as *A History of Landownership of Modern Egypt: 1800–1950* (Oxford: Oxford UP 1962). See also Baer's obituary in *Der Islam*, 61/1 (August 2009), 8–9. Bonne was also an economic historian and the author of *State and Economics in the Middle East: A Society in Transition* (London: Kegan, Paul, Trench, 1948).

might best make a scholarly contribution. Reports by his students describe a person who was more than usually open with his graduate students for someone of his age and academic training, holding seminars at his modest home in Talpiot near the old 1948-49 armistice line in Jerusalem and, on occasions, encouraging them to disagree with him.[32] In this, as in a number of his other scholarly activities, Baer was obviously echoing practices that he had come across in centers of Middle East study like Oxford, which he visited at least once in the early 1960s. He was also adapting them to his local environment in such a way as to ensure that he and his students could flourish intellectually while having access to a global network of scholarly support.

There are both strengths and weaknesses in running a center as a one-man show, as each of these cases evince. Given the traditional combination of weak central leadership and institutional inertia characteristic of most of the world's traditional universities, new initiatives require an extraordinary amount of energy, tenacity, and entrepreneurial spirit to succeed, allied with a missionary sense of the importance of the new enterprise to their country's general wellbeing. Success also seemed to require something of an authoritarian streak, as well as a capacity to play one's cards quite close to the chest. Not surprisingly, such a style of leadership, depending as it did on the personality of the man himself, was not to everybody's liking. Nor was it always flexible enough to respond to new challenges, particularly those of creating a new generation of successors. Albert Hourani, for his part, clearly recognized this situation; he retired early enough to be able to both concentrate on his own work and continue to act as a fatherly influence over a second generation of students, like myself, who took over the day-to-day burden of administration from him.

There were also occasions when the system of one-man direction either broke down through personal vanity and error or, in the absence of strong leadership, left a center rudderless and so without proper direction. Such was the situation at Harvard for many years after the retirement of Hamilton Gibb. The university proved unable to appoint a successor, and a series of interim directors either let things drift or exercised such poor judgment in the use of resources that they had to be removed from office. Nevertheless, it was also possible for the situation to right itself via the choice of a new man. At Harvard, Roy Mottahedeh was appointed. He then recruited new members like myself and set a new intellectual tone in which modern history rather than government or political science—with all their dangerous divisiveness when it came to a central focus on the Arab-Israeli conflict—became once again the master discipline.

---

32 Personal information from Yoram Meital.

Although the creation of new centers for Middle Eastern study was a sine qua non for the development of the new field, there were important scholars and freelance academic adventurers who played a valuable role in connecting these centers to the vital but often fluid and evanescent currents of the region's political, economic, and social life. For me, and for many people beginning the study of the Middle East in the 1960s and 1970s, the most influential and charismatic was the Oxford-educated, widely traveled, multilingual Fred Halliday, whose unrivalled range of contacts—mostly on the Left—spanned the Middle East, Europe, and the Americas. Fred had visited Persia, as it was then called, even before he went up to Queen's College in 1964. Later, he made a dangerous journey with a Lebanese fellow student at the School of Oriental and African Studies, Fawwaz Traboulsi, to observe the armed rebellion in Dhofar against the sultan of Oman in the late 1960s.[33]

This was the beginning of what Fred would later call "doing the work," which entailed going about the Middle East, networking, collecting information, and then putting it all in some larger political framework of a largely Marxist type. One result was the connections he developed with an astonishing number of activists and movements in and outside the region, making him a kind of point man or "go-to guy" for anyone wanting information about, or often access to, significant figures on the Left. He provided this wonderful service with diligence, openness, and good sense. He was, for example, the first person to put me in touch with American radical activists, like Joe Stork, who were in the process of founding the Middle East Research and Information Project in Washington in the early 1970s, as well as a series of Palestinian and Beirut-based intellectuals who were my own introduction to the Arab liberation movements of those violent days. It was he, too, who used my own domestic academic connections to find places in English universities for Arab student militants on the run from the security services in their home countries. Not that we were always in political agreement: Fred began too much to the left of me with regard to Middle Eastern politics, and then ended up too much to the right for my liking. But that was not the point—academic scholarship concerning the contemporary Arab world in Europe and the United States would have been a much more stultifying activity if it had not been constantly enlivened by Fred's extraordinary access to, and interest in, the hot news of the debates, dilemmas, and movements actually taking place on the ground.

---

33 Described in forewords to Fred Halliday, *Arabia Without Sultans* (London: Penguin Press, 1975) and *Revolution and Foreign Policy: The Case of South Yemen, 1967–1987* (Cambridge: Cambridge University Press, 1990).

The Field Gets Organized: Textbooks and Other Basic Readings

By the early 1960s, enough interest had been aroused for it to be clear that the study of the modern Middle East lacked the basic works needed for teaching and research. Most needed among these was a region-wide analysis of its history, its major political institutions, and of the basic features of its post-independence political practice in terms of competition for access to power and to economic resources. As the component parts of what had once been two great world empires, the Ottoman and the Persian, passed through foreign domination and parcelization to become independent sovereign states in the post-World War II world, what, to use a more contemporary term, was the "big picture?" And how did this region differ in terms of government and administration from those other states in sub-Saharan Africa, Asia, and the Far East that appeared to be experiencing a roughly similar trajectory at more or less the same time? There was one book that appeared to give some kind of a general history: George Antonius's 1938 *The Arab Awakening: The Story of the Arab National Movement*. But this was too obviously a personal work, written in the different world of pre-war French and British imperialism to be of much more than a minor historical significance in our search for the basic structures that stood at the heart of what we were striving to teach and understand. Much the same comment could be made about George E. Kirk's 1961 *Contemporary Arab Politics: A Concise History*, a self-styled rant against the forces of Middle East revolution that were carrying away previous hopes for a liberal constitutional order in Egypt, Syria, and Iraq.

Albert Hourani and a few of his graduate students like myself tried to educate ourselves by reading whatever was available, mostly books about the Middle East written within the conventional and, as it turned out, highly politicized paradigm of the passage from tradition to a democratic modernity. One week we would puzzle through Daniel Lerner's 1958 *The Passing of Traditional Society*, and then in another, Manfred Halpern's 1963 *The Politics of Social Change*. We believed such writers to be noble in their ambitions to provide a comprehensive account of the general processes of political and social change in a region that they had made some effort to get known personally, but we also recognized their writings as deeply flawed by their easy assumptions of Middle Eastern backwardness, compared with Western progress.

Fortunately, several good studies were emerging at the time. Some covered individual country politics, such as Patrick Seale's 1962 *The Struggle for Syria,* while others took up broader issues of national political economy

190

like Gabriel Bear's *A History of Landownership in Modern Egypt,* published in the same year. Nevertheless, it was only later that I, at least, understood how little these works contained about the growth and exercise of state power in a period when the major Western public concern was with the overthrow of democratically elected parliaments in military coups—as witnessed in J.C. Hurewitz's 1969 *Middle East Politics: The Military Dimension* and James Bill and Carl Leiden's 1974 *The Middle East: Politics and Power*. Even worse was their concern with what seemed to me the whole uninteresting question of whether the new regimes could be regarded as properly legitimate in the Weberian sense. I first came across this notion in Nadav Safran's 1961 *Egypt in Search of Political Community*; it was to be later amplified to include the whole Middle East in Michael Hudson's 1977 *Arab Politics*.

This lack of basic works was very much on my mind when I began teaching Middle East political—as opposed to economic—history at Oxford at the end of the 1960s; my lectures provided an inadequate substitute for those still-to-be-written book-length surveys. That is, until I was persuaded, as many teachers were, to write such a work myself. But this was also very much the temper of those times; 1970s Britain saw an explosion of interest by publishers in the type of general textbooks they believed could be used in the proliferation of both university and, often, high-school-level courses in some aspect of Third World or imperial history. Indeed, this was a heady period for academic writers, with publishers knocking at our doors with contracts in their hands, seeking new works to flesh out a rapidly multiplying list of series about this or that aspect of the modern world. Such contracts were often sweetened with douceurs in the shape of the kind of advances previously only available to the likes of novelists like Graham Greene.

Yet, like many such bonanzas, it was all too good to last, at least in its initial and overenthusiastic form. Contracts were easy to sign, less easy to honor. Delivery dates seemed impossibly far away until they suddenly were not. Advances spent on anything but buying writing time from teaching began to make the author feel perennially guilty. Friendships, too, came under great strain: the editors of the new series were often friends, and promises made much too easily inevitably led to mounting pressure to deliver, to the eventual response of "Yes, but only after a large number of other obligations had been dealt with first."

Two incidents come to mind that can be used as examples of the best and worst of those overheated times. The best involved a project I developed with my friend Bob Sutcliffe at Oxford in the late 1960s on theories of imperialism—interest had recently been revived in this subject by the

Marxist academic Tom Kemp. With a small advance from a publisher, Bob and I organized a series of weekly lectures by men who were also actively engaged in rethinking the subject, including two of the leading advocates of a theory-free approach to the expansion of empire: the authors of the 1961 *Africa and the Victorians*, Ronald Robinson and John (Jack) Gallagher. Such lectures had the great advantage of providing us with written or recorded texts to edit rather than having to wait until the authors themselves returned fair copy, a task we largely performed in Bob's country cottage in Wiltshire. As a result, we were able to produce a manuscript, published in 1972 as *Studies in the Theory of Imperialism*, more or less according to the time stated in our contract—a very rare experience then or now. Happily, the book also continued to sell well for a number of years, partly because it contained what we had always regarded as one of the weaker entries—a first sketch by Robinson of an influential theory of the role of intermediaries in the colonial process, which could be found nowhere else.

A much less satisfactory experience followed when, in a fit of misguided enthusiasm, I signed a contract with a publisher friend at Methuen sometime around 1981, not only to edit the Middle East component of a series called *The Making of the Modern World*, but also to produce the introductory volume, something I finally completed some ten years later. Just as embarrassing was the fact that I was unable to persuade several of my friends to produce their promised contributions; the only one who actually came through was Feroz Ahmad whose *The Making of Modern Turkey* was published in 1992.

The next decade or so witnessed a flood of new textbooks, most clearly based on many years of teaching, which made the choice for teachers something of an *embarrasse de richesse*. My own choice for undergraduates was William Cleveland's 1994 *A History of the Modern Middle East* on account of its straightforward, no-nonsense historical approach. Much later, James Gelvin's 2005 *The Modern Middle East: A History* became (and remains) my favorite for advanced courses due to its unique mixture of historical analysis, documents, and vignettes. The one book that I should have liked, but did not, was Albert Hourani's 1991 *A History of the Arab Peoples*, which seemed to me to depend much too much on an endless cycle of his notion of "the politics of the notables" while exhibiting a marked distaste for the politics of postcolonial populism.

What is obvious, though, is that almost all the textbooks follow a well-tried formula in which what Cleveland calls "The Struggle for Independence" follows "The Era of Transformation." This is then ensued by chapters that describe the modern period in terms of the authors' own political temperament: for some, a serious effort at state building, for others, what old-fashioned liberals like Albert Hourani famously characterized as "a disturbance of spirits."[34] What is also obvious is the almost entire absence of any real moment of revisionism, when the classic paradigm is finally challenged and then replaced. Such revisionism, as existed, was entirely devoted either to challenges to the Israeli national narrative or by contributions to the great debate concerning Western writings about the Middle East in the spirit of what Edward Said defined as "Orientalism." Nevertheless, these basic texts gave the field much of its coherence and collegiality, albeit in terms of a somewhat too-cozy feeling of warmed-over intimacy. They also made it different from those other fields of modern area studies, where attacks on the hegemony of the ruling paradigm were much more common.

More heat and dust was created, however, on the fringes of the field of Middle Eastern publishing. Here, determined attempts were sometimes made to prevent certain manuscripts from getting into print because of their supposed ideological content. One such event quite early on in my career was the battle to prevent the publication of Fred Halliday's 1974 *Arabia Without Sultans*, with its explicitly anti-imperialist, anticolonial stance. Halliday had developed this slant at least in part through his travels in rebel-held territory in Dhofar along the Yemeni/Omani border, which made him something of a marked man by the old colonial hands who served as readers of some of the important London publishers. Fortunately, Fred's putative publisher, Penguin, was going through one of its populist and progressive phases at the time and did not seem to need more than a few letters from so-called experts like myself to convince its editorial board that it was a work of academic importance.

Albert Hourani and I were also involved in a second set of less heated disputes through our presence on the advisory board—along with Michael Gilsenan—of what came to be called the Cambridge University Press's "Modern Middle East Library," established in the early 1980s. The first titles of this series dealt with relatively controversial subjects such as Helena Cobban's 1984 insider study *The Palestine Liberation Organisation: People, Power, and Politics* and Benny Morris's 1988 *The Birth of the Palestinian Refugee Problem, 1947-1949*. As far as I can remember, we chose such books because we felt they added some important new dimension to our field both in terms of subject matter and, in Morris's case at least, because his book was based so directly on material in the Israeli State and World Zionist Archives. But they certainly raised some hackles at the time on both

---

34 *A History of the Arab Peoples* (London: Faber and Cambridge, MA: Harvard University Press, 1991), chapter 6.

sides of the Israeli-Palestinian divide. Some later titles, for example, Gershon Shafir's 1989 *Land, Labor and the Origins of the Israeli-Palestinian Conflict: 1882-1914*, were also strongly criticized both before and after publication. Nevertheless, we never felt subject to any type of attempted censorship and were strongly supported by the members of the Cambridge University Press assigned to manage the series: Elizabeth Wetton and then Marigold Acland. The only major problem was the commercial one of how well each title might sell.

Conferences, Associations, and Collective Projects

Within modern Middle East studies, as no doubt was the case with other areas, there was a logic at work that moved from holding of international conferences—which helped define the field, its major concerns and players, and its relationship to the social sciences—to the creation of the professional associations deemed necessary to raise the field's profile in universities and to lobby for its interests before both governments and funding agencies. Simply to create lists of major events would be a tedious and meaningless activity, so let me just say that I found that the most formative collective occasions in terms of conferences and workshops were the two put on by P. J. Vatikiotis at SOAS in the 1960s on "Egypt" and on "Revolutions," followed by the large Middle East economic history conference that Avram Udovitch organized at Princeton University in 1971. All of these had the major function of identifying what used to be called the "state of the art:" the field's major preoccupation and its leading exponents in the United Kingdom, the United States, and certain parts of Europe, particularly France. Notable, too, at this stage, was the absence of any attempt at gatekeeping in terms of subject matter or approach. This was the same practice adopted by the early pioneers like Hamilton Gibb, in which one topic was viewed as being as good as another. What was lost, of course, was any notion of a general standard of either utility or value. In this area, the field as a whole has not advanced a great deal over the years, except perhaps in terms of the kind of conventional wisdom about quality created by the practice of critical reviews in the major professional journals.

There is also some evidence that it was this general absence of professional standards that led a group of senior US academics to come together in 1959 to create a scholarly association of their own, the Association of American Middle East Studies (AAMES). Later, in 1966, the Middle East Studies Association of North America (MESA) was formed, at the specific initiative of the Social Science Research Council-American Council of Learned

Societies Joint Committee on the Near and Middle East with support from the Ford Foundation. These new organizations appeared to follow such previous examples as the creation of the Association of African Studies in 1957: holding an annual meeting, the establishment of a small secretariat, the employment of a Washington lobbyist, and the inauguration of both a regular bulletin and professional journal. After an inaugural meeting in 1967 with only a dozen or so people present, MESA received a valuable boost from the huge political repercussions of the June War in the Middle East that same year. The creation of several copycat organizations overseas soon followed: British Society of Middle Eastern Studies (BRISMES), European Association for Middle Eastern Studies (EURAMES), and finally, World Congress for Middle Eastern Studies (WOCMES), which held its inaugural meeting in Mainz in 2002.

Like most other professional associations, MESA held annual conferences in large hotels in different cities, though it returned to Washington, its most popular venue, every three or so years. Nobody could describe these as important intellectual events, though some effort was made to ensure that the papers presented had been peer-reviewed, usually by the Middle East center of one or more universities in the host city. What mattered more was the opportunity the meetings provided to maintain old friendships, to gossip, to buy books, to observe the award of an increasing number of honors and prizes, and, perhaps most important of all, to get some sense of the latest intellectual trends: at one time questions of identity, at another the study of political transitions. There was also the possibility of engaging in a mild form of self-reflection. Each year's presidential address often concerned such important questions as the political relevance of Middle East studies, relations—and sometimes the lack of relations—with scholars in the region itself, and general issues of free speech and academic freedom. As a rule, historians and anthropologists dominated participation, with economists, sociologists, and political scientists generally preferring the greater theoretical rigor of their own professional associations.

Despite the obvious usefulness of such conferences, it is clear that any umbrella organization cannot represent the particular interests of all its members. Over time, such an organization also tends to conduct its business along certain well-tried lines, relying for new initiatives on its rotating system of one-year presidencies, the chairpersons of its standing committees, and the activities of its small permanent staff. One such initiative of which I believe the organization should be particularly proud was the 1990 establishment of MESA's Committee on Academic Freedom, which attracted members with a particular concern for the protection of freedom of speech in both Western universities and those in the Middle East.

Nevertheless, it also has to be said that the annual meetings were informed by a certain amount of clubby self-righteousness. This was produced, in part, by a pervasive feeling that the members' interest in questions of Arab and, especially, Palestinian rights made them particularly vulnerable to criticism in a country where Zionism and to some extent anti-Islamic prejudice was so strong and its exponents so unscrupulous and well organized. By the same token, many Israelis and North American supporters of Israel felt increasingly unwelcome. This feeling led eventually to the 2007 foundation of a rival Middle East association, the Association for the Study of the Middle East and Africa (ASMEA), based on the questionable assumption that, whereas MESA had become "irredeemably politicized," its own members could and would provide a "strictly scholarly and academic alternative."[35] As Zachary Lockman points out, this can be seen as part of a more general reaction by many conservative scholars to what they took to be the domination of the old professional associations by left-leaning political activists.[36] For me, personally, this was yet another example of a practice I had observed in England several decades before: both sides of any contemporary dispute accusing the other of sacrificing basic academic "truth" on the altar of politics. This was an annoying — because it is inevitably hypocritical — "game" that everyone was forced to play with some display of false sincerity. Of course, one might observe that such a statement is easy for me to make, as the two old universities at which I taught, Oxford and then Harvard, provided me with a much greater degree of protection against outside attack than my colleagues in less cosmopolitan institutions.

Almost any public choice one made — what to write, what conference to attend, even what colleague one wanted to hang out with — was an obviously political act, particularly during the emotionally-charged years of the 1967 and 1973 Arab-Israeli wars. I never participated formally in the fierce trench warfare among academics that ensued — taking refuge in the relatively less political practice of economic history. Nonetheless, my own friendship with Edward Said, as well as the complimentary things he had said about me in his 1978 *Orientalism*, meant that I was inevitably tarred with his brush and viewed by his opponents as dangerous.[37] Later, when I began to teach

---

35 Zachary Lockman, *Contending Visions*, 271.

36 Ibid.

37 For example, Martin Kramer's diatribe against Said and his supposed followers in *Ivory Towers on Sand: The Failure of Middle East Studies in America* (Washington, DC: The Washington Institute for Near East Studies, 2001).

Middle East politics, it seemed to me wiser to adopt the stance that the best course, in a situation in which everyone inevitably brought some personal baggage, was to be honest about personal opinions while doing one's best to postpone judgment until after you had presented the facts as you saw them.

Another important sign of the times was the 1967 establishment of the Association of Arab American University Graduates, or AAUG, at the initiative of two prominent Palestinian intellectuals, Ibrahim Abu-Lughod and Edward Said, as a direct response to the sense of Arab defeat produced by the June War. Open to any American university graduate of Arab origins, its initial remit was to try to counter the intense wave of anti-Arab and anti-Palestinian feeling at that time. To accomplish this goal, it strove to be at once an advocate for better understanding and for a calmer, more scholarly approach to thinking about the Arab world. It held annual meetings in the usual way and published a journal—*The Arab Studies Quarterly*, envisioned as "a platform for academic research to counter anti-Arab propaganda veiled by academic jargon"—while doing its best to counter what it took to be discrimination against Arabs who stood up for their cause.[38] Edward and Ibrahim were strong-minded enthusiasts, and for a while they gave the association a real presence in ethnic and communitarian politics in the United States. But, as generally tends to happen, they began to leave its core activities to others, as they got more closely involved in Palestinian politics in the Middle East.

My only direct association with this enterprise was an invitation to attend the AAUG's Detroit conference some time in the late 1970s to lend my name to the promotion surrounding the inauguration of the new *Arab Studies Quarterly*. Detroit, with its substantial population of Arab-Americans, was one of the few Arab-friendly cities at this time. I well remember an address from its black mayor who had obviously done some personal research on all things Islamic, Arab, and Palestinian. My own official presentation was much more routine: a call for Arab geographers and historians to preserve the names of Palestine's towns and villages before they were entirely renamed or otherwise obliterated by the Zionist project.

Looking back on all this now, I am struck, once again, by how difficult it is to organize and sustain collective intellectual projects outside the university, especially in the Anglo-Saxon world with its particular emphasis on individually authored work. Problems of finance are important, as are those of travel, but the main issue, as I have always seen it, is our lack of experience of working together. That is, at least in the humanities and the softer of the social sciences, where we are missing the background of

---

38 "About," *Arab Studies Quarterly*, http://www.plutojournals.com/asq/.

those who learned to participate in collective research techniques in the laboratories of their schools and colleges. This lack explains the reliance of any group on the one or two members with organizational energy and willingness to act as hosts, thus highlighting the importance of regular, predictable schedules, which make advance planning possible. This was how the Hull Group seemed to work in the United Kingdom, and it also proved a useful formula for the economic and business history group in both the United States and, later, in Cairo. There, with Abdel-Aziz Ezzel-Arab as our annual host, we got together to discuss the collection and use of Egyptian business records, often in association with the businessmen who had created them in the first place and who were able to see the value of what we were doing.

What remained lacking, the Egyptian business history project aside, were structures for sustained analysis of the Middle East in association with scholars living in the Middle East. There were many reasons for this. Some of the most significant were those set out by Salim Nasr, the Lebanese sociologist and Ford Foundation Program Officer in the Middle East, in an interview given in May 1997.[39] Nasr's list included the "weakness of (Arab) scholarly communities in general," "poorly equipped libraries," and "very limited resources to support scholarly research." To this list I would add the incentive structures in Arab universities that encouraged scholars only to study their own countries, and then never on a comparative basis. I would also mention the lack of any sustained intellectual dialogue between Arab academics working in the West and those at home. The one exception to the latter was the Center for Arab Unity Studies, which was established in Lebanon in 1975 by a group of concerned Arab intellectuals but then was forced to relocate to London a few years later. But even in this case, cooperation proved difficult. Although visits to the center's well-stocked library of books and newspapers in Beirut were encouraged, its founders were rightly suspicious of Western intentions toward the Middle East. This fact made formal cooperation difficult for many years until an uneasy trust could be established, generally on an individual basis.

Archives and Access to Archives

When I started my work in Middle East economic history, the easiest and most helpful archive was that contained in the British Public Record Office. Catalogs—based on the original official numbering of files—were good and

39 "Middle East Studies in the Arab World," Interview with Lisa Hajjar, *Middle East Research and Information Project*: 27/205 (Winter 1997), 205.

relatively accessible. The main limitation came from the employment of the so-called "Fifty Year Rule," which meant that in 1960 I could only request files up to the year 1910. This was no great problem for a nineteenth-century economic historian. Less useable official archives also existed in France, as well as in Cairo and Istanbul. But, for a while at least, London was the place to which many historians of the Middle East came first, ensuring that, like it or not, those who read them were presented with the views of what Gallagher and Robinson had already labeled the "official mind" of those who actually ran the British Empire. This tended to give one's work, as even Gamal Abdel Nasser's daughter Hoda was forced to admit, a kind of pro-British twist. Much the same was true of the somewhat less accessible French archives as they related to the colonial endeavor in Syria/Lebanon and North Africa.

Official archives also existed in the Middle East, but with several large drawbacks. For one, they appeared to have no history of their own, making it difficult to work out why most records were kept after they left the ministries that had created them, and under what system they were then housed. Nor was it usually possible to know from the catalogs what was actually available—access to the shelves themselves being forbidden. Rightly or wrongly, many of the archivists gave the impression that they did not know much about what they had in their charge. This supposition was given added strength by the stories told by the famous Ottoman historian Halil Inalcik, which suggested that he was often given a set of random files each day, perhaps one from the sixteenth century and another, unrelated one from the nineteenth, to prevent him from either witnessing the chaos that lay inside or making an official complaint.

As a rule, the Ottoman and Egyptian archives were also subject to the play of contemporary politics, with sensitivities about records relating to the Armenians in the former case, and a whole host of nationalist and anti-foreign prejudices in the latter. The situation in Egypt was made worse by the control exercised by the dreaded Central Agency for Public Mobilization and Statistics, established in 1964, which followed a blanket policy of asserting that almost any social or economic data was a national secret. This raised the already high level of suspicion concerning foreigners. It may also have something to do with the replacement of some of the older archivists who possessed an invaluable knowledge of Ottoman Turkish with newer government appointees who knew none. Then, at about the same time, huge numbers of records were simply removed from the Egyptian archives in support of a project—never to be completed—for rewriting the official history of Egypt to account for popular, anti-imperialist, and antimonarchical ideological currents then at the fore. This was all in the days before photocopiers and with one's bags or briefcases subject to a thorough search.

In such circumstances, those historians who prospered best were those who managed to secure a foothold in the archives by establishing a friendly and trusting relationship with an archivist. This, I think, was how the great French scholar André Raymond must have managed to work his way through the wills of artisans and merchants he used for his classic work on the fortunes of Cairo's productive classes.[40] And how Alexander Scholch came to write his classic work on the period of political and social turbulence that preceded the Urabi Revolt in 1882.[41] As for my own case, it took me four or five months before I could obtain permission to use the collection of records in Egypt's Abdeen Palace. I then had little idea how they were organized and what I might find by way of information about landownership and the production and export of cotton. The process was very much one of flying blind,[42] but it forced me to explore Cairo's many other collections, such as the library of the Jesuit order in Abbasiya and the many "scientific" societies established by Ismail Pasha, the country's ruler in the 1860s and 1870s.

The Field Strives to be Aware of Itself

One way of assessing the maturity of a new field is by measuring the extent to which it has become critically aware of itself, yet this is not as easy a matter to chart as might be supposed. Much of what appears critical in the early literature written from inside is concerned more with its shortcomings—its continued links with Orientalism, the paucity of contributions by social scientists, the lack of women's voices, etc.,—than with a wholesale evaluation of its particular strengths and weaknesses, including its independence from government. Indeed, some of my own early work on the subject falls very much into this category as well. Attempts to take a hard look at the field itself were also often sidetracked by what seemed to be the need to counter major ideological attacks on the associated fields of Islamic studies: for example, Samuel Huntington's enormously

---

40 André Raymond, *Artisans et commerçants au Caire au XVIIIe siècle*, 2 Vols (Institut Français à Damas, 1973/1974).
41 Alexander Scholch, *Egypt for the Egyptians: The Socio-Political Crisis in Egypt 1878–1882* (London: Ithaca Press, 1981).
42 Yoav Di-Capua, *Gatekeepers of the Arab Past: Historians and History Writing in Twentieth-Century Egypt* (Berkeley: UC Press, 2009).

influential *The Clash of Civilizations*, which appeared first as an article in 1993. More subtly, the end of the Cold War—which had been one of the major raison d'être for area studies in the first place—brought fears of loss of funds and of many types of university sponsorship.[43]

By the time these crises and intellectual conflicts had come and gone, and it was discovered that the field was now far too well established to require further defense, the need to account for its own particular history and to chronicle its achievements also seemed to have come and gone, at least at the level of serious books and articles. The one exception is Timothy Mitchell's trenchant essay on "The Middle East in the Past and Future," offered as a paper at two complementary workshops organized by the Social Science Research Council in 1997 and 1998.[44] More generally, it is my own feeling that, at least in the Anglo-Saxon academic world, the study of institutional history and of areas within it is generally left to biography and autobiography, as well as works commissioned for such anniversary celebrations as the fiftieth anniversary of a center for Middle East studies, for example those at Harvard (2004) and Oxford (2007).

The Field at Fifty: Some Reflections

Any attempt to evaluate how and when a field comes of age can only be done through the most arbitrary of exercises, depending as it does on an equally arbitrary set of definitions regarding the nature of academic fields in the first place, as well as a set of such insubstantial notions as "self-awareness" and that of a "critical mass" of interlocking networks of scholars who either knew each other or of each other, and who read each other's work and cited them regularly in their own books and articles. Fortunately, though, I do not feel myself alone in this enterprise. Some good work has already been done on the subject, particularly by Leonard Binder and Zachary Lockman, and many other old friends and colleagues who were willing to share their ideas with me.

Let me start with a critical look at Leonard Binder's 1976 contribution. At this stage, the field was still far from being fully formed. What he wanted, and found lacking, were two complex necessities: a general paradigm about "what is worth knowing, which problems require added

---

43 Samuel P. Huntington, "The Clash of Civilizations?" *Foreign Affairs* 72, 3 (Summer 1993).

44 David Szanton, ed., *The Politics of Knowledge: Area Studies and the Disciplines* (Berkeley and Los Angeles: University of California Press, 2004).

research, [and] how various subjects are to be defined," and a "corps of well-qualified scholars" with "disciplinary standards."[45] Of these, the first has still not appeared, which seems to me a very good thing in a field that still remains resolutely defined by object and practice rather than any one method of approach. But the second was almost certainly present by 1990 in the shape of one of Binder's other desideratum: "a community of understanding and purpose" consisting of a "corps of well-qualified scholars" with faith that, in some ways, we can know about "an alien culture."[46] Yet whether this was to be achieved in what he styles an "interdisciplinary" as opposed to a "nondisciplinary" manner of cooperation remained an open question in 1990, just as it had been at his time of writing. Moreover, the field as a whole still had not succeeded in reaching the last of Binder's desiderata: that Middle East scholars in the different disciplines be able not only to communicate with each other about Middle East matters but also to grasp each other's problems from the point of view of each person's relationship to his or her own discipline.[47] What the existing community of scholars had, though, was the capacity not only to reproduce themselves but also to expand teaching and research into new locations and new areas of knowledge. The result, according to one study, was that sixteen leading US universities awarded eighty-six Middle East–related PhDs annually by 1979.[48]

To these observations about criteria, I would add five of my own. First, by 1990, members of the field of modern Middle East studies had become self-conscious and self-critical in any number of ways. They interrogated the spatial and temporal boundaries of the field; examined the role of world empires like the Ottoman and the Persian, as well as the British and the French, in the creation of modern nation-states; and wrote histories that concerned themselves with groups and people beyond the elite, while pioneering the use of new sources like *waqf* documents and fatwas.

Second, the field had become mature enough to generate, and to welcome, its own forms of revisionisms. One example is Timothy Mitchell's critique of the notion of colonial modernity. Another is Talal Asad's concern with the study of religious discipline and practice rather than the old concern with ideas and innovation. Both of these works, for

---

45 Leonard Binder, "Area Studies: A Critical Reassessment" in Leonard Binder, ed., *The Study of the Middle East* (NY: John Wiley and Sons, 1976), 2, 4.
46 Ibid., 4, 11.
47 Ibid., 8.
48 Lockman, *Contending Visions*, 128.

the first time, were seen as making an important contribution in other historical fields as well.[49]

Third, the field of modern Middle East studies in both the United Kingdom and the United States became sufficiently detached from immediate questions of government policy and direct reliance on government funding. It outlived its origins in World War II intelligence and went on to produce genuine works of disinterested scholarship. It is true that many parts of the field's intellectual agenda still derived from notions of "relevance," which stemmed from immediate policy concerns, and that many of its students went on to work in government as experts. It is also true that it still required special clearance to look at many of the most recent foreign office and other reports. But looking at the books that were regarded as essential reading at that time—for example, Patrick Seale's *The Struggle for Syria* (1962), Malcolm Kerr's *The Arab Cold War* (1967), Hanna Batutu's *The Old Social Classes and the Revolutionary Movements of Iraq* (1978), Moshe Lissak and Dan Horowitz's *Origins of the Israeli Polity: Palestine Under the Mandate* (1978), Ervand Abrahamian's *Iran Between Two Revolutions* (1982), and so on—it would be difficult to argue that they were not works exhibiting the highest standard of independent scholarship.

Fourth, the field had become reasonably well funded, with sufficient money generally available from governments, universities, individual donors, and foundations, and, in the case of Europe, from the European community in Brussels, to create new posts, award traveling fellowships and scholarships, finance new research projects, and so on. Not that there ever seems to be quite enough funding, but I am also constantly amazed at how much can still be achieved for so little cost simply by putting a small group of people together for a weekend or so to discuss a subject of common interest, even without the prior circulation of papers.

Fifth, and last, there was the field's ability to absorb the great political shocks that rocked the Middle East: the Arab Israeli wars of 1967 and 1973, the Iranian Revolution of 1979, the Israeli incursion into Lebanon engineered by General Ariel Sharon in 1981, Saddam Hussein's occupation of Kuwait in 1990, the Allied invasion of Iraq in 2003 and so on, although sometimes its members were divided into different ideological camps. It helped that, for the most part, these same shocks entered the historical realm sufficiently quickly to become, on some later occasions, the subject for joint discussion and research. But not before they had created deep fissures between those

---

49 Mitchell, "Middle East in the Past," and Talal Asad, *Genealogies of Religion: Discipline and Reasons of Power in Christianity and Islam* (Baltimore: Johns Hopkins Press 1993).

living in the Middle East and those outside, as a result of the problems they posed for travel, exchanges, and in general, for keeping in regular contact.

I vividly recall how my colleagues and I experienced some of these major events and how we dealt with the political differences they generated. I was in Oxford when the June War of 1967 broke out and well remember my huge shock at the speed with which the much-vaunted Arab military was swept away, particularly the pre-dawn destruction of some four hundred aircraft, and the tears of some of my Arab friends. Soon I realized that this was a defining moment for my Israeli friends as well, the majority of them imagining, if only briefly, that they would find the Egyptian army in the suburbs of Tel Aviv the next day. In a flash, any pretense of objectivity, of imagining that there might be common ground, was swept away to the great detriment of true scholarship, with a writer's position on what came to be known as the "Question of Palestine" almost instantly revealed in the first paragraph of their work. In my own case, I took what small comfort I could from a retreat into the economic history of Mandate Palestine while being fully aware that, in some sense, I was a supporter of a losing team sustained not by the vast conspiracy theories which were rampant at the time but the hope that, bit by bit, the Egyptians and their allies would get their act together, recognize the glaring faults in their military apparatus, and prepare for another round. This, of course, is what they did, although under the new leadership of Anwar Sadat in the Canal Crossing of 1973. After that, and in the United Kingdom at least, the intensity of feeling about the Arab-Israeli conflict was much reduced, supporters on both sides rarely bothering each other very much in public events with only the occasional fanatic making use of an open seminar for a rant in the guise of a question. Here, the one exception I experienced was as a member of a Labor Party Middle East sub-committee in the late 1970s when a recommendation that policy shift slightly in the direction of Palestinian rights was ferociously attacked by two of the party's most left-wing MPs, Ian Mikado and another whose name I now forget, who turned up just for this one occasion.

The Iranian revolution posed much less of a problem as I knew no one who had a good word for the Shah. But I do remember telling a small group of celebrating Persian exiles in Oxford one evening that they had better enjoy themselves now for if there was one thing that the study of popular revolutions revealed it was that, try as their leaders might, it was extremely difficult to persuade the people to get out of the streets and go home again without the Napoleonic strategy of leading them off in a foreign war, a policy only thrust upon Tehran by the Iraqi invasion of 1990. I also benefitted from being able to talk to a wise friend and colleague,

Hamid Enayat, who explained to me the logic behind Ayatollah Khomeini's doctrine of "*vilayat-e faqih*" and how it had invaded the thinking of those pressing for a greater representation of religious doctrine in the newly-minted constitution. All this made the general Arab unwillingness to pay serious attention to what was going on in Iran both perverse and, I would say, fundamentally stupid, particularly when it came to ignoring the fact that, for better of worse, the Iranians had made a serious attempt to create a religiously-inspired constitution.

It may have been at this moment, too, that I first had an inkling that a few of my friends were fundamentally suspicious of Islam per se, even when it seemed to be on the side of revolutionaries bent on getting rid of a hated ancien régime. But, on the whole, this had little effect on the hatred of that avowed secularist, Saddam Hussein, who was generally regarded as a blood-thirsty dictator—although few went as far as my friend, Fred Halliday, to call him a "fascist," as he did at the time of Saddam's occupation of Kuwait in 1990, then the strongest word of condemnation in our vocabulary. I myself was prepared to humor Fred in this in that he at least had visited Iraq in the 1980s and discovered to his disgust how there was no area of independent thought, no possibility of making even the most innocuous criticism of the regime, a warning that prevented most of us from going there at all, something I sometimes regret in terms of maintaining contact with one of the countries that I was later required to talk and to lecture about.

Coming to the United States in 1993 to teach at Harvard was to have to operate in a more polarized environment with a more tenacious and well-funded Zionist movement in the Boston area. This included, for some years, an organization called Campus Watch which was alleged to send spies to attend the lectures and classrooms of those who were labeled as being on the Palestinian side of the dispute. For my first few years, this encouraged a certain amount of self-censorship, just in case. But then, miraculously as it seemed at the time, and for reasons I never quite understood, this was replaced by a general supposition that free speech of any kind should be respected on campus. Perhaps more insidious was the other kind of self-censorship I adopted concerning the choice of topics for my fortnightly *al-Hayat* articles in which, given the fact of the paper's Saudi ownership, I steered clear of any mention either of Islam or of Saudi Arabia, subjects about which I also had no particular expertise. As most of those I met were also adopting the same strategy, there was, I suppose, a general conspiracy of public silence in which the majority of my colleagues generally felt the same as I did without it being necessary to go into the matter in great detail. Looking back on it some fifteen years later, I realize that such a strategy

205

7 LESSONS BY WAY OF A CONCLUSION

Looking back on my nearly sixty years in Middle East studies, what are the major lessons I think I have learned apart from the obvious ones about the inevitable social conservatism that seems to come with increasing age? One is that, as a Briton, I have always been pleasantly surprised by the lack of ill will shown to me personally because of my nationality or, in the case of my military service, my role as an agent of a British colonial occupation. True, I was fortunate to come of age after the act of Indian independence in 1948 effectively put an end to almost all traces of the empire east of Suez, while Prime Minister Harold Macmillan's "winds of change" speech about the inevitability of African independence came just a little over a decade later. Nevertheless, it has always seemed to me that I must have been protected by the innate good sense of Egyptians and others by which they assumed that I, as an individual, was free of responsibility for my own government's errors, as indeed I largely was. Whereas I, as someone who knows something of the history of the matter, still think that the Balfour Declaration of 1917 was a great mistake while continuing to wince at all the examples of covert racism to be found in those who have been engaged in what Lord Cromer famously described as "the government of subject peoples."

That said, the choice of a vocation that involves the continuous study of the history and politics of another region of the world inhabited by largely non-English-speaking peoples does not seem to me as unproblematic as it did when I first began. Ideally, of course, such a journey should be embarked on as a junior partner of the local intellectuals and academic historians themselves. But this proved easier said than done, given their vestigial anti-colonialism, not to speak of the lack of local Egyptian and other independent research centers in the Nasser era. In my own case, the fact that, for a period of time, I probably knew more about the history of the cultivation of long-staple cotton than anyone else in Egypt was not enough to temper the feeling that I should be doing a better job of sharing this with other Egyptians. The best I could do, or so it seemed to me at the time, was to try to imagine passing all I wrote before some stern local critic of colonialism such as Anouar Abdel-Malek, making him both my conscience and my guide. Nevertheless, any traces of Western presumption or cultural ignorance must be counted as all my own.

Another stratagem, fitfully applied, was to try as best I could to rely less on asking direct questions — with their almost predictable answers — than on simply "over-hearing" conversations in buses, shared taxis, and elsewhere, relying on the fact that I obviously looked like a foreigner (*khawaga*) and people tended to assume that I could not understand what they were saying. In such a way I felt that I was getting closer to local urban opinion than I was by reading obviously censored newspapers or listening to official broadcasts. The actual village opinion was, of course, quite another matter, something I could only hope to learn from those few anthropologists who spent years just listening and learning.

A last and very obvious failure was my inability to interest anyone or any group in a discussion about what was going on either in the United Kingdom or, as I tried several times, in Europe during the early drive for economic unity. Here, it seemed to me, I could make an unambiguous contribution to local knowledge, only to run into the barrier posed by the fact that my interlocutors seemed to want to know only about what I thought about their country and not my own. Was this due to insecurity, politeness, or some other factor that I was destined, like so much else, to never properly understand? In any event, it was a salutary reminder that, whatever hopes or fantasies I might once have had about the matter, I would never, ever be able to think like an Egyptian. Or a Syrian or a Libyan or an Iraqi for that matter.

Did I choose the Middle East or did the Middle East choose me? Whatever the answer I soon realized that after writing a doctoral thesis about Egypt and an economic history of the whole region it was far too late to turn back. I had invested too much in trying to learn Arabic, in making important connections, in learning about the great cities, in writing books, and in sustaining significant friendships for that. Sometimes, I speculate about what it might have been like to study some other region instead, somewhere like Latin America where there might have been some possibility of knowing Spanish well enough to actually enjoy the poetry. But not only was I hooked on Cairo and the Nile much too early, I also have to admit that my life in Middle East studies has given me both a satisfying career and a set of experiences which I treasure even more now that I am unable to travel to the region with the ease that I once did.

EPILOGUE
MY SIXTY YEARS OF STUDYING THE
MIDDLE EAST: SOME FINAL THOUGHTS

There are obviously many reasons why someone of my age and class should want to spend his adult life studying the peoples and societies of countries other than his own. In my case these would include relatives who had been missionaries in South Africa, school teachers who had served abroad during the Second World War, and, most of all, my father, David Owen, who became one of the first members of the newly established United Nations in 1946. More interesting to me now is why I chose the Arab Middle East as my region and how I began to study it via an emphasis on its attempts to develop itself through a process of economic expansion and planned industrialization, for the reasons I have tried to set out in the early parts of this memoir.

What I was obviously unable to understand at the beginning, however, was where this study would take me and how difficult, if not impossible, it would be to abandon it for any other. As time went on, I began to see myself first as more of an imperial, then as a world, historian. Nevertheless, the Middle East always remained at the center of my academic concerns as well as a major source of my relationships with friends, colleagues, and students alike, a special space to be relished not just for what it was but also as a basis for comparison with other regions of the non-European world.

Lessons abound. One of the first was how academic interest in Egypt as a source of a major world crop, cotton, inevitably had to expand beyond libraries and archives into the homes, and in some cases, the fields, orchards, and market gardens owned by Egyptian friends. Part of this was due to my good fortune in meeting an Egyptian scholar of English literature, Mahmoud Manzaloui, whose family, before the Land Reform laws of the 1950s and early 1960s, had owned an *ezba*, a cotton growing estate, just south of Lake Manzala on the Egyptian coast. Getting there by train across the fields of the Delta was one thing, looking at copies of his estate records with their careful record of payment to those employed, some seasonally, some on an annual basis, was another. And lastly, the sight of Mahmoud, mounted on a horse and throwing sweets to the little children of the *ezba*'s crowded streets on the Muslim holiday of Eid al-Adha yet another, completing a set of experiences that encompassed almost the entire process of growing and exporting Egypt's major agricultural resource before it dwindled largely into insignificance at the end of the twentieth century due to a combination of competition and loss of rural land to the needs of urban housing.

Another form of what might be termed academic "mission creep," was the expansion of my Oxford history courses from the history of the Egyptian economy to that of the entire region, then from economic analysis itself to a form of political economy focused on the structures involved in the exercise of direct power. The former took me both up the Nile to the cotton-growing regions of northern Sudan as well as to an Iraq where the unruly spring floods I encountered in 1968 still played havoc with the standing crops.

I am also well aware of the good fortune that accompanied the whole enterprise, notably being able to meet, and often befriend, a great number of Egyptian and other inhabitants of the region who provided me with key insights into aspects of its special trajectory including their own example of notable pieces of historical revision. As I have remarked before, it proved unexpectedly easy for a foreigner like myself to spend time with newsmakers like President Abdel Nasser's old confidant, the journalist Mohammad Hassanein Heikal, anxious to find what a fellow-commencement speaker at the American University of Cairo was like. It helped too that mid-century London was full of Arab exiles, coming and going according to the dictates of ever-changing political fortune, sometimes as students, sometimes as budding journalists. Then there was the enormous piece of good fortune I had in mid-1988 in meeting Jamil Mrowe in Beirut just as he was about to re-launch his father's journal, *Hayat*, for which I have been writing op-ed pieces to an Arab-reading audience ever since.

These were also times when political links of an anti-imperialist, anti-colonialist type easily crossed international borders, helping to make young activists like me temporarily brothers-in-arms against the Eden Government of 1956 that launched the Suez attack or the Israeli one of 1967 that threatened the whole of the Arab Middle East. In this way, lasting friendships were made, providing, inter alia, a list of persons to be phoned or, later, emailed if there were particular questions I wanted to ask about what had just happened in Beirut or Cairo or Damascus. And, in return, and particularly as I got older, I could offer what I hoped were useful comments on longer-term trends, on international comparisons, or simply, what it was like to be in Cairo during Evacuation Day in 1956, Amman during Black

September 1970, Libya before, during, and after Qaddafi or the Gulf before oil. It was as if all I had to do was show interest for the questions to start and a discussion begin.

And now that my visits to the Middle East are coming to an end, I have begun to ask myself whether the particular version of Middle East studies that I learned and helped to develop should not be coming to an end too, transforming itself, along with African, South Asian, and all the other area studies, into a version of global history, albeit with certain key political, cultural, religious, and other variations. I believe students should still try to live in the region for at least a year or two, to learn several of its major languages, and where possible, work in some of its major government archives. They should do so without fetishizing the whole experience as it so often was in the past, because it remains valuable as a source of authority for those like me wanting to make large claims about why the study of the Middle East still matters. This is all the more important as the region keeps throwing up new challenges to our understanding of how to explain phenomena like the present prevalence of civil wars and the emergence of new and well organized militant groups like the Islamic State. But if I have one single over-arching concern, it is that this local specialization must be balanced by a parallel understanding of how the region, as well as its various parts, fit into the larger process of global history.

CPSIA information can be obtained
at www.ICGtesting.com
Printed in the USA
BVOW07s0158141116

467652BV00006B/11/P

9 781939 067234